W9-ANW-937

The Passion of
Thérèse of Lisieux

I have seen a saint die, yes, I who am speaking to you, and it is not as one imagines. It is not as we read about in books. One must stand firm for one feels the soul's armour crack.

Georges Bernanos

To my Carmelite Family and all whose lives in touching mine have inspired and encouraged me in my journey through life, and also to Margaret Burger who typed the final draft of this manuscript onto a computer word processor, I dedicate this translation with gratitude.

Sr Anne Marie Brennan ocd

Guy Gaucher

The Passion of Thérèse of Lisieux

with a new introduction by
Benedict J. Groeschel, CFR

A Crossroad Book
The Crossroad Publishing Company
New York

This printing: 2017

The Crossroad Publishing Company
www.CrossroadPublishing.com

Original title *La Passion de Thérèse de Lisieux*
© Edition du Cerf, 1973, Desclée de Brouwer Quatrieme
Edition—revue et corrigée

English translation by Sr. Anne Marie Brennan, OCD,

English edition © 1989 by St. Paul Publications, Homebush

Introduction © 1997 by Benedict J. Groeschel, CFR

Printed in the United States of America

Library of Congress Cataloging-in-Publication Data

Gaucher, Guy, 1930–
    [Passion de Thérèse de Lisieux.   English]
    The passion of Thérèse of Lisieux / Guy Gaucher.
        p.   cm.
    Translation of : Passion de Thérèse de Lisieux.
    Includes bibliographical references.
    ISBN 0-8245-0987-0
    1. Thérèse, de Lisieux, Saint, 1873–1897.   2. Christian saints—
France—Lisieux—Biography.   I. Title.
    BX4700.T5G3813   1990
    271'.971'024—dc20   89-48603
                                                                                CIP

Contents

1

Introduction

When I received the request of the publisher to write a brief introduction to *The Passion of St. Thérèse of Lisieux*, I was delighted. I am by no means an expert on St. Thérèse but in recent years have grown in my admiration of this remarkable spiritual figure, especially in my personal devotion to her. I have good reason to believe that I have often experienced her assistance in my work, particularly with fellow members of the clergy. Repeatedly I have had evidence of her assistance—mysterious evidence, like finding a large, stemless golden rose in the middle of a big city street while with a priest friend who at that moment had risen from prayer before a shrine to this saint in a Carmelite convent a few feet away. Like many others burdened with care, unexpectedly in front of him was this traditional sign that the devout speak of when they have received assistance from St. Thérèse. And assistance was on its way. The world can scoff, but too many have had such experiences for one to intelligently ignore such phenomena.

Like most of those who have a devotion to St. Thérèse, I had read a few different editions of her autobiography, most recently the translation of Ronald Knox. But I was not well informed about the final circumstances of her final illness and especially about the last hours and moments of her earthly life. When I first came across *The Passion of St. Thérèse of Lisieux,* I had no idea that the author was a Carmelite and that he had been made Auxiliary Bishop of Bayeux and Lisieux. This adds a certain authority to his book.

As I turned the pages of this remarkable volume I was astonished by what I had not known about St. Thérèse. A few weeks before I read Bishop Gaucher's study, another bishop, my friend Auxiliary Bishop Patrick Ahern of New York and a Thérèsian expert in his own right, had brought up the idea of Thérèse being named a Doctor of the Church. I was unimpressed at the time. I think of the Doctors as those great geniuses like Thomas and Bonaventure or women of a prophetic stature like Catherine or Teresa, but not our own little Thérèse. I thought to myself, "Don't ruin it for me by making this humble and holy soul what she is not."

But Gaucher's book turned me around. Doctors of the Church should speak loudly to their own times. Despite her sheltered life, Thérèse is a genuinely modern person with all the baggage of our times. She struggles with skepticism and even nihilism. Cardinal Cahal Daly has said that even as a believer she expressed the experience of nihilism characteristic of this age more profoundly than Nietzsche. Her own description of the black thoughts that came to her in the months before her death are unsurpassed expressions of the nihilistic experience precisely because she is a believer.

> It seems to me the darkness, borrowing the voice of sinners, says mockingly to me, "You are dreaming about the light, about a country fragrant with sweetest perfumes; you are dreaming about the eternal possession of the Creator of all these things; you believe that one day you will walk out of this fog which surrounds you! Dream on, dream on; rejoice in death which will give you not what you hope for, but even deeper night, the night of nothingness." (Ms C p. 213)

The more I read and studied Gaucher's book, which led me on to other sources, the more it dawned on me that this young nun was not only a spiritual prodigy but also a person who like the "Doctors of the Church" has so very much to say to us a century after her death. This is because there are so many aspects to the message of Thérèse of Lisieux. Perhaps each one who gets to know her writings learns something a little different, something very personally suited to one's own needs. To me, Thérèse is a most powerful witness to the relevance and necessity of personal devotion for the Christian of our age. We need to hear an intelligent, cultured, informed person say to Christ, "I love you." We are so preoccupied with historical reconstructions, with the scholar's view of Jesus of Nazareth, that we no longer speak in deep personal ways to our Savior, who is present in our lives. This personal devotion made Thérèse willing to endure trials, to be faithful and generous, to be globally concerned about the human race from her little Carmel. Her last words, "My God, I love you," are exactly the profound expression of devotion that our psychologically jaded and selfist world needs to hear.

As the Church stirs back to life in France after decades of confusion and little faith, and as the first signs of the long-awaited second spring come to the English-speaking world, what better way to mark this event than the recognition of Thérèse of Lisieux. I have gone from being a skeptic about Doctor Thérèse to being an ardent enthusiast.

Reading *The Passion of St. Thérèse of Lisieux* is a profound way of entering into the experience of the Church coming back to life. The enthusiasm of more than a million people gathered in Paris for World Youth Day and the remarkable celebration of the Pope's announcement of the conferral of the doctoral status will echo down the twenty-first century. Bishop Gaucher will give you, as accurately as possible, the chronological events of the new Doctor's life during her final illness. He will do his best to coordinate these events with the physical effects of her terminal illness. Often we do not realize what she is saying or experiencing without a chronological and medical framework. In addition, he will "sketch a portrait of Thérèse in the face of death from all the authentic documents that are available in print at the present time." Reading and re-reading this work has proved to be a powerful experience for me and for many with whom I have spoken.

Cardinal Newman, who may be the other Doctor of this age, was sharply critical of those who would not go out of their way to witness the marvelous or the mysterious. He taught that beauty and power are the surest roads for coming to the truth. This is entirely clear in his contemporary Thérèse, whom he never heard of, although she surely heard of him. Get to know Thérèse and you will rediscover that truth is found in beauty and power.

Thérèse was a great missionary of her age. For this reason, the doctorate was officially proclaimed by Pope John Paul II on Mission Sunday, October 19, 1997. She is a powerful intercessor for the foreign missions. Many missionaries have celebrated her incredibly spiritual power of intercession. She never fulfilled her own desired vocation of being a missionary contemplative in the Carmel of Hanoi, but she has affected many in the non-Christian world.

Anyone interested in Thérèse should carefully study the last moments of her life. These last moments are similar in many respects to the death of Joan of Arc, whom Thérèse loved and respected. They both spoke to their Savior in the last moments of darkness. Their lives are shining examples of beauty and power. Power is made perfect in weakness and beauty is made transcendent in suffering. This mysterious fact of life becomes incandescently clear in the life of the young nun from the Carmel of Lisieux. Allow yourself to get to know her. She will teach you the Gospel of Jesus Christ. Ponder her life, her words, her deeds and her death and you will see that she has changed you. This is the sure sign of someone who can be called a Doctor of the Church.

Benedict J. Groeschel, CFR, 1997

Foreword

'I can nourish myself on nothing but the truth'.[1]

On 20 July 1895, Sister Thérèse of the Child Jesus and of the Holy Face wrote to her aunt:

> I love reading the lives of the saints, the account of their heroic deeds sets my courage on fire and rouses me to imitate them: but I must admit that sometimes I have envied the happy lot of their relatives who had the good fortune to live in their company and enjoy their holy conversations. (LT, 20/7/1895)

Two years before, Sister Thérèse seemed to describe her own story, but the roles would be reversed: she herself would be the saint, and her own sisters, without realising it, the recipients of her last conversations.

'The happy lot' of those privileged witnesses has become ours since the publication of the _Last Conversations_. Thanks to them, we can live in daily 'company' with a saint, hear her words, know what she did during a long illness that was filled with the unexpected, and we can be present at her agony and death. This is without doubt a privilege that is unique in the annals of christian sanctity.

Blasé users of the cinema, tape-recorders and world-wide media, we are no longer surprised when we see famous people reappear on the television screen a few moments after their death. The next day, newspapers publish their last words. The great ones have sometimes taken the precaution of bequeathing their writings to National Libraries . . .

It was just the opposite with the Carmelite from Normandy who was consumed by tuberculosis, died 30 September 1897, and became, according to Pius X, 'the greatest saint of modern times'. Her one concern was that she might live 'unknown and counted as nothing'.[2] She even wished to leave her obscure monastery and go to live in a Carmel in Hanoi where she would be truly 'unknown'. Now by a strange chain of circumstances we have documented information about her that is exceptional for the period. Let us recall briefly a few facts.

The first which claims our attention, a fact unique in the history of the Lisieux Carmel and extremely rare in the Carmelite Order, concerns those two exercise books of memoirs that Thérèse wrote at her superior's order. They could have disappeared without leaving a trace.

Why have most of the apparently insignificant letters and notes of this child and young Carmelite been kept? At the beginning of 1893 her sisters asked her to write some poems and small plays for times of recreation. Could they have known that she would reveal the inmost depths of her soul in those poor verses?

Then there is something else that is unusual: the face of this unknown person has come down to us, thanks to the forty-seven negatives that were taken at a time when photography, especially in Carmel, was looked upon as a modern invention. Now, forty-three were taken within the enclosure.

Finally, during the last months of Thérèse's life, when she became seriously ill, the Martin sisters' affection prompted them to keep a systematic account of everything that in any way concerned their little sister. Mother Agnès resolutely made herself her 'historian' after Mother Marie de Gonzague, who was then prioress, had ordered Thérèse to continue writing down her memoirs. Each day, at her sister's bedside, 'Pauline' took notes. Was she aware of the historical significance of what she was doing? Not at all. For her it was simply a matter of keeping as many memories as she could of that 'angel' who was going to leave her loved ones so prematurely. It is true that some thought had also been given to the writing of the customary 'circular', a biographical account that is sent out to the Carmels after the death of a nun, but it was not without some misgivings that, after Thérèse's death, this circular had become a large volume of 475 pages. We know the extraordinary success *Story of a Soul* attracted when two thousand copies were published on 30 September 1898. The speed with which Thérèse, as she had so often promised, extended her activity after her death to the whole world obviously encouraged the keeping of everything that was connected with her.

With the exception of the Benedictine Abbey where she went to school, the places where she had lived, which enable us to situate with greater accuracy the context of her life, escaped the destruction of two world wars. In June 1944 Lisieux was a furnace, and yet not one record was burnt. Sometimes it was only a matter of a few metres!

The unusual longevity of the main witnesses of her life[a] made possible for fifty years the explanation of obscure points and the accuracy of countless details.

Thus the convergence of all these facts has enabled us to have unparalleled documentation that has not yet been fully explored or classified.

The writing of Thérèse's last manuscript (Manuscript C) was interrupted at the beginning of July 1897 by the progress of the tuberculosis, and the last months of her life would have remained in obscurity but for the notes that Mother Agnès of Jesus took down each day. These documents,

---

a   Sister Marie of the Sacred Heart died 19/1/1940 aged 80 years; Mother Agnès 28/7/1951 at 90 years; Sister Geneviève 25/2/1959 at 90 years.

together with the novices' reminiscences, were used to write Chapter XII of *Story of a Soul* and intended to complete the theresian autobiography. When the *Manuscrits autobiographiques* replaced *Story of a Soul* in 1956, Chapter XII disappeared. At the time many of the Saint's friends said that, as *Novissima Verba* was out of print, the account of Thérèse's illness, agony and death would no longer be available to modern readers. The *Derniers Entretiens* have filled that gap, but by placing the testimonies of all the witnesses side by side they are inevitably incomplete.

Moreover many would be discouraged by the detailed apparatus of a critical edition, and so, after having worked in the team which published the *Derniers Entretiens*, we have tried to write an account that follows Thérèse's last days which readers might find more accessible, but no less historical.

The present book therefore hopes to attain two objects:

1. On the one hand, to follow as closely as possible in chronological order Saint Thérèse's biography during the last months of her life, from 4 April to 30 September 1897.

To write this biography it is necessary to follow the stages of pulmonary tuberculosis. Only within this medical context can the true value of the patient's words and actions be fully appreciated. Until now biographers, for want of knowledge as to all the documents, have scarcely brought out the medical aspect. Certainly we know that Thérèse endured great suffering. This has been said. But her sufferings remain in a sort of halo reminiscent of Epinal's painting: 'a young consumptive', smiling as she lay dying, and unpetalling roses over her crucifix. The truth was quite otherwise. Sister Thérèse of the Child Jesus walked a way of the cross, and it is now possible to follow each station, thanks to the wealth and accuracy of the documents.

2. On the other, we have tried to *sketch a portrait of Thérèse in the face of death* from all the authentic documents that are available in print at the present time.

Undoubtedly it is becoming to remain modest in this area. The *Derniers Entretiens* do not change our understanding of the mature Thérèse. But we cannot overlook the unpublished facts which they bring out and which enable us to be more accurate with regard to this or that trait of her human or spiritual physiognomy. This final stage of the illness did not mark the close of Thérèse's life, for the theresian dynamism only really came to an end on 30 September 1897 at twenty minutes past seven. Until her last breath, Thérèse searched, progressed, discovered. In suffering, in the face of death, her deepest self is fully revealed. The written testament, Manuscript C, receives its authentification from the 'last conversations', the lived testament which, according to Mother Agnès and Sisters Geneviève and Marie of the Sacred Heart was Thérèse of Lisieux's real passion. They show how this saint lived, suffered and died, and how little the truth conforms to accepted ideas.

Our Method is inspired by the principles that Thérèse herself clearly set down, and which constitutes the golden rule for all historical work. They are expressed in two sentences of the *Last Conversations.*[b] The first, spoken in August, 'I can nourish myself on nothing but the truth'[3]; the second, a few hours before her death, 'Yes, it seems to me I have never sought anything but the truth.'[4]

A hagiographer herself, Thérèse was not satisfied with statements about principle. When she wrote two plays on Joan

---

b   There are two editions of the *Derniers Entretiens*. The first, a two-volume critical edition published in French. The second, a shorter version, *J'entre dans le Vie, Derniers Entretiens (Paris: Cerf-Desclée de Brouwer, 1973)* that has been translated into English by John Clarke o.c.d. under the title, *St Thérèse of Lisieux, Her Last Conversations (I.C.S. Washington, 1977).* Translator's note.

of Arc, she did not wish to improvise or invent something according to her own fancy. Yet no spectator in the community audience would have protested about this or that liberty being taken with history. What did it matter! Thérèse went to the library to consult Henri Wallon's book which, for her and in the circumstances, was an authoritative source. She also gave the basis that she would have used to write about the life of Mary at Nazareth: 'I'd first make people understand how little we do know about her life. We shouldn't say unlikely things, or things we don't know anything about! ... It was not as they tell us, as they imagine ... I must see her real life, not her imagined life ... they (sermons) should present her as imitable, bringing out her virtues, saying that she lived by faith just as we do, and give proofs of this from the Gospel.'[5]

Let us notice the word *proofs*. Thérèse used it in the sense of textual criticism. She confided: 'In Holy Scripture, isn't it sad to see so many different translations. If I had been a priest, I would have learned Hebrew and Greek, and wouldn't have been satisfied with Latin. Then I would have known the real text dictated by the Holy Spirit.'[6]

She had loved a biography of Théophane Venard based on his correspondence. 'He is the one who is speaking and not "someone else telling the story and making him speak".'[7]

Indeed, if Thérèse had little appreciation for the sermons that she heard on the Virgin Mary, the hagiography of her day would not have given her any more satisfaction.

If some of the saints were to return to earth, I wonder how many would recognise themselves in what has been written about them.[8]

Such principles herald the most radical requirements of modern hagiography. We wish to be as faithful to them as possible by using Thérèse's own words and what is contained in the documents. There is a wealth of material for the short period that interests us here. Thérèse wrote forty-five letters and notes, six poems and Manuscript C. By comparing these dated texts in chronological order and studying the vocabulary, we are able to follow the development of the sick nun's thought and spiritual life.[c] Words taken from the *Derniers Entretiens* have been included in this framework which is chronologically accurate. It has not always been possible to date them all precisely, but such an occasional error does not affect the whole picture.

This book does not therefore contain theological or spiritual reflections. They can only follow at a later stage, based on facts and not on subjective reflections. First of all we have to listen, to look, to ponder in order to 'rediscover that unique human being, Sister Thérèse of the Child Jesus, as she really was', and to be with her again in her actual daily life situation as an invalid. It is a modest, but necesary objective, and must serve as our basis if we are not to build upon sand. Perhaps, somewhere, the power of truth will awaken in some hearts, in silence, the word Saint Thérèse meant for them, with more efficacy than a glowing commentary.[d]

Exactness does not exclude fervour. After three years of daily contact, one is never 'tired of little Thérèse',[9] her personality remains fascinating and mysterious. We dare to say that we have written this book only in the hope that it

---

c   The widespread custom of quoting Thésèse words out of context, without regard for their chronological order, has altered the perspectives so much that we are not afraid, twenty-five years after Mgr Combes masterly work, of stressing the importance of the time element. (The Processes set a bad example by giving only very minor attention to the chronology, as was customary at that time). When our quotations follow one another, they are always in their chronological order, as far as it is possible to date them.

d   If Georges Bernanos' name appears several times in the third part, it is not to embellish our text with literary citations, but because *Novissima Verba* was his bedside companion. His human and poetical sense enable him to understand and have a special insight into the agony and death of the one who revealed to him the way of spiritual childhood.

may awaken the same admiration in new friends of Saint Thérèse of the Child Jesus and of the Holy Face and that, in its own way, it will help, on the eve of the centenary of her birth, to 'break the statue'.[e]

---

e   The name of Gilbert Cesbron's play on Thésèse (1947) published in *Il suffit d'aimer (Livre de poche no. 2862).*

Part I

'The giant's course' of an 'unknown person'

True wisdom consists in 'desiring to be unknown and counted as nothing'. I desire that 'my face be truly hidden, that no one on earth know me'. (Ms A.p.152)

I desire the Cross! ... I love Sacrifice! ... I await your call, I am ready to suffer. To suffer for love of you seems a delight to me. Jesus, my Beloved, for you I wish to die. (1894)

Chapter 1

The Lisieux Carmel in 1897

1897: Félix Favre was presiding over the destinies of the Third Republic in a France shaken by a continuing Affair: for two years, the former Captain Dreyfus had been enduring his punishment on Devil's Island. Small-time French investors were sending their savings to Russia where a young man of twenty-seven, Vladimir Ilich Ulyanov, called Lenin, was soon to be spoken about. Countless fire-works were being set off to celebrate the franco-russian alliance. William II was making bellicose statements. Yet there was a feeling that conflicts between Europeans would come from elsewhere. Captain Marchant was making his way towards the Nile.

A 'strange flying-machine', flown by Clément Ader, had risen some three hundred metres above the ground near Paris. In that city, the Lumière brothers were operating a film projector they had invented. Parisians preferred to go and applaud Edmond Rostand's new play, _Cyrano de Bergerac_.

In the Holy Land, Viscount Charles de Foucauld arrived incognito. He would work as an odd-job man for the Poor Clare nuns at Nazareth.

In Lisieux, a town of 16,200 inhabitants in 1896, Thérèse Martin had been living within the enclosure of the Carmel for eight years and eight months under the name of Sister Thérèse of the Child Jesus and of the Holy Face. The small monastery with its poor red brick walls, situated on a piece of low-lying damp ground, had nothing to attract the attention of an age that would later be called 'beautiful'.

If, some years before, it had been spoken of in the region, it was precisely because it had sheltered members of the Martin family. But after the father's death, in 1894, other gossip had fed the Lisieux chronicle. There had been a controversy that had been followed, not without a certain amusement, between the staunch Catholic, Isidore Guérin, a first-class chemist, and his former employee, the anti-clerical Henry Chéron, who would later have a notable political career. In *Le Normand*, the former defended religious and monarchical values against the latter who had founded *Le Progrès Lexovien*.

On 15 August 1895, M Guérin, Thérèse's uncle and a benefactor of the Carmel, had accompanied his daughter, Marie, to the threshold of the monastery where she met again her four first-cousins.

Would Teresa of Avila, the great reformer, have allowed one fifth of one of her communities to have consisted of members of the same family? We would doubt it after reading what she wrote to the prioress at Seville, about a postulant, 22 July 1597: 'It does not suit us at all for the present to take the youngest. First of all, on account of her age, but also because no monastery should accept three sisters, still less ours, where the numbers are so few.' What would she have said of four sisters and a cousin?

This community consisted then of twenty-four religious, including the four lay-sisters and five novices. An extern sister formed the link between the enclosure and the outside world. The last of the Martin sisters, but the third to enter, 'little Thérèse', as she was referred to in Lisieux, and is still called today, had only one companion younger than herself, the novice Sister Marie of the Trinity. The term 'little Thérèse' was not used to mean a frail young girl, for her 162cm made her the tallest of the Martin sisters. One of the rare photographs taken within the enclosure without her Carmelite veil shows a beautiful young woman, with an open, determined face. The profound gaze seems to be caught up elsewhere. Some of the sisters, including the prioress, found her 'very pretty'. According to her contemporaries she was 'usually smiling', but her face, which was extremely mobile, eluded the negatives which needed several seconds of exposure.

If Sister Thérèse occupied a rather unusual place in the community it was not because she had been given special treatment on account of the circumstances surrounding her entrance. On the contrary: in September 1893, three years after her profession, according to the Constitutions, she should have left the novitiate. But, 'out of humility and also zeal for the good of the novices', she asked to remain there. She therefore held a somewhat unique position in the novitiate. Mother Agnès explained the reason:

> When I was elected prioress in February 1893, I was obliged to make Mother Marie de Gonzague novice mistress. But lest the novices suffer, I asked Sister Thérèse of the Child Jesus, who was then twenty and the senior novice, to look after her two companions, Sister Marthe and Sister Marie-Madeleine (who had entered six months earlier). Both were lay-sisters. In actual fact she had charge of the novices. Mother Marie de Gonzague herself had chosen her to be her assistant and it was her duty to instruct them when necessary.

It was a difficult and very delicate situation that continued until March 1897. When Mother Marie de Gonzague was elected prioress, she confirmed Sister Thérèse in her office of assistant. 'Novice Mistress', without having the official title, Thérèse was aware of the insecurity of her position.[a]

---

a   Because of the prioress' fickleness, Sister Thérèse did not have a moment's security in this so-called Office, which was taken from her and given back again every two weeks or so. In this situation, any peace the novices enjoyed was due solely to the Servant of God's prudence. If Sister Thérèse's influence was too strong, Mother Prioress was offended and said she had no right to be giving us advice, that she was overstepping her instructions. *St. Thérèse by Those Who Knew Her*, Christopher O'Mahony, ocd, Veritas Dublin, 1975. p.120.

She calmly accepted the consequences and devoted herself wholeheartedly to the five religious then in the novitiate.

She also held the office of assistant-sacristan and helped with art work. In March 1896, she asked for a duty that had never attracted anyone: to help the sister in charge of the linen room, Sister Marie of Saint-Joseph, 'a poor sister whom no one could get along with'. Even the best thought this task beyond their strength.

Such were Thérèse's external duties. She was the last of the Martin family and she found herself last in Carmel. For, outside the novitiate, she was truly the youngest in the community. A solemnly professed choir sister for seven years, she did not have a voice in the chapter as her two sisters were already members of it. Sister Geneviève was to describe her sister's unusual situation in the following passage:

> Even at the end of her life when she enjoyed a certain influence in the community, no one ever thought of giving her her right to sit on the chapter. It is true that she could not have had the right to vote, but she could have been a member of the chapter. Instead, like sisters deprived of membership as a punishment, she used to make her accusations with the novices, after the lay-sisters, and withdraw humbly from the meeting.

Her youth and her self-effacement did not prevent her from exercising a real influence. The discreet, but very efficacious role she played in the novitiate bore fruit beyond that limited group. Thérèse's relationship with each member of her community would require a detailed study that would be very interesting. But as the last months of her life were spent practically cut off from most of the nuns, it is better to concentrate here on her ties with those who were around her bedside.

1. Sister Thérèse and Mother Marie de Gonzague

Thérèse's relationship with Marie de Gonzague alone would provide ample material for a book. Let us just look at 1897.

She who was called in the world, Marie Davy de Virville, stood out without possible rival in the community. This was not only because, at that time, a prioress had considerable powers. Her undeniable human qualities made her a striking personality. Held in high esteem by the Guérin family, consulted in the parlour by many priests, possessing sound judgement in the opinion of the prior of the Abbey of Mondaye, she showed this quality in her judgement of Thérèse's worth, and by entrusting her with important responsibilities. Her changing moods and fits of jealousy do not change this fact: she had practically given charge of the novitiate to 'this young religious' and, 30 May 1896, she had insisted that Thérèse become responsible for a second spiritual brother. The objections of the twenty-three year old sister were in vain. The prioress, it is true, was responsible for this correspondence, but each time that she herself wrote to Fr Roulland, or the seminarian Bellière, she praised their spiritual sister whom she called the 'Carmel's treasure'. Intuitively Mother Marie de Gonzague must have sensed in this young Carmelite an unyielding purity. Before this 'child', she felt that the depths of her soul were laid bare, like the novices who thought that Sister Thérèse had the gift of reading souls. This was why the young sister could 'remonstrate' to her prioress with tact and prudence in June 1896 about the painful elections of March of the same year.[1] 'In the end she had confidence in her alone,' said Mother Agnès. Sister Marie of the Trinity testified at the Apostolic Process that Mother Marie de Gonzague had said to her on several occasions: 'If a prioress were to be chosen out of the whole community, I would not hesitate to choose Sister Thérèse of the Child Jesus in spite of her youth. She is perfect in everything. Her only drawback is having her three sisters with her'.

From the confidences contained in Manuscript C, which was addressed to Mother Marie de Gonzague, we see a clear expression of Thérèse's sentiments towards her prioress.[b]

The child, a would-be 'postulant', who used to visit her sister, Pauline, in the parlour, must have idealised this lovable prioress whom she saw through the grille and who sent such affectionate little words to her 'Thérèsita'. Once in Carmel, Sister Thérèse, like Sister Marthe and some of the other nuns, must have had to struggle against succumbing to an all too human affection for the prioress. At fifteen, with 'a heart thirsting for love', Thérèse could have become attached to Mother Marie de Gonzague 'like a dog attached to its master'[2]. But, unfortunately, Thérèse was quickly to experience a cruel deception that resulted from the discovery of her defects, her capricious way of governing the community and, later, the sufferings inflicted on her 'little mother', Pauline, when the latter became prioress.

In 1897, still very clear-sighted and full of charity, Thérèse loved Marie de Gonzague with an almost maternal love. How could she not suffer to see her often still living on a level that was so natural (hence her veiled remonstrances)? She loved her truly, not only with a love inspired by faith — for God spoke through her — but also with a purified affection.

2. Thérèse and her sisters
Mother Agnès of Jesus

Let us again confine ourselves to a study of the relationship between the two sisters for the period that interests us.

---

b   At the end of 1895 she wrote: 'Without doubt, I loved our Mother very much, but with a pure affection which lifted me up to the Spouse of my soul!'. Mother Agnès said: 'She even told me that she truly loved Mother Marie de Gonzague and when she wrote, 'Beloved Mother' and 'Dearest Mother', which I found in the exercise book of her life, these words expressed the real feelings of her heart'. 'Dearest Mother' appears 21 times in Manuscript C and 'Beloved Mother' 39 times.

In April 1897, it seems very clear that, in the community, Mother Agnès was the one who knew her sister best. Not that Thérèse had given her a detailed step by step account of her rapid spiritual growth, but when Mother Agnès read the brown exercise book she had received on 21 January 1896 – and which moreover she had only read later – she saw her little sister's transformation. She whom she had encouraged on the way of perfection from her earliest years, whose homework and letters she had corrected, whom she had welcomed to Carmel, had become unconsciously a spiritual teacher. During Mother Agnès' term of office (February 1893 - March 1896), anyone else, except her sister, would have taken the legitimate opportunity at that time of renewing the intimacy with the one who was then 'her mother twice over'. 'Of all the sisters, she was the one I saw least of during my term of office ... I sometimes said to myself: "It is a long time since I have spoken to her!"'

Pauline's eyes were opened when she read the little exercise book of memoirs (Manuscript A). Thirteen years later she recalled her reaction: 'I said to myself: "And this blessed child, who wrote these heavenly pages, is still in our midst! I can speak to her, see her, touch her. Oh! how unknown she is here! And how I am going to appreciate her more now!"' And so the roles were gradually reversed, and Mother Agnès, in her turn, sought counsel from her daughter.

However she did not know her completely. Not only did she not know about certain depths of her being, but she was also ignorant of such an important fact in her life as the two haemoptyses of April 1896, for example. When Thérèse told her on the evening of 30 May, Mother Agnès was stunned by the bitter discovery of the extent of the disease: her sister was going to die. The older sister's reaction resulted in the writing of Manuscript C, and the later 'conversations' which she left for posterity.

When Mother Agnès obtained the prioress' permission to sit by her sick sister's bedside each day, she was thirty-six.

During her term of office, she showed her ability to govern as prioress, and had not remained under Mother Marie de Gonzague's influence as the latter had more or less consciously hoped she would: not without suffering and making concessions, she knew how to govern. But her keen sensitivity often caused her to waver. Thérèse was to do all she could to alleviate the pain of her 'little mother' who was faced with her sister's approaching death.

Sister Marie of the Sacred Heart

After Mother Agnès, the one who knew her god-child best was Sister Marie of the Sacred Heart. But what contact could she make between the little girl who used to come to her in tears to tell her about her scruples and the postulant who gently but firmly refused the help she believed she was offering her? She had spent more than three years with her in the novitiate and was in a position to judge her maturity. Was she not the one who, by her insistence, was responsible for Mother Agnès asking Thérèse to write Manuscript A? And it was at her request that Thérèse wrote her famous letter in September 1896 (Manuscript B). What confidence she must have had in her little sister's interior life! From that time she sensed the intensity that lay hidden beneath the apparent monotony of her god-child's life. But willingly, she remained discreet and in the background.

Sister Geneviève

Thérèse's relationship with Sister Geneviève, the inseparable Céline of Les Buissonnets, was quite different. Yet what a change had taken place since those years! Where was the tender intimacy they had known in the Belvedere? What had happened to the loving confidences we find in the letters of 1888-1894? When Céline, at twenty-five, entered Carmel, 14 September 1894, she was placed under her younger sister's 'strict' direction.[c] Day by day, the postulant discovered the way that her 'little Thérèse' had been following for six years. How could she not be sad at seeing herself stumbling along so far behind? An abyss seemed to separate them. When Thérèse fell seriously ill, Sister Geneviève realised that she was going to lose her surest guide, the one who was teaching her with watchful patience her 'little way' that was so suited to her whole fiery temperament. Fortunately, her work in the infirmary allowed her to continue to be near her mistress each day, and because the first infirmarian, Sister Saint-Stanislas, willingly relinquished 'her rights' with regard to the patient. Thanks to some notes that Sister Geneviève took at that time, we know how Thérèse continued her work of formation as long as she had the strength to do so.

But the *Last Conversations*, written down by Céline, hardly give us a hint of the sufferings that she caused her sister. An oral tradition in the Lisieux Carmel going back to Mother Agnès, Sister Marie of the Sacred Heart and her contemporaries tells how the novice did indeed often try the saint's patience. The little 'vinegared salad' that Thérèse speaks of in Manuscript C came from Céline. She describes it as a 'delicious feast', but at the time, it made her cry. 'And I who wanted her here so much! . . .' she said to Mother Agnès. In the infirmary, she still suffered from little negligences on the part of her infirmarian, whom she exhorted, often in vain, as we know, to be gentle, simple, humble. How is this surprising? With admirable frankness, Sister Geneviève would recount much later her weaknesses and struggles. She only entered into the spirit of her sister's way 9 October 1897, through a sudden grace of conversion that finally opened her eyes and changed her heart. Nine days after her death, Thérèse kept her promise and accomplished in a moment what she had not been able to do in three years.

c   'She was sometimes strict with the novices' (Sister Geneviève). Thérèse knew that she had this reputation. Cf. Ms.C.p.238.

3. Thérèse and her novices

In the novitiate, Thérèse enjoyed real prestige. Instinctively, all the novices who, with the exception of Sister Marie of the Trinity, were older than she, perceived their mistress' deep spiritual life. This does not mean that there were no difficulties, sudden outbursts, revolts and tearful reconciliations with the one who was not put off by these storms.

Family ties did not make her task easy. We have seen this in the case of Sister Geneviève. It was the same with her cousin Marie Guérin who became Sister Marie of the Eucharist. To be initiated into the religious life by one's former playmate when one is impulsive and also scrupulous can cause many problems. Not without difficulty, Thérèse won her cousin's confidence. In the letters that Marie wrote to her family giving them a report of Thérèse's health, we find proof of her admiration for her mistress and also of her attachment.

Sister Marthe was also faithfully devoted to Thérèse to the extent that she refused to leave the novitiate in order to stay with her. She owed not a little to the struggle that Sister Thérèse, who was eight years her junior, had made her undertake to become free from Mother Marie de Gonzague's overpowering influence. But this contrary lay-sister of 'mediocre intelligence' did not facilitate Thérèse's duty.

There were even difficuties with Sister Marie-Madeleine of the Blessed Sacrament who was 'intelligent, capable and active', but very withdrawn. She never gave her full confidence to her guide.

As for Sister Marie of the Trinity, she had come from the rue de Messine Carmel in Paris and found it hard to adapt to the Lisieux Carmel in June 1894. Her profession, 30 April 1896, was a great victory for Thérèse. Even on her sickbed, she supported, corrected and consoled her 'doll', as she sometimes called her. She was the youngest in the novitiate and when her mistress fell seriously ill she was relieved of her infirmary duties so that she would not run the risk of contracting the disease.

Sister Geneviève was not afraid to say at the Diocesan Process: 'Sister Thérèse was not spoilt in the choice of her novices; they were far from being on the way to perfection like those whom her intercession sends us today. One was really uncouth and sullen, and ignored her instructions and advice. Another was rather stupid and had no vocation to Carmel, she exhausted the Servant of God's zeal and energy, apparently in vain. A third was so difficult to train that if she remained in Carmel, it was due only to her young mistress' patience. Such was the difficult kind of ground she had to cultivate.

4. Relations with her community

As we cannot study in detail Thérèse's relationship with each of her sisters, we shall just look briefly at her position in the community in 1897.

How did she see her sisters? We have only to read attentively Manuscript C to find a very accurate description. Reflecting on fraternal charity, she asked herself how Jesus had loved his disciples: 'Ah! it was not their natural qualities which would have attracted him'.[3] In fact, in the Carmel of Lisieux these qualities were somewhat lacking. On the intellectual level, the standard was rather low. Some sisters had done some studies.[d] Several had worked as domestics or had come from their farm to Carmel.[e]

d Mother Marie de Gonzague, Mother Agnès, Sister Marie of the Sacred Heart, Sister Geneviève, Mother Hermance, Mother Marie of the Angels, Sister Thérèse of Saint-Augustine, Sister Marie of Jesus, Sister Marie of Saint-Joseph, Sister Marie of the Trinity, Sister Marie of the Eucharist. We must not forget that Thérèse herself left school at thirteen and then followed individual studies. This was in keeping with French custom in the C19th.

e Sister Saint-John the Baptist, Sister Aimée of Jesus, Sister Marguerite-Mary, Sister Marie-Madeleine.

The lack of culture, the temperamental differences and the setting did not encourage human relationships. Thérèse realised that, if one does not have 'enemies' in Carmel, there are 'feelings'. 'You feel attracted to one sister, and with regard to another, you would make a long detour to avoid meeting her. And so, even without realising it, she becomes a subject of persecution.'[4] We naturally avoid 'imperfect souls'. 'When I speak of imperfections, I am not speaking of spiritual imperfections since even the holiest souls will be perfect only in heaven; but I want to speak of the lack of judgement, up-bringing, the touchiness of certain characters, all these things which don't make life very pleasant'. Thérèse was speaking from experience. In June 1897 she no longer had any illusions, for she adds: 'I know very well that these moral infirmities are chronic, that there is no hope of a cure ...'[5]

In March 1896, Sister Marguerite-Marie was admitted as a patient to the Bon-Sauveur at Caen for the second time, and in June returned to her family. Sister Thérèse of Jesus, of Polish origin, and Sister Marie of Saint-Joseph, the neurasthenic sister in the linen room whom Thérèse wanted to help with her work, were both to leave the community in 1909. Then there was Mother Hermance of the Heart of Jesus, a difficult patient who made her infirmarians want to flee from her. If we include Sister Thérèse of Saint-Augustine who had 'the faculty of displeasing me in everything, her manner, her words, her character, everything about her seems very disagreeable to me', we see that Thérèse's natural sympathies, apart from the four members of her family, would have extended to only a few sisters. In such a setting we can also appreciate the sentiments she expressed in this reflection: 'The goods which come directly from God, inspirations of the mind and heart, profound thoughts, all these are a form of riches to which we are attached as if they were ours and which no one has the right to touch ...'[6]

If Thérèse was aware of the human condition of her community, the sisters for their part, at that time, were divided in their opinion about her. We say 'at that time'. In fact all the evidence given at the Processes has to be used with a good deal of discernment. Firstly, because these witnesses were partial.[f] Secondly, because without questioning the witnesses' sincerity, Thérèse's death and subsequent triumph had 'influenced their ideas'.[g] Without denying the interest of this evidence, we have to try to recapture the real situation of the saint according to the oldest documents that relate the contemporary facts. For after Thérèse's death many eyes were opened and genuine conversions took place. The dead sister even seems to have gone out of her way to favour in a special way those who had had little appreciation of her during her lifetime.

On the whole, the majority of the nuns held her in high regard. Thérèse knew this, and, in June, said that she was 'showered with praises'. She describes herself, not without a certain humour, as following 'the road of honours'.[7] Sister Geneviève said at the Diocesan Process that 'some of the senior nuns seeking her advice, used to go to her, like Nicodemuses, in secret'. Mother Hermance, the sick nun, had a 'high regard for her virtue' and used to correspond with 'the little Louis'. Sister Saint-John of the Cross was one who sought her good advice. Sister Marie-Emmanuel was of the same opinion as Mother Marie de Gonzague and 'would have liked her to be prioress if she were not only twenty-two'.[8]

The community was unanimous in its appreciation of Thérèse's poetical ability and talents. The pious plays that she wrote and performed had aroused the enthusiasm of the

f   Nine of the twenty-three nuns gave evidence at the Diocesan Process (1910): seven had died and three had left the convent since 1897. Eight gave evidence at the Apostolic Process.
g   Refers to Sister Saint-Vincent de Paul who changed her opinion about Thérèse. Sister Geneviève emphasised that this 'was immediately after (her) death, before outside opinion could have influenced her ideas'.

nuns. She was often asked to write little poems for special occasions.

Thérèse knew all this. If she 'was seen by the community as a religious full of faults, incapable, without understanding or judgement' she would hardly have been of use in the novitiate.[9] But at the same time she was not unaware of the reservations held by some of the sisters. In May, thinking of what good the sisters would see in her if they were asked, she said: 'One would say, 'She is a good little soul'. Another would say: 'She is very gentle, very pious, but . . .' Several would find me very imperfect, which is true'.[10] In the infirmary, Thérèse was soon to hear the echo of those reservations.

On the whole the community's attitude was positive. 'In the eyes of creatures I succeed in everything. I walk the road of honours insofar as this is possible in religious life,' she wrote in June. She compared her Carmel to a 'delightful oasis' where she lived happily under the 'motherly care' of Mother Marie de Gonzague. If she would have to leave it for the missions 'it would not be without pain', she wrote to her prioress, for 'here, I am loved by you and all the sisters, and this affection is very sweet to me'.[11]

5. Outside relationships

Outside her community, Thérèse's contacts were limited to the priest who heard her confession regularly, the extraordinary confessor, the retreat preachers, her family whom she met in the parlour and with whom she corresponded, and her two spiritual brothers who had recently come into her life.

Abbé Youf, the Carmelites' chaplain and ordinary confessor, had a high regard for Thérèse. All the evidence is unanimous on this point. But he does not seem to have played a decisive role in her spiritual evolution, nor did he even help her effectively during her trials. In April 1897, aged fifty-five, he was sick himself and feared death. He only survived his penitent by eight days.

The family group consisted of Léonie Martin, Uncle Guérin and his wife and their daughter Jeanne who was married to the doctor, Francis La Néele.

How would Léonie, who had made three unsuccessful attempts to enter religious life, not have admired the determination of Thérèse who had entered the convent at fifteen? Scarred by her difficult childhood and these repeated failures, she was living with the Guérins who surrounded her with affection. Yet for them all she remained 'that poor little Léonie'. Thérèse was the only one who encouraged her in her vocation to become a Visitandine and sent her letters worthy of a spiritual director.

The Guérin family loved the sensitive and affectionate 'little Thérèse'. But, for Uncle Isidore, the striking personality of the family was Pauline. The little youngest one appeared so shy and retiring in the parlour! She also kept up a correspondence with the La Néeles and repeatedly expressed her hope that Jeanne would one day become a mother. Francis was to look after Thérèse in the infirmary.

She had met Fr Roulland in the parlour, 3 July 1896, after his Ordination to the Priesthood and followed the progress of his apostolate in China. As for the seminarian Maurice Bellière, still not strong in his vocation, he begged his sister for help. Both held 'such a large place' in the Carmelite's life! Under Mother Marie de Gonzague's watchful control, Thérèse, whatever she herself had to say on the matter, became more and more a counsellor to these two young men.

At the end of this brief survey, we can say that, except for her three sisters, no one really knew Thérèse. It can even be said that, despite what she did say to her sisters, the

Martin sisters only knew her imperfectly. How can we be surprised at this? She had always wanted to live unknown and hidden. She succeeded. Furthermore, her contacts were reduced to a very limited circle. And so it was that, in April 1897, no one would have thought that in less than five years, this young smiling and lovable Carmelite would be known throughout the whole world.

But, the rapid progress of her illness at the end of Lent focused everyone's attention on her. Yet how could Thérèse's health have been able to deteriorate to such a serious extent without those around her noticing it sooner?

Chapter 2

Early symptoms of the disease
(June 1894 - April 1897)

'I have iron health, though the good God can break iron like clay'. (LT, 18/7/1894)

Let us examine the documents which mention explicitly Thérèse's health during this three year period.[a]

The climate of Lisieux, and in particular that of the Carmel, situated on the banks of the Orbiquet, was hardly suitable for a young adolescent who had a rather weak throat, was subject to winter colds,[b] and who had suffered earlier from 'difficulty in breathing'.[c] To an unfavourable geographical position must be added the very strict regime of the Carmelite life at the end of the C19th: the continual cold that made Thérèse suffer 'even to the point of dying from it',[1] the poor food, the prolonged fasts[d] and lack of sleep.

a   We hope that one day a doctor will make a detailed study of Thérèse's health from her birth till her death.
b   'She was sick every winter. A slight cold would bring on a high temperature and great difficulty in breathing' (Mother Agnès). This note concerned Thérèse's childhood for Mother Agnès wrote: 'Later, this passed completely. In Carmel she seldom caught a cold.'
c   'I am worried about my little Thérèse. For several months she has had difficulty in breathing that is not normal. As soon as she begins to walk a little quicker, a strange whistling sound can be heard in her chest.' (LT, 12/11/1876)
    'My little Thérèse is sick. I am worried about her. She frequently suffers from colds that cause difficulty in breathing. It usually lasts for two days.' (LT, 8/1/1887)
    Céline recounted, referring to play-time at the Abbey between 1881 and 1885: 'As a child, Thérèse could not run because she easily became short of breath.'
d   Thérèse did not fast until she was twenty-one (2 January 1894).

35

Conditions not helpful to the physical growth of a young girl between fifteen and twenty. Nevertheless, during the severe 'flu epidemic' of the winter of 1891-92 which claimed the lives of three sisters in the community, Thérèse, in the strength of her seventeen years, was almost the only one left on her feet to carry out the most arduous tasks.[2]

It was only in June 1894 — she was twenty-one and a half — that we have the first evidence that she was given medical treatment. It is possible that she had been sick before this date, as many complaints can pass unnoticed by others. 'She had a weak throat and often suffered from it,' Mother Agnès noted in 1909. 'At Carmel they are waiting to see Francis on Sunday to ask his opinion about Thérèse who has a continual sore throat, huskiness and chest problems. They would have liked Francis to examine her, but that could be rather difficult because of Dr de Cornière . . .' These lines of Marie Guérin written to her sister, Jeanne, 28 June 1894, introduce us to the two doctors who cared for Thérèse during her last illness.

Dr de Cornière was the Carmel's official physician. He was fifty-six and had given his services free to the nuns since 1886. He was a friend of Mother Marie de Gonzague and the Guérin family and had known Thérèse for a long time. He would hardly have been in favour of her entering the monastery. It is easily understandable that, when Dr Francis La Néele, thirty-six, came to the parlour to visit his cousins by marriage, the temptation was great — for Mother Agnès was prioress — to ask him to look at Thérèse. But the Martin sisters did not want to provoke any 'awkward situations'. However, it was a delicate situation and was still causing difficulties three years later.

In June 1894, Céline, who was soon to join her sisters in Carmel, was again concerned: 'Above all, take good care of yourself,' she wrote to Thérèse, 'it is a moral obligation'. The next day she received a somewhat ambiguous answer. 'But above all do not be alarmed, I am not ill, as a matter of fact,

I have iron health, though the good God can break iron like clay'.[3] Why this last phrase? Did Thérèse have a premonition of an early death? Céline must have pondered on the meaning of those sibylline words, 'Jesus will take one of us', that she had read a few lines before.

Mother Agnès in her turn told Céline: 'Sister Thérèse of the Child Jesus is no worse, but she is still subject to sore throats which flare up in the morning, and again about 8.30pm in the evening. Then her voice becomes husky. We are doing our best to care for her'. Céline was sent to help in the infirmary shortly after she entered Carmel, 14 September. According to her own account – long overdue, but as expected – she cauterised Thérèse's throat with silver nitrate.

In October, Marie Guérin expressed the concern of the family, and especially of the uncle who was a pharmacist:

I hope my little Thérèse takes care of herself. Yesterday I found her voice noticeably changed. I have spoken to Francis about her. It is absolutely necessary for her to look after herself properly. At present it is nothing serious, but it could become so at any time and then there would no longer be any cure to help her. She can very well get better now, if she takes constant care of herself. She needs, above all, frequent gargles. (I do not know what the word is,[e] it is not in the dictionary). My little Thérèse must obey the doctor's instructions. Francis specialises in these diseases.[f] I believe what he says and have confidence in him. He cured M. Féroulle of a 'very serious' complaint. He will also cure my little Thérèse ... P.S. Papa insists that Thérèse be well cared for. When I spoke to him of her he seemed worried.

e   Marie used a word from the Norman dialect, 'gillette'.
f   Dr La Néele therefore had made a diagnosis. What was this 'very serious complaint' of which M. Féroulle was cured and which could become incurable? At the time, did Francis have tuberculosis in mind? This is a simple hypothesis on our part.

The year 1895 seemed to bring an improvement. We make this simple deduction from the fact that Thérèse's health is not mentioned in the documents. No reference is made to it in Manuscript A, except perhaps in the last lines?[g] But this silence must not be taken as conclusive proof, for does not Thérèse, when she is very near death, remain very discreet about her health in her letters and last manuscript? There is another significant indication in something said to Sister Thérèse of Saint-Augustine, who recalled it in these words: "'I am going to die soon.' When Sister Thérèse said that she was enjoying perfect health.' According to this witness, Thérèse said that she was going to die 'not in a few months, but in two or three years', because 'of what was happening in (her) soul'. But we do not know if her health was as 'perfect' as it outwardly appeared.

Why then did she say in a poem given to Mother Agnès, 7 September:

Mother, Love gives me wings . . .
Soon I will fly away
Towards the eternal hills
Where Jesus deigns call me.

But to this foreign shore
Without leaving the court of heaven
I will come down to my Mother
To be her angel for her turn.

Heaven would hold no charms for me
If I could not console you
Changing your tears to smiles . . .
And share all my secrets with you . . . etc.[h]

A month later, Thérèse thanked Francis La Néele who had gone to a lot of trouble to find remedies for her. We do

g   Is this only a presentiment or is it based on symptoms she alone knew about when she wondered if the 'little flower will be picked in its youthful freshness?' (Ms A p.181).
h   This poem contains many themes found in the Last Conversations: coming down from heaven, consoling her loved ones, etc.

not know what these were, but a letter written 14-17 October 1895 shows that all was not well.

Winter passed. Thérèse observed the Lenten fast (19 February - 5 April 1896) 'in all its rigour'. 'Never had I felt so strong, and this strength remained with me until Easter'.[4] Suddenly, two nights in succession, she suffered her first 'coughing up of blood'.[5]

We know how she persuaded Mother Marie de Gonzague to let her follow all the austerities of that Good Friday. Sister Marie of the Trinity, the assistant-infirmarian, was the only one who shared her secret. Her account is as follows:

> That Good Friday she fasted on bread and water like the rest of us. Besides, she continued to take part in the house-cleaning. When I saw her washing a tiled-floor, looking so pale and worn out, I begged her to let me do her work for her, but she would not hear of it. That evening she took the discipline with us for the space of three Misereres. Then, returning exhausted to her cell, she had another 'coughing up of blood' at bedtime as she had had the night before. (Cf Christopher O'Mahony, op.cit p.243).

According to the same sister, the prioress had the patient examined by her cousin: 'The prioress, Mother Marie de Gonzague, first had her examined by Dr Francis La Néele who did not attach any great importance to this serious accident. Consequently, this prevented her from receiving the treatment and care that she needed'. The blame seems to lie on this doctor who, two years before, had diagnosed an illness that could become incurable. How could he have disregarded two serious haemoptyses? It is hard to believe that a competent doctor, warned about the possibility by a relative, would do so. Mother Agnès, perhaps, gives us the answer in her account, thirteen years later, of that visit at which she was not present. She only learnt of the haemoptyses of April 3 and 4 1896 the following year. 'She was not examined thoroughly. She put her head through the little grille in the oratory and the doctor had to make his examination like that. He was not able to make a proper assessment and said that nothing serious had happened: perhaps a small blood-vessel in the throat had broken, or even that her accident, without her even realising it, may have come from her nose.'

This is undoubtedly the explanation for Dr La Néele's attitude. Under these circumstances and conditions (could it still be called an 'examination'?) he was not able to estimate the danger. Thérèse does not seem to have helped very much. We have only to read Manuscript C (written two years later) to find evidence of 'something like a *bubbling stream* mounting to my lips' that she had *'coughed up'*. These underlined words rule out the possibility of a small broken blood-vessel in the throat and still less of a nose-bleed.[i] At the oratory grille, the patient must not have used these words which would have alerted any doctor.

Mother Agnès wrote: 'When pressed with questions, she admitted that she had suffered very much from hunger during the whole of Lent, in the evenings after Matins'. She thought, she said, that everyone suffered like that from the fast. She had a swollen gland in the neck that the doctor attributed to weakness.

In June, a simple phrase in one of Sister Marie of the Sacred Heart's letters is precious, despite its brevity: 'Sister Thérèse of the Child Jesus is not worse, on the contrary'. This clearly shows that she was not well. In fact, 'a little persistent dry cough' tired Thérèse 'during the course of the summer' and caused pains 'in the chest'. She received treatment. In July: 'Very often she is still a bad colour. She no

i   In some cases the patient begins to cough, a warm liquid rises to the throat and the blood spurts out in such a way that the tubercular patient does not feel that he or she is spitting, but rather vomiting blood. Dr Dieulafoy, *Manuel de pathologie interne*, Masson et Cie, diteurs, 1897 p.297.

longer has chest pains, and has stopped coughing. There is certainly an improvement'. And Sister Marie of the Eucharist adds: 'Our Mother looks after her so well that this is not surprising'.

Nine days later, the patient herself confirmed the good news to Léonie: 'You ask me about my health. As for that, darling Sister, I no longer cough at all. Are you satisfied?' One hopes that she was, for the next phrase, still enigmatic, would surely have upset her: 'This will not stop the good God taking me when he will'.[6]

On 15 July, if we accept this humorous account as evidence, there must have been a brief examination by Dr de Cornière: 'If I tell you that I am in marvellous health, you won't believe me, so I shall let the famous Dr de Cornière speak for me. I had the signal honour of being presented to him in the parlour yesterday. This illustrious person, after having honoured me with a glance, declared that I looked well! . . .'. Thérèse, always ready with a witty retort or joke when it comes to doctors, does not say any more.

Was this the same visit that Sister Marie of the Trinity spoke of? Nevertheless, her cough persisted, and Dr de Cornière came about July in the following year. He also said that it was nothing serious for the present. He prescribed tonics, used a cauterising remedy, 'pointes de feu', to relieve the pains in her side and ordered massages to help the circulation.[j] 'She was given meat for a few weeks', Mother Agnès added.

---

j   All this is not very clear. It is difficult to see why all this treatment was prescribed when the cough had stopped and there was an improvement. It is extremely hard to set down the treatments Thérèse received in 1896 and at the beginning of 1897. The evidence at the Process was given twelve or fifteen years after it had happened. A study of the prescriptions would be interesting, but, in Thérèse's case, they were not all written down. Some are missing. However, we can follow fairly clearly the main stages of the disease.

During the severe winter of 1896, Mother Marie de Gonzague 'ordered' Thérèse to use a foot-warmer heated by live coals to keep her alpagates warm.[7]

In November, when the question was raised about Sister Thérèse's departure for a Carmel in Indochina, a Novena was begun to Blessed Théophane Vénard to obtain 'her complete cure'. At the time, she was attending all community exercises, even Matins. But, 'precisely during the Novena' she started coughing again. From that time 'I've gone from bad to worse', Thérèse told Mother Agnès in May 1897.[8]

This corresponds with a letter of Sister Marie of the Eucharist to her father where she mentions having visited a sick nun in her cell who had been given a vesicatory 'the evening before'. Written in a humorous vein, (the sick nun's name is not given, she is referred to only as the 'church-mouse' as she seemed so poor), it is already a health report like those of 1897. We see here Thérèse (for everything points to her) eating a plate of veal offered by the Guérin family. Sister Geneviève had reason to write, 10 January 1897, to Brother Simeon: 'We are very concerned about her weak chest'.

Lent began 3 March. Very weakened, Thérèse tried to follow the community exercises to the limit of her strength. 'She confided to me that often during the office she had to do violence to herself to recite the psalms and remain standing, and that, tempted to go out, she encouraged herself with these words: "If I die, someone will see it."' (Words of a soldier going to capture an enemy flag).[k] But Thérèse could not keep going under these conditions. Before the end of Lent, she fell seriously ill. This would have been at the beginning of April. Is it not symbolic that the first letter that mentions Thérèse's last illness was dated precisely

k   Sister Marie of the Trinity.

42

4 April, Passion Sunday,[1] and the anniversary of her first haemorrhage?

Only this Passion was to last much longer than the liturgical time. It would continue for exactly one hundred and eighty days.

From that date, Thérèse could no longer continue as if her illness did not exist. The sisters had grown accustomed to seeing her pale, to her long coughing fits.[m] Now she would become more and more separated from community life, living in her cell, then in the infirmary. Her life as a Carmelite – at least exteriorly – would consist in being sick.

But who was this nun living in isolation? Without claiming to pierce the well-guarded secret of her profound personality, we can at least, thanks to her own writings, trace the main stages of her spiritual growth from 1895, and so be in a position to understand better her deepest sentiments at the time when she became that seriously ill person.

[1]   Sister Marie of the Eucharist postdated her letter by one day.
[m]   One day, she was seized during the meal by a fit of violent coughing. The Mother Prioress, tired of listening to her, said rather sharply: 'Go out, Sister Thérèse of the Child Jesus.' We do not know at what period in Thérèse's life this incident occurred.

Chapter 3

'How she is unknown here!'

Let us follow Thérèse in what she herself called her 'giant's course'[1] from the last months of 1894 until April 1897.

This period has been chosen, not at random, but for several reasons. Firstly, because it corresponds approximately with the first symptoms of the disease that we have just summarised. Now, during this thirty-month period Thérèse's presentiments became a conviction: she was soon going to die. During these thirty months a series of important graces enabled her to climb a steep and rapid road. Immense desires were born within her. More and more she had but one goal: To love Jesus to folly, to make him loved, to die of love for him.

Then, during this time – from the end of 1894 till the beginning of 1895 – she discovered the scriptural basis for her little way thanks to Céline's note-book of biblical texts. Her basic intuitions confirmed by scripture, Thérèse could now go forward.

Finally, the year 1895 was an exceptional year in her life. It was a year of plenitude, a year of graces. It was indeed providential that Mother Agnès, at Sister Marie of the Sacred Heart's suggestion, had ordered Thérèse to write down her childhood memories precisely that year. Having reached this summit, she could look back and see her life in the light of God's Merciful Love. Yet, when she put the points of suspension on page 84 of her manuscript, she had not reached the end of her course.

In the pages that follow, we have decided against classifying and grouping together in logical themes Thérèse's aspirations and sentiments. On the one hand, we would have had to cover the same ground several times. On the other, we would have impoverished the 'theresian élan' which becomes progressively more profound, fired as it is by the same intertwining passionate desires. It is better to proceed like Thérèse and follow the course of time, even if it entails repeating the same themes at each stage, just as they come up in her correspondence, her manuscripts, her poems, her plays, or in the evidence of her companions. What does it matter if we experience a certain surfeit ... The result will show that this young girl was not merely repeating pious formulae, but was expressing completely her whole being which was thirsting for love. We will see the approach of death for a weakened body, but also and above all, the impetuous rush of a lover towards her Beloved who gives way to her searching.[a]

We are dividing this spiritual journey from 1895 till 1897 into four main stages.

1. From the scriptural confirmation of the little way to the act of oblation to love (End 1894 - 9/14 June 1895)

Since her discovery in Céline's note-book of Old Testament texts which gave the scriptural basis for her 'way of confidence and love', Thérèse advanced swiftly and joyfully along her road. At the beginning of that year, a year so rich in diverse graces, she was asked to write her Memoirs. She would soon set down her 'thoughts on the graces that God had given her'.

a   Thérèse had wanted to write a commentary on the Song of Songs. (Sister Marie of the Trinity's evidence at the Apostolic Process). This is a normal attraction for a mystic, but says much for Thérèse's maturity.

I find myself at a period in my life when I can look back over the past. My soul has matured in the crucible of exterior and interior trials. Now, like a flower strengthened by the storm, I can raise my head and see the words of Ps 22 realised in me. (Ms A p.15)

In December 1894 - January 1895, Thérèse also wrote her third play which she performed successfully for the community 21 January, taking the role of Joan of Arc. Thirty months later, she would say to Mother Agnès: 'I have re-read the play that I wrote on Joan of Arc. You will see in it my thoughts on death; they are all there'.[2] That play therefore requires attentive reading. In taking the leading role, Thérèse identified herself with her heroine. In writing it, she 'foretold'[b] her own end, her agony, death and victory.

Faced with death, faced with martyrdom, Joan in her prison appears at first overwhelmed ('to die at twenty!') and abandoned by all. As a counterpoint to each of her plaints, the Archangel Gabriel puts before her an episode of Christ's passion. Joan takes courage: 'Oh! how consoled I am to see that my agony resembles that of my Saviour . . .' However her attitude appears to be more one of resignation than of voluntary acceptance. In her turn, St.Catherine comes to console her, quoting a long passage from the Book of Wisdom on the death of the just man, and in particular, of the just man who dies prematurely.

Transformed, the prisoner rises up and cries out:

I accept martyrdom, Lord, for love of you
And I no longer fear death or fire
For my soul aspires to you, Jesus.
My one desire is to see you, my God,
To take up my cross and follow you, my Saviour.
I ask only to die for love of you.

b   Where does the border between consciousness and unconsciousness lie in the projection of desire and the foretelling of future events?

I want to die that I might begin to live —
I want to die to be one with Jesus.

She accepts to wear a white robe to her execution: 'It seems to me that by wearing it, I will resemble my Beloved Saviour more closely'.

Thérèse therefore described Joan of Arc's passion as an identification with the passion of Christ. She herself, in the months that were to follow, hardly took her eyes from the Crucified.

About a month later, 26 February, Thérèse composed spontaneously fifteen verses during a day when there was Exposition of the Blessed Sacrament. This reveals an impetus that she received from an exceptional inspiration. It was moreover the first time that she had written a poem without being asked to do so. Without any doubt, Thérèse's deepest aspirations were expressed in the poem '*Vivre d'Amour*',[c] as we can see by the following two verses:

To die of love is sweet martyrdom indeed
It is the one I wish to suffer.
O Cherubims! tune up your lyres . . .
For I know that my exile will soon be over . . .
Flame of Love, consume me unceasingly.
Passing life, your burden weighs heavy upon me! . . .
O Jesus, make my dream come true:
    To die of Love! . . .

My hope is to die of Love when at last
    my chains shall be broken.
God will be my reward, for I want no
    other gifts of his love.
I want to be set on fire with his love.
I want to see him, to be one with him forever.
This is heaven for me . . . this is my destiny:
To live for Love!

---

c   This poem was to have a glorious destiny and would be regarded as the theresian manifesto. Numerous copies were made and sent to Abbé Bellière, to Brother Simeon in Rome, to Dr de Cornière etc.

'I know that my exile will soon be over ...' This 'know' seems to us to be a kind of presentiment, a spiritual intuition, that agrees with the already cited testimony of Sister Thérèse of Saint-Augustine: 'What I experience in my soul makes me feel my exile is nearly over'.

Yes, something was happening in Thérèse's soul. In a letter written to Léonie during these months, she acknowledges 'the lights Jesus gives (her)',[3] and reassures her sister who was still wavering in her vocation. On the same day, she gave Céline a poem for her birthday. Lyrically, and at length, she recalled their childhood together. Was she speaking of Céline? Or was it Thérèse? When reading this verse of the poem, one would be inclined to say it was the latter.

> I will sing with the angels,
> These praises of sacred love ...
> May I soon soar up to join their ranks.
> O Jesus, may I die one day
> Of love!

June 9 of the following year marked a decisive moment in the theresian story. On Trinity Sunday, during Mass, she was inspired to offer herself to Merciful Love. The next Tuesday, June 11, kneeling with Sister Geneviève in front of the Virgin of the Smile, she recited the prayer she had composed. Of that important event we shall include here only that section of the Offering which refers to her ardent desire for martyrdom and to die of love:

> In order to live in one single act of perfect Love, I OFFER MYSELF AS A SACRIFICIAL VICTIM TO YOUR MERCIFUL LOVE, asking you to consume me incessantly, allowing the waves of infinite tenderness within you to overflow into my soul, and that thus I may become a MARTYR of Your LOVE, O my God! ... May this MARTYRDOM, after having prepared me to appear before you, finally cause me to die and may my soul take its flight without any delay into the eternal embrace of YOUR MERCIFUL LOVE. (John Clarke, *Story of a Soul*, p.276).

Three days after this lyrical and passionate offering, Thérèse, in the choir, received a great grace:

> I was just beginning the Way of the Cross when suddenly I was seized with such a violent love for God that I can't explain it except by saying it was as if I had been totally plunged into fire. Oh! What fire and what sweetness at the same time! I was on fire with love, and I felt that one moment, one second more, and I wouldn't have been able to sustain this ardour without dying. I understood, then, what the saints were saying about these states which they experience so often. As for me, I experienced it only once and for a single moment, then fell back immediately into my habitual state of dryness. (Last Conversations, 7.7.2).

Let us note that it was *while she was making the Way of the Cross* that the seal of acceptance was seemingly placed on her offering by this fire. Thérèse was to live in hope. Death was going to come. She would die of love. But when?

'Ever since I was young, God gave me the feeling that I would die young', Thérèse told Mother Agnès 13 July 1897.[4] Five days later, she wrote to Abbé Bellière: 'I have never asked God to let me die young. It would have seemed to me cowardice. But *from my childhood* (the emphasis is ours) he has given me the deep conviction that my course here would be brief'.[5] We must not forget that it was about this time that she saw in the stem broken close to the roots a symbol of her life. She thought that the good God 'seems to be saying by this that he'll soon break the bonds of his little flower, he will not allow her to fade away on this earth!'[6] Presentiments, or physical symptoms that we do not know about?

2. From the act of oblation to the entrance into 'the tunnel' (June 1895 - April 1896)

On 12 August, Thérèse gave Sister Marie of the Trinity a poem for her twenty-first birthday: *'Mon Ciel ici-bas'*, later published under the title *'Cantique à la Sainte Face'*.

Oh! to console you I wish
To live uknown on this earth!
Your beauty that you know how to hide
Unveils all its mystery to me
To you I wish to soar aloft! ...

The young and laughing Marie of the Trinity would scarcely have wanted to 'soar aloft' at that time! So it is necessary to say something about these poems and plays that so often may provoke a smile.

The sisters who asked Thérèse to compose verses for various occasions, (a birthday, feast, reception of the habit, liturgical feast, etc.) were not able to know that they were thereby forcing the saint, at a crucial time in her life, to cast her interior fire into a ridiculous mould. The result, which seemed to them 'delightful' or 'sweet', because Thérèse couched her thought in the pious religious clichés of her day, in reality concealed burning confidences. Thérèse never lied, and at each stage of her interior adventure she put her whole heart and soul into these verses.[d] To the sisters, who were in admiration of her poetical talents, 'To die of love' may have seemed simply a pious allegory. But the one who wrote it meant it literally. The facts we shall now relate prove it. Far from disregarding these poetical efforts, (and some of them are not without literary merit), we attach great importance to them. These verses hold secrets that we can decipher, thanks to the historical evidence. If we read them in the order in which they were written, we can follow the theresian ascent, her aspiration towards death, that is, towards Divine Life.

Marie Guérin entered Carmel 15 August and found herself placed under her cousin's direction. The latter gave her a

---

d   The proof is that during her illness her poems would spontaneously come to her lips: she sings them or recites a verse which fits the situation. Vivre d'amour; 5.8.7, 14.9.2. Jésus mon Bien-Aim; 2.8.4. Pourquoi je t'aime, Marie; 10.6, 23.8.2, 11.7.1, 23.8.9.

little poem expressing the postulant's sentiments. In fact, it was a programme of life worthy of an experienced Carmelite. We hear in it, above all, the voice of Thérèse:

> Jesus, in Carmel I wish to live
> Since your love has called me to this oasis.
> There I wish to follow you,
> To love you, to love you and to die ...

In October, Thursday 17 to be precise, an unexpected event crowned Thérèse's joy: the prioress, Mother Agnès gave her a spiritual brother, Abbé Maurice Bellière, a seminarian. One of her great and seemingly impossible desires was fulfilled: to have a brother a priest. Overjoyed, she immediately wrote a prayer of thanksgiving and petition for her brother:[e] 'O Jesus, I thank you for granting one of my greatest desires: to have a brother a priest and an apostle ... you know, Lord, that my one ambition is to make you known and loved; now my desire will be realised'.

Sister Marie of the Sacred Heart received later a poem bearing her name which had inspired it. When she read it at the time did she see the secret contained in the last verse?

> To contemplate your glory
> I know I must pass through fire,
> And I choose for my purgatory
> Your *burning* love, O Heart of my God.
> My exiled soul, on leaving this life,
> Would want to make an act of perfect love
> And then, taking flight to its heavenly Fatherland,
> Enter your Heart, without any detour!!!

More important still is the long poem of thirty-three verses, based on the theme: '*Jésus, rappelle-toi*!' that Thérèse wrote

---

e Eighteen months later, she would tell Mother Marie de Gonzague: 'It would be impossible to put my happiness into words ... I felt that this part of my soul was renewed. It was as if someone had struck for the first time musical strings which had been left forgotten till then.' (Ms C p.251)

at Céline's request. It is impossible here to give it the detailed exegesis it deserves. With reluctance, we shall have to be content to just mention Thérèse's thirst for love (verse 25), to live by faith (verse 27), to love with Christ's own heart (verse 33), and, of course, to die a martyr, to die of love:

> Remember, Jesus, Word of Life,
> That you loved me unto death.
> I also want to love you unto folly,
> I also want to live for you ...
> You know, O my God, that I desire only
> To make you known and one day to be a martyr ...
> Grant my desire, O my Divine King,
> Make me die of love.

It was about this time that the Carmelite finished writing Manuscript A and it obviously contains the same aspirations. Each word in these final lines must be weighed:

> And now I have no other desire but to *love* Jesus unto folly. I no longer desire suffering or death, and still I love them both; it is love alone that attracts me. I desired them for a long time; I possessed suffering and believed I had reached the shores of heaven, that the little flower would be gathered in the springtime of her life.[f] Now, abandonment alone guides me. I have no other compass!.[7]

Thérèse therefore had wanted to die,[g] she had believed that she would die ... then she no longer seemed sure. She abandoned herself. She loved:

> My dearest Mother, you allowed me, to offer myself to God in this way (9 June 1895) and you know the rivers or rather the oceans of graces which have flooded my soul. Ah! since that happy day, it seems to me that *Love* penetrates and surrounds me, that at each moment this *Merciful Love* is

f   When did Thérèse believe that? We can only hypothesise.

g   'I have never asked God to die young; it is true I have always hoped that this would be his will.' (Ms C p.215). Text written beginning June 1897.

renewing me, purifying my soul and not leaving any trace of sin in it, and I have no fear of purgatory. (Ms A p.181)

She ends with a query:

How will this 'Story of a little white flower' end? Perhaps the little flower will be plucked in her youthful freshness or else transplanted to other shores ... I don't know, etc. (ibid)

The year 1895 ended with this admission of ignorance.

By January 20 of the following year, Thérèse had completed a substantial amount of writing. For the traditional feast of Saint Agnes, the prioress received the exercise book of memoirs, a poem, (*Les Répons de Sainte Agnès*), and a play that was performed in her honour entitled, '*The Flight into Egypt*'. This latter is the story of some likeable robbers, told in fanciful language, who were completely ignorant of the true God, but who were converted when they met the Holy Family, and their child was cured of leprosy.

Another great joy came to Thérèse, 24 February, when her Céline made her profession, and received the veil on 17 March. On the evening of the same day, Marie Guérin received the habit. Everything was working out for their young novice mistress: one by one all her desires were being granted. Was not this living proof that her great aspirations − to love Jesus, to die of love − would one day be fulfilled? After having known years of trials, her spiritual road was becoming clearer.

But the first cloud appeared in that serene sky 21 March 1896. Amazed, Thérèse learnt of Mother Marie de Gonzague's difficult election.[h] The latter entrusted her with the novitiate under the conditions that we already know.

Several days later, during Holy Week, the young Mistress 'coughed up blood' twice. For anyone else, these two

h After seven ballots.

haemoptyses would have seemed a disaster. Not so for Thérèse, she rejoiced. That red handkerchief announced her approaching death. We must re-read the text in which, fourteen months later, she described the event. When recalling the details, Thérèse experienced the same joy:

> Oh! how sweet this memory is to me! . . . I thought that perhaps I was going to die and my soul was flooded with joy. However, as our lamp was out, I told myself I would have to wait until morning to be certain of my good fortune, for it seemed to me that it was blood that I had coughed up. The morning was not long in coming. When I awoke, I thought immediately that I had something cheerful to learn, and so I went to the window. I could see that I was not mistaken. Ah! my soul was filled with great consolation; I was interiorly persuaded that Jesus, on the anniversary of his own death, wanted to have me hear his first call. *It was like a sweet and distant murmur which announced the Bridegroom's arrival.* (Ms C p.210)[i]

Before she experienced such moments, she had already reached the summit. Mistress of herself, detached from her lot, ready to die, she was, above all, stretching forward towards the encounter. But events had to take their course. Calvary was still a silhouette in the distance. Her going up to Jerusalem began only with a sudden and unexpected trial – the entrance into darkness at the very moment when the Church celebrates the light of the Risen Christ.

> At the time I was enjoying a faith that was so living and clear, that the thought of heaven filled me with happiness, and I was unable to believe there were really impious people who had no faith. I believed they were speaking against their own innner convictions when they denied the existence of heaven, that beautiful heaven where God himself wanted to be their Eternal Reward. During those very joyful days of the Easter season,

---

i These lines reveal Thérèse perfectly, her courage, her simplicity, and above all, her authenticity. What novelist would have dared invent these details to extol his hero? (After 'coughing up blood' in the dark, went to bed and *slept?*)

Jesus made me feel that there were really souls who have no faith, and who, through the abuse of grace, lose this precious treasure, the source of the only real and pure joys. He allowed my soul to be invaded by the thickest darkness, and the thought of heaven, which up until then had been so sweet to me, to be only a cause of struggle and torment. This trial was to last not a few days or a few weeks, it would end only at the hour set by God himself and ... this hour has not yet come. I would like to be able to put into words what I feel, but alas! I believe this is impossible. One would have to travel through this dark tunnel to understand its darkness. (Ms C p.211)

Thérèse would try however – in June 1897 – to describe her trial with the help of images:

When I want to rest my heart, wearied by the darkness which surrounds it, by the memory of the luminous country to which I aspire, my torment redoubles; it seems to me that the darkness, borrowing the voice of sinners, says mockingly to me; 'You are dreaming about the light, about a country fragrant with the sweetest perfumes; you are dreaming about the *eternal* possession of the Creator of all these things; you believe that one day you will walk out of this fog which surrounds you! Dream on, dream on; rejoice in death which will give you not what you hope for, but even deeper night, the night of nothingness'. (Ms C p.213)

She preferred not to continue this description of the darkness that obscured her soul for, she said: 'I fear I might blaspheme ... I fear that I have already said too much'. (ibid)

We can never stress too much the place this trial had in the last months of Thérèse's life. The great majority of the sisters remained unaware of this secret Passion. Even those who did know of it did not suspect its intensity. What a contrast there was between that little girl who wrote such loving poetry, and that abyss of darkness that made her contemporary with the atheists of her century. She was aware of this situation herself:

I may perhaps appear to you to be exaggerating my trial. In fact, if you go by the sentiments I express in my little poems composed this year, I must appear to you as a soul filled with consolations and one for whom the veil of faith is almost torn aside. It is no longer a veil for me, it is a wall which reaches right up to the heavens and hides the starry firmament. When I sing of the happiness of heaven, of the eternal possession of God, I feel no joy in this, for I sing simply what I WANT TO BELIEVE. (Ms C p.214)

We must understand clearly that Thérèse, when she wrote those lines, had been living in the tunnel fourteen months. She had pondered deeply on this trial of dereliction; she understood that it was a purification for herself[j] and a means of redemption for 'sinners' with whom she shared the 'bread of sorrow'. But it was only April 1896. We must try to imagine what it would have been like for her to suddenly find herself in darkness after the waves of light of the preceeding months. Who could help her when she did not dare express her thoughts fully? How could she still hope 'to die of love' when she was like one thrust down into hell? Where was her Beloved leading her? Had he deceived her? For the first time were her hopes going to be ridiculed? Thérèse could not not ask herself these questions. She had not yet reached the stage when she would see her trial 'as a great grace'.

3. From the entrance into darkness to the discovery of her vocation (April - September 1896)

On 10 May, a dream restored her confidence. The Foundress of Carmel in France, Anne of Jesus, assured her of the affection of the inhabitants of heaven. Thérèse expressed her preoccupation in a spontaneous question: 'Oh Mother! I beg you, tell me whether God will leave me for a long time on

---

j   'Now it (this trial) is taking away everything that could be a natural satisfaction in my desire for heaven'. (Ms C p.214)

earth. Will he soon come to get me?' The reply pleased her: 'Yes, soon, soon, I promise you'.[k]

A second typically theresian question followed: 'Is God pleased with me?' 'He is pleased, very pleased!'[8]

Twenty days later, there was another consoling sign. Mother Marie de Gonzague gave Thérèse a second spiritual brother, Fr Roulland of the Foreign Missions of Paris. The Carmelite saw herself confirmed in her desire to sacrifice herself, and pray for missionaries and the people who were to receive the Good News. The next day, 31 May, Trinity Sunday, she gave to her novice who bore that name a poem that does not need any commentary:

> ... My Beloved, take my whole life.
> I want to suffer, I want to die for you ...
>
> Lord, you have told us yourself:
> 'Greater love hath no man
> Than to give his life for those he loves',
> And you, O Jesus, are the One
> I love above all others.
>
> It is late, already it is evening,
> Come and guide me, Lord, along my way,
> With your cross I am climbing the hill,
> Stay with me, Pilgrim from Heaven.
>
> Your Love is my only martyrdom.
> The more I feel it burn within me
> The more does my soul desire you ...
> Jesus make me die of Love for you!!! ...

Whatever the reasons, or the occasions surrounding the composition, all the poems of May, June and July 1896

---

k   Let us note this adverb 'soon' that Thérèse uses. From this time it will reappear frequently in her poems and correspondence to refer to her departure. This dream had a lasting influence. She spoke of it again in May 1897, and had Mother Anne of Jesus' relics in the infirmary.

develop the same themes: an intense desire to love, to die of love, to save souls through the hidden life. Sometimes there is a brief allusion to the trial of faith, as in 'Mon ciel à moi' (7/6/1896). For the feast of the Sacred Heart, Thérèse wrote *'Ce que je verrai bientôt pour la première fois!'* For Fr Roulland's Ordination, Sunday 28 June, there was another poem *'Jeter des Fleurs!'* which, after extolling the salvation brought to sinners, ends with the following:

I will soon be in heaven
Strewing flowers with the little angels.

It was also most probably at this time that she wrote a prayer of 'Consecration to the Holy Face' — that hidden Face, that veiled Face[1] — in which she expressed her desire to slake 'the thirst of love' of the Condemned and to give him 'souls, especially souls of apostles and martyrs, so that through them, we might inflame with your love the multitude of sinners'.

For the feast of Our Lady of Mount Carmel, she dedicated a poem about the missions to the Virgin, (having Fr Roulland in mind):

You have united me forever
To a missionary's work
By the bonds of prayer,
Suffering, and love.

I crave for suffering,
I love and desire the Cross.
To help save a single soul
I would die a thousand times! ...

That same 16 July, she heard Abbé Lechêne mention in his sermon the possibility of persecution: 'He seemed to us

---

1 A theme dear to Thérèse which keeps recurring in her letters: the hidden face of Jesus, veiled during his Passion like her father's in the vision at Les Buissonnets (Ms A p.45). Source of Thérèse's desire to be hidden like Jesus. cf LT 18/7/1890; 7/9/1890; 8/9/1890; 19/10/1892; 20/2/1893; 23/7/1893; 2/8/1893; 24/2/1896; 9/1/1897; etc.

already poised for martyrdom'.[9] During these months of 1896 this idea of martyrdom seemed to haunt Thérèse. 'Martyrdom was the dream of my youth and this dream has grown with me within Carmel's cloisters . . .'[10] she was soon to write. In fact, the hazards of the policy against the Religious Congregations was such that, at times, the Carmelites could have easily believed that they might shed their blood. In September, in a passionate search for her vocation, Thérèse expressed the desire for martyrdom at the apex of her many desires. 'But above all, my Beloved Saviour, I would shed my blood for you even to the very last drop'.[11] That same month she was overjoyed when she heard a talk on the sixteen Carmelites of Compiègne by Mgr de Teil,[m] the postulator for their cause of Beatification. But Thérèse knew the teaching of traditional theology: 'Martyrdom of the heart is no less fruitful than the shedding of blood'.[12]

It was time for the annual retreat. Thérèse was to receive positive lights on her vocation. Thanks to her god-mother's insistence, she wrote the famous letter that was to become Manuscript B.

A new stage. What is striking in this text — a jewel of spiritual literature — are the writer's pressing questions. One would say that she never rested, she was ever searching, never satisfied. A saint had assured her that God was pleased with her and that her life would be short. Anyone else would have

---

m   In 1909 Mgr de Teil would become vice-postulator for Thérèse's beatification cause. 'Once she came to me, her face radiant, and said: "Our Mother just told me of the persecution raging on all sides against religious communities . . . What joy! God will answer the most beautiful dream of my life! . . . When I think that we are living in the age of martyrs! . . ." ' (Sister Marie of the Trinity).
During her pilgrimage to Italy, inside the Colosseum, Thérèse had asked for the grace of martyrdom and had 'felt in the depths of her heart that (her) prayer had been heard'. (Ms A p.130) Same desire reading the life of Théophane Vénard 21/11/1896: 'Martyrdom! . . . It has been the dream of my youth . . .' cf. also Profession note 8/9/1890.

been satisfied with that. But these signs were not sufficient for her. Her very vocation was not enough: 'To be your *Spouse*, to be a *Carmelite*, and by my union with you, to be the *Mother* of souls, should this not be enough for me? And yet it is not so . . .'[13] After enumerating all the vocations that attracted her, warrior, priest, deacon, apostle, doctor, martyr, she finally found herself meditating on a passage from Saint Paul:

> At last my mind was at rest. *Charity* gave me the key to my *vocation*. I understood that LOVE CONTAINED ALL VOCATIONS, THAT LOVE WAS EVERYTHING, THAT IT EMBRACED ALL TIME AND ALL PLACES . . . IN A WORD, THAT IT WAS ETERNAL! Then, in the excess of my ecstatic joy, I cried out: O Jesus, my Love . . . At last I have found my *vocation*, . . . MY VOCATION IS LOVE! Yes, I have found my place in the Church and it is you, O my God,who have given me this place. In the heart of the Church, my Mother, I shall be *love*. Thus I shall be everything, and thus my dream will be fulfilled'. (Ms B p.194)

The inspiration and lyricism contained in this pen-line is exceptional. She finished with a synthesis of the little way, and once again expressed the already asserted hope of becoming the prey of Love.[n]

Happily (for us), the recipient answered her god-daughter immediately and asked for a further explanation. In the letter of 17 September, a real continuation of Manuscript B, Thérèse clearly explains her thought. She only taught what she was living: 'My *desires* for martyrdom *are nothing*, they do not give me the boundless confidence I feel in my heart. What pleases God . . . is to see me love *my littleness and poverty, the blind hope I have in his mercy*. It is trust, and nothing but trust that must bring us to Love . . . Since we see the *way*, let us run together!'[14]

In that way, Thérèse was to continue to run.

n   Ms B. p.187. 'This retreat which will perhaps be the last', wrote Thérèse at the beginning of her letter to Sister Marie of the Sacred Heart.

4. From manuscript B to the last relapse
(September 1896 - April 1897)

During the month of November when the winter was very severe, Thérèse fell ill. She would not be leaving for the Saigon Carmel. Her zeal for the foreign missions was no less ardent:

> We must help the apostles
> By our prayers and love.
> Their battle-fields are ours,
> Each day we struggle for them.

L'Ame d'un Missionnaire which Fr Roulland had sent her, and above all the life of Théophane Vénard that she had read, as well as her correspondence with her spiritual brothers, had enkindled Thérèse's missionary fervour. In the room where she worked, she had pinned onto the wall the map of Su-Tchuen, Fr Roulland's mission station. She assured him of her close collaboration through prayer and sacrifice. 'I am your little Moses'.[15] She asked for him 'the incomparable favour of martyrdom' and, for herself, the increase 'in her heart of the desire to love (Jesus) and to make him loved'.

She reminded Abbé Bellière who was only at the formation stage that a 'Carmelite who was not an apostle would be losing sight of the goal of her vocation and would cease to be a daughter of the seraphic Saint Teresa who would have given a thousand lives to save a single soul'.[16]

At the beginning of the last year of her life, Thérèse confided to Sister Geneviève that she expected to die that year. Once again, a poem allows us to know her deepest sentiments at that period of her life. For Mother Agnès she set down the reasons for her joy. We find once again her apostolic desire:

> My joy is to struggle unceasingly
> That I might give birth to the elect.

the desire for death:

> For a long time now I have wished to live,
> Lord, if that would please you,
> In heaven where I would follow you,
> If that would give you pleasure.

but especially abandonment in love:

> Love, that fire of the Fatherland,
> Does not cease to consume me.
> What is life or death to me?
> Jesus, I find my joy in loving you ...

The letter that this young girl of twenty-four wrote to the old brother Simeon (eighty-three years old) contains a clear declaration: 'I think my course here below will be short ... If Our Lord comes for me first, I promise to pray for your intentions'.[17] She adds her usual prayer: 'One thing I beg you to ask for my soul is the grace to love Jesus and *make him loved* as much as this is possible for me to do.'[o]

At the beginning of February, Thérèse wrote a poem without being asked to do so. *A Théophane Vénard* expresses her friendship for the thirty-one year old martyr who was to be her inseparable companion during those last months. Since she had read his letters, everything about him attracted her; his youth, his martyrdom at Tonkin, but even more, his soul, his sentiments, especially his cheerfulness: 'My soul is like his'. 'I have read Théophane Vénard's life which interested and moved me more than I can say, as a result I have written some verses which are quite personal.' She expressed her desire to go to the missions, 'if God calls me there one day ...' and above all, like Théophane, to be 'gathered up' 'soon'.

Another young saint attracted her attention: St Stanislaus Kostka, a novice of the Society of Jesus. He was the subject

---

o   Same wish, repeated twice, in letter to Abbé Bellière 24/2.

of her last play and she projected her own aspirations into this historical character who became her mouth-piece:

Oh! how happy I am ... soon I will contemplate Jesus no longer under the appearance of a weak child but in all the splendour of his glory ... I have no regrets about anything on earth, but I do have one desire, a desire so great that I could not be happy in heaven if it were not fulfilled. Tell me, Mary, if the blessed can still work for the salvation of souls. If I cannot work in paradise for the glory of Jesus, I prefer to remain in exile and go on still fighting for him!

The Virgin answered in the affirmative. Then he asked her 'if he could return to earth' and 'protect those still fighting'. Another affirmative reply was given.

It is not difficult to see here Thérèse's desire which was to be repeated more frequently from this time until her death. On 24 February, she wrote to Bellière:

You have promised to pray for me *all your life*. No doubt it will be longer than mine: and you are not allowed to sing with me: 'It is my hope, my exile will be short!' But neither are you allowed to forget your promise. If the Lord takes me soon to himself, I ask you to continue saying the same little prayer daily, for in heaven I shall want the same thing as on earth: to love Jesus and make all love him. Monsieur l'Abbé, you must find me very strange. Perhaps you regret having a sister who seems so anxious to go off and enjoy eternal rest, leaving you to work on alone ... But you need not worry, the only thing I desire is God's will, and I confess that if I could no longer work for his glory in heaven, I should prefer exile to the Homeland. I do not know what will happen, but if Jesus brings to pass what I feel lies before me, I promise to remain your little sister up above. Our union, far from being broken, will be closer than ever; then there will be no more enclosure, no more grille and my soul can fly to the remotest missions. Our roles will still be the same: for you the weapons of the apostolate, for me prayer and love.

Her last Lent began 3 March. Thérèse's thoughts were orientated more and more towards this posthumous mission.

From March 4 to 12, she made a Novena in honour of St.Francis Xavier and told Sister Marie of the Sacred Heart: 'I have asked for the grace to do good after my death. I am sure now that my prayer will be granted because one obtains all that one desires through this Novena'.p She also prayed to St.Joseph for this intention.

In the middle of Lent, a short note to Mother Agnès hides beneath the usual humorous style an announcement that was both heart-rending and happy: her affection would remain unchanged after her death: 'Yes, but when I am up there, my little arm will reach very far, and my little Mother will hear about it . . .'.[18] To Fr Roulland she confided that she certainly would not be going to the missions although her superiors knew that she had the vocation for it, 'the scabbard is not as strong as the sword!'.[19] She asks him to pray for her as she 'was leaving this exile', and concludes: 'I want to save souls and forget self for them. I want to save them even after my death'.[20]

March 25 was a day of joy: Thérèse saw her last novice, her cousin Marie, make her profession. Her work of formation was completed. She gave the newly professed sister some verses on the theme of spiritual combat that ended with these lines:

> With a smile I will brave the cannonade
> And in your arms, O my Divine Spouse,
> With a song I will die on the battle-field
> Weapons in hand!

Yes, during these days Thérèse fought valiantly to remain on her feet in suffering, to sing in choir when she had dragged herself from her cell to the chapel. But no one can go on

p   Let us remember that, thirty years later, 14.12.1927, Pope Pius XI made St. Thérèse of Lisieux principal patron, with St.Francis Xavier, of all missionaries, men and women, and of all existing missions in the whole world.

indefinitely beyond the limit of their strength. At the end of Lent, (the beginning of April), Thérèse fell seriously ill.

Let us just summarise the growth of Sister Thérèse of the Child Jesus and of the Holy Face during this thirty month period.

Her little way was confirmed by the Word of God. Thérèse offered herself to the Merciful Love which had created her, chosen her and freed her from her limitations and weaknesses. This Offering included the desire to die of love according to St. John of the Cross' description, for Love can only be repaid by a wholehearted loving response, by love alone. In April 1896, Thérèse was given proof that she would die soon. She would suffer so that she might follow Jesus to death. Overflowing with graces and joy, she entered suddenly into darkness to share the night of atheists. Tried to the very foundations of her hope, she accepted to walk that unexpected road. She did not doubt that her great desire to die of love would be granted. But how would it come about? Far from waning, her desire to 'save souls' intensified. The more she became aware of the approach of death, the more she wished to expand her activity. She went so far as to believe that when she was dead she would do more.

She is characterised by a reckless daring, a fighting spirit, an intrepid conviction based on experience and absolute trust in God. 'I know in whom I have placed my trust,' said the Apostle Paul.

Without a director – except Jesus alone – this twenty-four year old Carmelite discovered a short-cut to the sanctity that had always been her objective. Eagerly, she made it her own. There remained then only to die doing God's will.

During this whole period, her meditation became more profound: the Isaian texts on the Suffering Servant often occupied her thoughts. These themes recur in all her writings of this time.

Now, this living flame of Love was consuming her unseen in the midst of her most ordinary everyday duties. It was so hidden that her twenty-three companions were scarcely aware of it. What a contrast there was between what she *was* and what she *seemed* to be to her sisters! 'Ah! God alone knows the depths of the heart ... Creatures are so narrow in their thoughts!'.[21] So that everyone's attention might be focused on her, the disease had to strike her down at the moment when the whole Church was entering into the liturgical season of Passiontide. Less than a year before, she had written these lines:

With your cross I am climbing the hill,
Come, Lord, and guide my steps along the way.

If we wish to know better who this Carmelite was whom we are now going to watch climb 'the hill', we must follow her route. The *Last Conversations* only make sense if we know the 'giant's course' of this 'unknown person'.

___ Part II___

'I'm a very sick "little girl".
Yes, very sick!' *(L.C. 17.8.2)*

____ Chapter 1 _____

The stages of the tuberculosis

To write a biography of Sister Thérèse of the Child Jesus and of the Holy Face beginning in April 1897 consists mainly in following the stages of her illness. There are several distinct phases or periods.

1. The gradual withdrawal from community life (April - May)

The medical journal for the months of April and May provides little information. Letters, written by witnesses at the beginning of April, mention a feverishness that flared up each afternoon, digestive trouble, a cough that persisted despite several vesicatories. 'My Sister Thérèse of the Child Jesus is not very strong,' wrote Sister Marie of the Eucharist on the 3rd. That tells us little. A recurrence of haemoptyses, about the 25th,[a] revealed the gravity of her condition. On the 25th precisely, Sister Geneviève did not hide from Brother Simeon that 'everyone expects the Divine Master to pick this flower that is so beautiful'.

Thérèse herself makes no mention of her health in the letter she wrote to Abbé Bellière that same day. In a way, this is understandable, since she was still living the community life with, no doubt, some mitigations and permissions

---

a 'She coughs up blood in the morning.' We read in a letter dated 28 April, which seems to indicate that it was not the first time that day.

that exempted her from work that was too heavy, such as the washing at the end of the garden. The work that she had asked for — to help Sister Marie of Saint-Joseph in the linen room — would end about 18 May, if we follow the dates given in the *Yellow Note-Book*.[b] But she continued to sew, at least until 4 June, as she did not want to waste her time. On Thursday 26 May, she did not take part in the Rogation Procession in the garden.[c] On the 28th, although she was running a temperature, a sister asked her to do some painting, as a distraction. Some days before her cousin's Veiling Day, she spoke with her, but it was about this time, at the end of May, that she was relieved of her care of the novices.

When did she stop going to the choir for the Divine Office? It is hard to say. A note, written by Sister Geneviève, indicates that Thérèse was seen saying her Breviary in the garden. This could have been either 6 May or 30 May.[d] If we compare this with a remark of Mother Agnès in the *Yellow Note-Book* for 18 May, it seems we must opt for the first date. Therefore it seems likely that Thérèse had to give up going to the choir at the end of April.

With regard to her presence in the refectory, a conversation of May 27 would seem to imply that she was still going there at that date.[e] After 15 June, we can be sure that she no longer went down to the refectory. It was in May also that Thérèse had to give up going to the community exercise of recreation.[f]

b   All my duties were taken away from me'. (LC 18.5.1)
c   cf. *L.C.*, 26.5.1
d   *Conseils et Souvenirs*, published by Sister Geneviève p. 222.
e   'Did you notice during the reading in the refectory . . .' (LC 27.5.7)
f   'You were not at recreation this evening . . .' (LC 1.5.2.). By comparing Sister Marie of the Sacred Heart's evidence about 'this shower of roses' with an entry in LC 9.6.3., it would seem Thérèse was still going to recreation on 9 June. Can we rely on the chronology of the Yellow Note-Book here?

This gradual withdrawal from community life is easily explained when one realizes to what extent she was forcing herself to keep going during this period.

> One day, when she had been to Mass and received communion — although shortly before, she had received a vesicatory (blistering), I began to cry and was unable to go to the Divine Office. I followed her back to her cell, and I shall always see her seated on her little bench, her back supported by a partition of rough boards. She was quite exhausted and was gazing at me with a sad but very gentle expression! My tears redoubled, and, knowing how much I was causing her to suffer, I begged her pardon on my knees. She said simply: "It is not too much to suffer to have communion! . . . " To repeat the phrase is nothing; you had to hear her say it. (Mother Agnès) LC 21/26.5.6 p.256.

Although it is difficult to date the following evidence of Sister Marie of the Trinity, it must belong to this period:

> The last day that she could stand on her feet she came to the evening recreation. The Servant of God, having difficulty in breathing and running a temperature, came into the recreation room and came and sat on her heels next to me. She whispered to me: "I have come near you so that you can *guard* me. I feel that I have not the strength to carry on a conversation. Look as if you are talking to me so that others won't come to speak to me. I do feel so sick, but I don't want to tell Mother Agnès yet, she would worry so much! . . . Last evening it took me more than half an hour to get up to our cell, I had to sit down on almost every step of the stairs to get my breath. When I finally reached our cell, I had to make an unbelievable effort to undress. I thought at the time that I would never make it . . . if you only knew how powerless we can become through illness!" . . .

The prescriptions for the end of this month of May include vesicatories, cough syrup,[g] sedatives, 'pointes de feu' (a

---

g   'She was coughing very much at this period, especially at night. She was obliged to sit up on her "paillasse" (straw mattress) to lessen the suffocation and to enable herself to breathe'. Mother Agnès added that Thérèse preferred to remain in her cell instead of going down to the infirmary: 'Here they don't hear my coughing, so I don't disturb anyone'.

cauterizing remedy). Thérèse herself refers to these 'expensive remedies'.[1]

Gradually she entered into an even greater solitude. She continued to recite alone her 'little Offices of the Dead',[2] to sew and to go from her cell to the garden when the weather was fine. She was still walking around.[h] The frequent coughing spells do not seem to have caused haemoptyses in May.

The nuns, seeing her walking in the cloisters thought that, with treatment, rest, and spring sunshine, Sister Thérèse would return, more or less soon, to community life. She herself, although she thought that if she had said nothing no one would have discovered that she was sick,[3] was not under this illusion. What she slipped into three poems she wrote proves this. '*La rose effeuillée*', (19.5.1897) written at the request of a Carmelite in Paris, is clear, even in its title:

> Jesus, for love of you, in the eyes of men,
> I have wasted my life and my future,
> Seen as a *rose* forever *wilted*
>   I must die! . . .
>
> *For you* I must *die*, Supreme Beauty,
>   What a happy lot!
> *In shedding my petals* I wish to prove my love for you.
>   O my Treasure! . . .
>
> Beneath your *little feet*, I want to live in secret
>   here below,
> And I want still more to lighten your final steps to
>   Calvary! . . .

Meditating on Mary in the Gospels, in the month that is consecrated to her, Thérèse recalls 'the night spent in anguish'.

---

h   In a letter written May 28, Thérèse says that she had just met Sister Saint-John the Baptist.

Mary, is it then a good thing to suffer on earth?
Yes, *to suffer in loving*, is the *purest happiness!*
Everything Jesus has given me he can take back.
Tell him that he does not have to ask me ...
He can also hide himself, I will wait for him
Until that day when faith will be no more ...

She concludes her Marian poem with these lines:

Soon I will see you in heaven.
You came and *smiled on me* in the morning of my life,
Come and smile on me again, Mother, for it is
evening! ...

(*Pourquoi je t'aime, Marie*)

Like Thérèse, let us emphasise again those lines which sum up her whole attitude during these months: 'To love is to give all and to give oneself'. Abandonment was her habitual disposition. It is the '*Fruit délicieux de l'Amour*', as she expressed it in the title of a poem she gave to Sister Thérèse of Saint-Augustine on 31 May.

The same sentiments are to be found in some letters and notes of these two months, but never a word about her health. In a letter to Sister Anne, who had returned to Saigon, we find this unexpected sentence:

Oh Sister, please ask Jesus that I, too, may love him and make him loved. I want to love him, not with an ordinary love, but like the saints who committed follies for him. Alas! how far I am from resembling them! Ask Jesus too, that I may always do his will — for that I am ready to cross the world ... and I am also ready to die. LT 2/5/1897.

She wrote at length to her spiritual brothers so that she could pass on to them her 'way of trust and love', her reflections on martyrdom, for she had just learned of Fr Mazel's death, and her ardent desire for a universal mission.

Her conversations often centred around her approaching death or heaven. She lived in expectation. All 'hope' of a cure did not seem lost.[i] Could one say whether or not this word was bad news for Thérèse? For 'if she had had her choice, she would have preferred to die'.[4]

But, at the beginning of June, her condition became worse.

2. The writing of the last manuscript (June to the beginning of July)

Events moved quickly. On Saturday evening, May 30, Mother Agnès learnt of the haemoptyses of the preceding year. On the night of June 2, she suggested to Mother Marie de Gonzague that she ask the sick nun to continue her Memoirs. She also obtained permission to stay with her sister in the evenings in her cell: the 'last conversations', properly so called, were about to begin. For Thérèse's writings, together with Mother Agnès' notes, would make it possible to write a substantial circular to send out after her death.

On Wednesday 2, Marie Guérin's Veiling Day, Thérèse (undoubtedly) went to see her family in the parlour. But the next day, a vomiting attack and pains in her side gave concern to those around her. Then on Saturday 5, she was suffering so much that she felt as if she was going to die,[5] and the same day the dismayed community began a Novena to Our Lady of Victories. Dr de Cornière visited the patient and prescribed a milk diet that was to begin during the next few days. Now, 'that cannot go on for too long', said Thérèse, who was 'indeed seriously ill'. However, the following day, Pentecost Sunday, Sister Marie of the Eucharist took her for a ride in the garden in M. Martin's wheel-chair.[6]

From this time Thérèse usually spent her days in her cell. She had to go downstairs to go out into the garden. She was

---

i   'Let no one believe that if I were to be cured it would throw me off my course etc.' (LC 27.5.5)

76

still walking round a little, since we have the account of her coming up to Sister Marie of the Trinity in the grotto of the Holy Face.[7]

From about June 10 until the beginning of July, her condition remained stable. Whether 'in bed', or 'sitting in the pretty little white armchair',[8] Thérèse wrote out of obedience. Not without difficulty, for she was always being interrupted, especially when she was outside. The hot June sun blazed down on the 'hay-makers'. Nearby, beneath the shade of the chestnut trees, Thérèse tried to concentrate. In vain. Humorously, she relates her adventures 'in the groves of Carmel' and mimics 'the good sisters', who interrupt her 'out of charity':

> In order for me to express my thoughts, I have to be like the solitary sparrow, and that is rarely my lot. When I begin to take up my pen, behold a sister who passes by, pitchfork on her shoulder. She believes she will distract me with a little idle chatter: hay, ducks, hens, visits of the doctor, everything is discussed; to tell the truth, this doesn't last long, but there is more than one good charitable sister, and all of a sudden another hay worker throws flowers on my lap, perhaps believing these will inspire me with poetic thoughts. I am not looking for any at the moment and would prefer to see the flowers swaying on their stems. Finally, tired of opening and shutting this famous exercise book, I open a book (which doesn't want to stay open) and say resolutely that I shall copy out some thoughts from the Psalms and the Gospels for the feast of Our Mother. It's true that I am not sparing in these quotes. Dear Mother, I would amuse you, I believe, when telling you about all my adventures in the groves of Carmel. I don't know if I have been able to write ten lines without being disturbed, etc. (Ms C p.228)

What a delightful scene! A nun, looking well, out in the sun, writing to keep herself busy while the other nuns toss hay in the nearby little field. Who would have thought that she was suffering from a mortal illness? Her coughing could be heard, that was true, but who knew about the pains in her side which came and went, or that increasing weakness which she hid beneath a smile?

She alone, since June 9, knew that she was going to die. On that day, she wrote to Abbé Bellière: 'I am taking advantage of a moment when the infirmarian is out of the room[j] to write you a short word of farewell. When you get it, I shall have come to the end of my exile ... Oh! my Brother, how glad I am to die! ...'[9]

She also bade farewell to her sisters. She gave them a memento card on which she had copied out some of Théophane Vénard's last words before his martyrdom.[k] She put everything in order. On Pentecost Monday, June 7, she let Sister Geneviève photograph her 'in view of her approaching death!' There were three different poses. The photographer thought she looked too sad in the first one, she moved during the second and, while the third was being taken, the gardener, who was working in the nearby courtyard, heard her beg her sister: 'Oh! hurry up, I'm exhausted'. The final result was hardly any better: 'When the novices saw me they cried that I had put on my grand look. It seems that I am ordinarily more smiling'.[10]

Throughout June she continued to write, treating freely of topics suggested to her: fraternal charity, the novitiate, her spiritual brothers ... Dr de Cornière came to see her on the 11th, 22nd and 24th.[l] On Wednesday 30, Thérèse, still shy in the presence of Uncle Guérin, went to the parlour for the last time. Her uncle was preparing to go on vacation to his property at La Musse, near Evreux.

---

j   Mother Marie de Gonzague had forbidden Thérèse to speak about her correspondence with her spiritual brothers.

k   A letter about 10/6. The Yellow Note Book says 4 June but this must be an error as Mother Agnès says: "during the Novena" and that commenced on 5th.

l   He must have made other visits, but there is no record of them.

She was still on her feet at the begining of July, but, 'at the end of her strength'. In the afternoon of the 2nd, the first Friday of the month, she went for the last time to adore the Blessed Sacrament in the oratory.[11] The doctor prescribed a kind of condensed milk diet that she found 'a horror to take'. But she could keep it down when she could not digest ordinary milk. The fears of June (a month that was full, since Thérèse had written down what could be called her testament) suddenly became a reality, when a sharp decline in her condition threw the community into a state of consternation.

3. The period of haemoptyses (6 July - 5 August)
Thérèse in the infirmary

The patient's mental faculties were not affected, as can be seen by Manuscript C, but her weakness increased. She had to abandon the little black note-book. After writing thirty-six pages Thérèse had to give up using pen and ink and continue with a pencil. That pencil which would often be used in the infirmary to write notes and letters. But, a few days later, even it became too heavy, and fell from her hand. This says much about her physical condition when we know her will power.

A period, very characteristic of the disease, began on Tuesday July 6 which was to last until Thursday August 5. For twenty-nine days, almost without a break, Thérèse lost blood day and night, often several times during the day and night.

The month of July therefore takes on a particular intensity for both patient and those around her because of these distressing haemoptyses.[m] It is difficult to give the exact

---

m 'The coughing up of blood is one of the most important symptoms of pulmonary tuberculosis and this is what alarms patients most. Haemoptyses occur at all stages of the phthisical tuberculosis, but especially as an early symptom, and then towards the end when the cavities are forming. They are caused by the rupture of small aneurisms that have formed in the pulmonary alveoli. The patient can die within minutes.'

number of these coughings up of blood, and so we would say that there were about twenty. Yet, how could you count as 'one' haemoptysis this evidence of Sister Marie of the Eucharist, when she says: 'She was coughing up blood, or rather vomiting it all through the remainder of the day'[12]

We do not hesitate to spell out this litany of health reports. In its monotony it is more eloquent than any commentary:

Wednesday July 7: 'Yesterday, she coughed up blood twice ... these are particles of blood that look as if she is vomiting some liver, and all through the remainder of the day, she was coughing up blood.'[13]

Thursday 8: 'It's now two days since she vomited blood or even spat it.'

Saturday 10: 'Last night (at midnight, according to Mother Agnès) she was seized with a coughing fit, and it was stopped by giving her a lot of ice.'[14]

Wednesday 14: 'She coughed up some more blood.'

Saturday 17: 'She coughed up blood at three in the morning.'[15]

Tuesday 20: 'She coughed up blood again this morning. It has become a regular affair, happening every third day in the morning.[n] She'll cough up a generous glassful in a quarter of an hour.'[16]

Saturday 24: 'Little Queen coughed up blood twice during the day.'

Tuesday 27: 'She coughed up blood again twice.'

Wednesday 28: 'She is coughing up blood every day.'

n   To be precise – 14, 17 and 20 July.

Thursday 29: 'She coughed up blood in the morning and at three o'clock in the afternoon.'

Friday 30: 'She is coughing up blood every day now, even two or three times a day. It was continuous this morning.'[17] 'This evening, she coughed up blood again.'

Saturday 31: 'Last night she coughed up blood again ... She did not cough blood until three o'clock this afternoon when she had a fit of coughing.'

Sunday August 1: According to a letter dated August 5: 'Today is the first day since the 28th that our little patient has not coughed up blood.' Haemoptyses must have therefore occurred on Sunday 1, Monday 2, Tuesday 3 and Wednesday 4.

The period of haemoptyses ceased August 5.

We said a commentary was not needed. It suffices to describe her physical condition. But, before going into the details, we shall look at the witnesses' reports of Dr de Cornière's diagnosis which will enable us to follow the progress of the disease. He visited the patient at least eighteen times during this period.

Tuesday, July 6, was a turning point. A very high fever preceded a serious recurrence of haemorrhaging which greatly alarmed those round her. 'To mention the state the community is in,' wrote Sister Marie of the Eucharist, 'there are tears, sobs and grief on all sides'.[18]

The next day the doctor called twice. 'It is not tuberculosis,' he said, 'but rather an accident which has caused serious lung congestion'. Thérèse was burning with fever and had to take ice continually. She also had to submit to mustard poultices and two dry-cups. A state of extreme weakness followed on Thursday 8: 'She isn't able to raise her hand to her mouth, it just falls by her side'.[19] The doctor found the right lung still congested. He said that in

81

her state 'only two per cent recover'. She was put on a condensed milk diet, but still had difficulty in eating and vomited frequently.

In the evening, she was brought down to the infirmary on a mattress.[o] Her condition was such that some thought the time had come to administer the Last Sacraments. The doctor and superior did not think so. They did not believe that death was imminent. It is true that, when they visited her, Thérèse made an effort and found the strength to joke with them.

On Sunday evening, July 11, the doctor thought that she could still go on for some weeks if she could get some nourishment.[20] On the 20th, he found several cavities and said that the top of the right lung was also 'damaged'. He said: 'She's lost unless a great miracle takes place'.[21]

July 27-28 saw the beginning of the 'great suffering'. Until then, Thérèse said that she had had 'only inconveniences to put up with, not sufferings'.[22] These 'inconveniences' included feverishness, coughing, perspiring, coughing up blood, bringing up the milk and her emaciation. On Friday 30, in the evening, she reached crisis point. She was suffocating and given ether to help her breathe, but it brought little relief. At six o'clock Canon Maupas finally gave her the Last Sacraments. It was thought that she would not live through the night. In the next room everything had been prepared for the imminent burial: candles, holy water, paillasse. The suffering (violent pains, suffocation) was to

o   The morning before, the doctor 'forbade her to make any movements' and he would not even 'allow her to be taken down to the infirmary until the wound in her right lung was healed' (LC p. 272). It is strange that Sister Marie of the Eucharist does not mention this transfer in her letters of July 9 and 10. She only told her father in her letter of July 12, without giving the precise date. In this case, it is wise to take it as being July 8, as this is the date given in both the *Green and Yellow Note-books*.

continue however until August 5-6. The crisis of the preceding days was caused by the progress of the tuberculosis in the right lung. But then, contrary to all expectation, Thérèse's condition stabilized.

Before describing it, we shall return for a moment to Thérèse during the period of the haemoptyses.

On July 8 she was brought down to the infirmary which was on the ground floor. From that day she was to live in a small room five by four metres. From her iron bed surrounded by high brown curtains on which she had pinned her favourite holy pictures, she could not see, except by leaning over, the window which looked out on to the garden. On her left was the door of the room where Sister Geneviève, the infirmarian on duty, would rest. A little further along there was another door which opened on to the cloister. Between these two doors, against the wall, stood the statue of the Virgin of the Smile which had also been brought down on July 8 from the little room in front of Thérèse's cell where it had been kept. The patient was full of joy at seeing it again and her gaze often rested on it. This statue, which had played such an important role in her life, would be with her now until she died.

Sister Stanislaus, the first infirmarian, and 'Bobonne' (Céline, whom Thérèse sometimes called by this name) bustled about her. Mother Agnès, 'the little mother', was often at her bedside. Mother Marie de Gonzague and Sister Marie of the Sacred Heart freqently came to see her, and also Sister Marie of the Eucharist who called in for news that she then dispatched to La Musse. The other nuns rarely came to the infirmary, for Thérèse's condition hardly allowed prolonged visits. She was still getting up for two hours a day, at least on those days when she was not coughing blood.

What did she do? It was no longer possible for her to write her 'little life'. The last pencil-written words[p] (apparently after she had been moved to the infirmary) at the top of page 37 in her black exercise book are: 'through confidence and love'. She made a truly heroic effort to write to Abbé Bellière who was on holiday and who begged her help so insistently. She wrote yet another letter of farewell to Fr Roulland on July 14, two to her family on the 16th and the 24th or 25th, as well as several notes to her sisters. The lines clearly written in 'a shaky hand' reveal her determination. Such an effort must have taken much time and courage.

She read a little. *The Imitation of Christ*, her constant companion, the Gospels which never left her, St.John of the Cross ... She spoke when it was possible for her to do so. One third of the words contained in the *Yellow Note-Book* belong to this period. Mother Agnès, who thought that the end was near, questioned her often, and asked for more precise details about certain matters in her Memoirs. The sick nun therefore gave her many confidences. Her manuscript was unfinished and she knew that she would not be writing any more, so she made various important recommendations to Mother Agnès.

The spiritual event of July was undoubtedly the reception of the Last Anointing and Holy Communion as Viaticum. On the days when death seemed near, her joking increased, for, contrary to Dr Dieulafoy's description of tuberculosis patients, Thérèse did not become panic-stricken. 'She will die laughing,' wrote Sister Marie of the Eucharist to her parents. But the time to die had not yet come.

p On this same page, Mother Agnès wrote in ink: 'Sister Thérèse of the Child Jesus wrote these last lines in pencil in her infirmary bed (July 1897). We do not know which day.

4. Condition stabilises (6 - 15 August)

The haemoptyses ended, but the fever and difficulty in breathing remained. After the alarm of July 30, there was a lull, which did not mean an improvement. 'Her condition has stabilized' is the repeated report in the letters to La Musse. Before rejoining his wife at Plombières, Dr de Cornière said that the sickness was spreading to the left lung. He prescribed some remedies for use during his absence and recommended a doctor from Lisieux to replace him.q

M. and Mme Guérin, for their part, after much hesitation, consulted their friend, Dr de Cornière, and decided to leave for Vichy where Uncle Isidore was going to cure his gout.

In fact, Thérèse enjoyed a relative respite. She was surprised that she had a craving for 'all sorts of good things'.[23] On Tuesday 10, she again asked for the pencil that had been refused her on the 5th. This time it was given her and she was able to write a last letter to Abbé Bellière. She told him that she was quite ready to go and wrote down what would be given to him as an 'inheritance'. He called them his 'relics'.[24] On the 12th, she wrote to Sister Marie of the Trinity on the back of a small picture for the latter's twenty-third birthday. But these days of remission were not to last.

5. The great sufferings (15 - 27 August)
A. *The tuberculosis attacks the left lung*

On the evening of the feast of the Assumption, Thérèse had great difficulty in breathing and she suffered greatly from

---

q   In her evidence at the Deposition (1908), Sister Geneviève gave another version: 'The community doctor who had left for the South, entrusted his little patient to Dr. La Néele, our cousin by marriage'. Mme Guérin's account, contemporaneous with the facts, seems more accurate. However this doctor was never consulted.

sharp pains in her left side. She also had swelling in her legs. This marked a new stage in her illness.

In the early hours of Monday 16, the pains in the left lung were so severe that Sister Geneviève, alarmed, lit a blessed candle. Thérèse's distress ceased, but the pain continued.

The next day it was realised that she could not remain in that state without seeing a doctor. Mother Marie de Gonzague gave permission for Dr Francis La Néele, who had returned from Caen, to enter the infirmary. In the letter he wrote to his father-in-law on the 26th, he gave the following diagnosis – the only one written by a doctor that we possess – : 'The right lung is completely lost, filled with tubercles in the process of softening. The lower part of the left lung is affected. She is very emaciated, but her face still does her honour. She is suffering very much from intercostal neuralgia'.[25] In the evening following this visit, Sister Marie of the Eucharist also wrote to her father: 'Francis told us that the tuberculosis[r] has reached its final stage'.

On Thursday 19, Thérèse received Holy Communion for the last time. She offered it for the Carmelite priest, Father Hyacinthe Loyson,[s] who had left the Church and married. From then on she was deprived of the Eucharist, because she was unable to fulfil the conditions necessary for the reception of this sacrament. (They were very strict at that time). Also, the long and involved ceremonial upset her nerves, and she could no longer take any more.

She began coughing again. The nights became almost unbearable. They seemed endless! During Friday August 20,

r   This was the first time that this word had been used. Perhaps the date of this letter, August 17, should read, August 27 (cf. p.286 Translator's note).
s   Hyacinthe Loyson (1827-1912), ordained 1851, Carmelite (1859), Advent preacher at Notre Dame, Paris, (1864), broke with the Church in 1869 and set up, in 1879, the 'French Catholic Church'.

Thérèse could not hold back little cries. The next day, the diary reads: 'Great suffering, suffocation, coughing'. It was hard to believe that the suffering had not reached its limits. Yet it was only the beginning.

B. The tuberculosis attacks the intestines: gangrene feared (22 - 27 August)

The most painful period of the whole sickness then began with renewed suffering which was to last for six days.

There is abundant medical information for Sunday August 22. Thérèse was in an 'excessive state of weakness'. She was suffering 'all over': in both her sides, in her joints. She 'groaned', 'coughed', could hardly breathe. When she tried to speak she had to stop between each word for breath. Sister Marie of the Sacred Heart described it in the following words: 'It is a day of continual suffering'. Thérèse knew this: 'People do not know what it is to suffer like this. No! They would have to experience it'.[26] She said that she had 'several sicknesses altogether'.[27]

Then those terrible pains in the intestines began, which were to overwhelm Thérèse with sufferings and humiliations. 'Her stomach was as hard as a rock. She was no longer able to perform bodily functions except with terrible pains'.[28] The next night was the worst night she had spent so far.

Francis La Néele had gone with his wife on the national pilgrimage to Lourdes, and so both doctors were absent when their presence would have been most useful. On Monday 23, the patient was given enemas, but to no avail. On August 24, 25 and 26, she was racked by pains that made her cry out. At each breath she suffered violently and she could not stop herself from groaning. Nothing gave her any relief. When she was seized with a coughing spell, she thought she was sitting 'on iron spikes',[29] for two small bones had pierced the skin.

It was during this period that Thérèse uttered her most poignant cries. They can be understood only in the context in which they were made. Mme Guérin's letter to Jeanne La Néele, in its medical realism, reveals the state of those who were caring for Thérèse: 'For four days now, they have given her enema after enema'. They feared gangrene.[t] It seems most likely that it was at this time that Thérèse gave the advice about not leaving any poisonous medicines within a sick person's reach:[u] 'If I had not the faith, I would have committed suicide without a moment's hesitation.'[30]

In the afternoon of Friday 27 there was a sudden relief. The next day her bed was moved, and placed in the centre of the room from where the patient could see the garden through the window. That pleased her greatly. She was now in front of the Virgin of the Smile and she could see the statue through the opening in the bed-curtains.

When they thought she was dying, she was to have another nineteen days remission. She was extremely weak, yet took an interest in what was going on around her as if she had regained her taste for life.

6. An unexpected remission (28 August - 13 September)

The words 'remission' or 'improvement' are only used by way of comparison. They simply mean that the sufferings

t   Sister Geneviève was to give more details at the Apostolic Process: 'The physical sufferings she endured were atrocious, for the tuberculosis had spread from the chest to the intestines which became gangrenous. Her extreme emaciation caused the formation of sores. We were powerless to give her any relief, and she remained without alleviation because Mother Marie de Gonzague left the patient for a month without a doctor.
u   In the Green Note Book we read: "On 22 August ... she asked that poisonous drugs not be left near her and she advised that they never be left near patients suffering this intense pain which could 'make one go out of one's mind' and, not knowing what they are doing, they could very well take their own life".

of the preceding days had ceased. The fever, the thirst,[v] the difficulty in breathing, the weakness, had been her daily lot since the beginning of July.

Three days after this unexpected alleviation Thérèse could be seen on the cloister in a folding bed. Sister Geneviève took the opportunity to take her photo for the last time, as she was unpetalling roses over her crucifix. The bed was then pushed to the little door that opened into the nuns' choir and, from there, she prayed for the last time before the sanctuary.

Dr La Néele, back from Lourdes since Wednesday 25, was summoned to Caen by Mme Guérin's telegram and again entered the enclosure on the 30th. He said that the left lung was half gone. (Thérèse therefore had only half a lung with which to breathe. She had exactly one month to live). As he was leaving, Francis remarked rather curtly to Mother Marie de Gonzague that his cousin's sufferings were such that she should have seen a doctor every day. He returned the next day and said that she 'could die turning in her bed'.[31] On September 8, he visited her for the fourth and last time and, to Thérèse's great surprise, said that she was like a ship that neither advances nor goes back. He predicted that she would not have an agony.

During these days, Thérèse seemed to come back to life. She was astonished and humiliated that she had all sorts of cravings for food. Mme Guérin did her utmost to satisfy the patient's desires. They were the last movements of an organism that was exhausted, but still young. On September 2, Thérèse fancied some roast meat and thick soup, but she ate the meat with distaste.[32] She preferred the Apple-Charlotte, and, still more, a chocolate éclair which she had unexpectedly asked for. Sister Geneviève had passed on her

v 'Every morning her tongue was so dry that it looked like a rough file, a piece of wood.' (Yellow Note Book) request.[33] On Monday 6, she ate with enjoyment some chicken, and on the 16th, some artichokes that M. Guérin had brought along specially, as well as some cream cheese which gave her indigestion.[34]

In that late summer the patient showed interest in the September fruit and flowers. She was brought some to celebrate the seventh anniversary of her profession on Wednesday 8, and on the 11th, she still had enough strength to weave two crowns out of cornflowers which she gave to the Virgin of the Smile. It was also for Mary that she wrote four lines in ink with a trembling hand — they were the last lines that she was ever to write.[35]

On Friday 10 September — most probably his first visit since returning from holidays — Dr de Cornière was 'puzzled' by his patient's state. Then the following day, her condition deteriorated. This remission of nineteen days marked the beginning of the end.

7. The end (17 - 30 September)
A. The continued deterioration of the left lung

'This is a bad sign', said Dr. de Cornière when he saw the recurrence of swelling in Thérèse's feet on Sunday 12 and the following days. On Tuesday 14, he gave her about fifteen days to live. This time he was right. The patient was so weak that when the strong Sister Aimée of Jesus lifted her up in her arms while the bed was being remade, it was feared she would die.[36]

Yet until the very end, Thérèse was to baffle her entourage: in the afternoon of that same Saturday, September 18, she had a new lease of life. She showed interest in the altar cloth Sister Geneviève was embroidering beside her bed. She admired the bright red virginia creeper that was climbing up above the chestnut trees. She was pleased when she saw her features reflected in the chalice of Father Denis who celebrated his first Mass at the Lisieux Carmel on Sunday 19.

The next day, Mother Marie de Gonzague was asked to come and see the patient's extreme thinness. She was very shocked and said: 'What is this little girl who is so thin?' 'A skeleton', replied Thérèse who could still joke.[w] However the following day she asked: 'What is the agony? It seems to me I'm in it all the time!'.[37] These days brought with them intense suffering and a crisis caused by the extreme difficulty she had in breathing. The escalade continued: the tuberculosis was attacking the remaining part of the left lung. Thérèse could only express herself by signs. The doctor could not understand how she was still living. On the Sunday before she died, she said: 'My life hangs only on a thin thread'.[38] How could she in fact live on when her lungs were gone? 'Mama! . . . earth's air is denied me, when will God grant me the air of heaven? Ah! never was it so short! . . .' (her breathing).[39]

This time she had indeed reached the end of the road.

B. The agony (Wednesday 29 - Thursday 30 September)

We must confront this agony, or better, enter into it.
Bernanos.

In the morning of Wednesday 29, Thérèse appeared to be in her agony and there was a painful rattling in her throat. From six until seven o'clock, the community gathered in the infirmary to recite in Latin the prayers for the dying. Thérèse was suffering atrociously − her 'nerves' were on edge, but she remained lucid and smiling. From time to time she was given a spoonful of morphine syrup.

---

w   In the French there is a play on words. The prioress had said: 'Qu'est-ce que c'est qu'une petite fille aussi maigre?' Thérèse had replied: 'Un quelette!' ('un quelette' is a skeleton).

At noon she asked the Mother Prioress: 'Mother, is this the agony? . . . I will never know how to die!'.[40] Mother Agnès read to her some passages from the office of the day — it was the feast of Saint Michael — and translated for her the prayers for the dying that had been said in the morning. Dr. de Cornière visited her for the last time. Mother Marie de Gonzague assured her: 'Yes, my little child, it will be to-day'. Throughout the whole day she was suffocating.

In the evening, Abbé Faucon heard her confession, for Abbé Youf himself was seriously ill. The extraordinary confessor was deeply moved by this final meeting.[x] After Matins (about half past ten), the mother prioress again went in to see her and refused to let her remain alone during the night as Thérèse had asked. Sister Geneviève and Sister Marie of the Sacred Heart would take it in turn to stay with her.

During that terrible night, she prayed much to the Blessed Virgin, and so as not to awaken her sister who had fallen asleep, she made the effort to hold a glass in her hand.

On the morning of September 30, Sister Marie of the Sacred Heart went to get Mother Agnès, who was sleeping near by in the cell off the cloister. During the community Mass, the three sisters stayed with Thérèse. She was gasping for breath and could only say these words as she looked at the statue of the Virgin: 'I prayed fervently to her! It is sheer agony without any consolation! . . .[41]

In the afternoon she rallied, and about half past two, to everyone's surprise, she sat up in bed, for she had not been able to do that for several weeks. According to Sister Marie of the Trinity's account: 'Thérèse cried out in a voice rendered loud and clear by the acuteness of her pain: 'My

---

x   He was to testify at the Process. 'On leaving the infirmary, he said: 'What a beautiful soul! She seems to be confirmed in grace'. (Mother Agnès).

God, have mercy on me! ... Mary, help me! ... My God, how I am suffering! ... The chalice is full ... full right up to the brim ... I'll never be able to die!' Mother Marie de Gonzague encouraged her.

About three o'clock, still sitting up in bed, she put out her arms in the form of a cross to obtain some relief, resting them on the shoulders of Mother Agnès and Sister Geneviève who supported her. She had strange pains in the whole of her body. The prioress placed a picture of Our Lady of Mount Carmel on her knees. Then the community left and Mother Agnès remained on with her alone. She has left us the following account:

> I was alone by her side. It was about half past four. Her face changed all of a sudden and I understood it was her last agony. Mother Prioress returned and the whole community was soon assembled. She smiled but did not speak again until just before she died.[y] For more than two hours, a terrible rattle tore her chest. Her face was flushed, her hands purplish, she was trembling in all her members and her feet were as cold as ice. Large beads of perspiration stood out in drops on her forehead and ran down her cheeks. She was having more and more difficulty in breathing, and in order to breathe, she sometimes uttered little involuntary cries.[z]

Sister Geneviève wiped her forehead and placed on her lips a small piece of ice. Thérèse smiled at her.

At six o'clock the Angelus rang. She looked for a long time at the Virgin of the Smile. She was still holding her crucifix firmly in her hands. A few minutes past seven, Mother Prioress allowed the community, which had been there for more than two hours, to leave. The prioress remained with

y   'She did not speak any more after 5.00pm' (Sister Marie of the Sacred Heart). All the words of September 30 were therefore spoken between two o'clock and five o'clock.
z   This account is taken from the *Green Note-Book* of Mother Agnès.

the three Martin sisters. Thérèse addressed her last words to her:

> Mother, isn't this the agony? ... Am I not going to die?'. 'Yes, my poor little one, it's the agony, but God perhaps wills to prolong it for several hours'. 'Well ... all right ... all right! ... I would not want to suffer for a shorter time! ...

We shall let Mother Agnès describe what followed:

Her breathing suddenly became weaker and more laboured. She fell back on the pillow, her head turned towards the right. The infirmary bell was rung and, to allow the nuns to assemble quickly, Mother Marie de Gonzague said in a loud voice: 'Open all the doors'. Hardly had the nuns knelt at her bedside when she pronounced very distinctly her final act of love: 'Oh! I love him ...' she said, looking at her crucifix. Then a moment later: 'My God ... I ... love you!'.

We thought that was the end, when, suddenly, she raised her eyes, eyes that were full of life and shining with an indescribable happiness 'surpassing all her hopes'. Sister Marie of the Eucharist approached with a candle to get a better look at that sublime gaze which lasted for the space of a 'Credo'. The light from the candle passed back and forth in front of her eyes did not cause any movement in her eyelids. ... It was twenty past seven.

Then she closed her eyes and the whiteness of her face, which had become more accentuated during the ecstasy, returned to normal. She appeared ravishingly beautiful and had a heavenly smile ...

We did not have to close her eyes, for she had closed them herself after the vision. Mother Prioress then had the community retire, and Sister Aimée, Sister Marie of the Sacred Heart and I prepared the Servant of God for burial. Her face had a childlike expression and she didn't seem any more than twelve years old.

When she was dressed and lying on her paillasse, according to the custom of Carmel, before lifting the body, we placed in her hand, together with her crucifix and rosary, a palm branch, and next to her, on a small table, we put the statue of the miraculous Virgin.

The Servant of God retained the expression she had when she died. Her head was turned towards the right and her smile was so marked that we thought she was only asleep and having a happy dream. Her limbs were supple until the coffin was closed.

The following day, Friday, in the afternoon, her body was taken to the choir where it was placed in front of the grille until Sunday evening[a] when, because there were some signs of decomposition, the lid was closed. The Servant of God was however still beautiful, but the veins in her forehead had swollen and the tips of her fingers were a purplish-blue.

Sister Thérèse was buried in the late morning of Monday October 4 1897 in the town cemetery, on the hill overlooking Lisieux.

Thirteen years later, September 6 1910, that tomb was to be opened by order of the Church authorities. The Diocesan Process had begun with a view to the eventual Canonization of Sister Thérèse of the Child Jesus and of the Holy Face.

a   'On Sunday, October 3, I took another photograph, in the afternoon when she was exposed on the bier surrounded by flowers. But this picture showed her features to be elongated and, curiously, her blond eyebrows appeared dark brown, almost black. She was still majestic, but we could no longer recognize her'. (Sister Geneviève CSG p.244)

'My little life is to suffer, and that's it!'

'I have suffered very much here below, you must make it known to souls.'[1]

We have followed her journey and reached this summit, and it is not without hesitation that we write the following chapter on Thérèse's sufferings. What remains to be said? Is it necessary to say any more? However, we have taken to heart her own words: 'You must make it known to souls', and have decided to make a synthesis of the principle psychosomatic sufferings she endured during the last one hundred and eighty days of her illness.

Only those who have experienced the unrelenting pain of physical suffering can understand the slow undermining of a twenty-four year old body. 'One must suffer in order to know'.[2] When Thérèse first became ill she was not unacquainted with suffering. But she was more familiar with moral suffering. The great trial of her life belonged to the past: the cerebral paralysis of her beloved father that had touched the innermost recesses of her being. Nothing could ever equal that abyss of sorrow into which she had been plunged at fifteen. It lasted from the time of her postulancy until 1892.[a] A person who comes through such a trial victorious at that age has matured.

But she had had almost no experience of physical suffering. She was to say: 'Ah! to suffer in my soul, yes, I can suffer

a   Thérèse entered Carmel 9 April 1888 and learned of her father's disappearance to Le Havre in June. His paralysis spread and necessitated hospitalisation in the mental institution of the Bon Sauveur at Caen, from 12 February 1889 until May 1892, three years of martyrdom. M. Martin died at La Musse 29 July 1894.

much ... but as for bodily suffering, I'm like a little child, very little. I'm without any thought, I suffer from minute to minute'.[3]

If we add that we wish to establish the true facts, as opposed to the legend which still circulates, of a 'rose-water' Saint Thérèse who did not know what it was to suffer, then the reader will understand why we have included this chapter: 'It wouldn't be so encouraging to souls if they didn't think I suffered very much'.[4]

1. 'I didn't expect to suffer like this'[5]

Before Thérèse was finally confined to bed she suffered from several ailments. They were bearable in themselves, that is true, but we must not disregard the effort she made to follow the austere Carmelite rule.

In April and May we have seen her dragging herself along to follow community exercises, to perform various duties, to be of service. These were tasks which, when a person is enjoying perfect health, require energy, patience and self-control. What must they have demanded of one who had had a vesicatory, a session of 'pointes de feu', who was burning with fever, suffering from indigestion and fits of coughing?

A. Fever and profuse sweating

For six months Thérèse suffered from a fever which fluctuated.[b] Sometimes her back was 'burning like fire'. At the same time she was perspiring so much that she became

___

b 'We never took her temperature, but judged it by the high colour of her face which was naturally very pale. She must have had a high fever in April 1897.'

dehydrated. 'Last night, before her vomiting spell, she was perspiring so much that her pillows were soaked through and we had to change her'.[6] 'During the night she perspires so profusely that her mattress is soaked right through'.[7] On September 30 she perspired so much that, after her death, 'her mattress, pillows and all her clothing were wet through'. And, as a consequence, 'she suffered continually from thirst'.[8] But to mortify herself she still did not ask for that extra drink: 'If I listened to myself, I would drink too often'.

B. Digestive troubles

Thérèse suffered frequently from nausea, often losing her meals, even before she became bed-ridden. When the haemoptyses began and she could not get sufficient nourishment, the doctor prescribed milk. But, by an unfortunate circumstance, Thérèse had never liked milk. She could not digest it. Yet, from July 3 she had to take a kind of condensed milk which she found even more repugnant. She forced herself to take it, but usually could not keep it down. However, courage was never lacking. When Mother Agnès asked her if she would drink a cup of it to save her life Thérèse drank it down in one gulp![9] On August 23 this trial finally ended: 'We've stopped giving her the famous milk diet. It's impossible to push it any further. The poor little thing believes she is being poisoned, and it required courage like hers not to have said this before. We were only noticing her very great repugnance when taking the cups'.[10] Thérèse had kept to that diet for sixty-nine days.

The remedies of her day were no more attractive than the milk diet. Despite the fact that the 'Elixir of Huxan' looked like 'a delicious red-currant liqueur', it was a 'very bitter medicine to take'. We shall not go into details about the 'snail syrup' which was one of dear old Sister Stanislas' somewhat dubious concoctions: 'As long as I can't see their horns', Thérèse said, drinking it with a laugh.

99

C. Respiratory troubles

As the tuberculosis spread through the lungs, Thérèse suffered pains first in her right shoulder and arms, then in her left side.

Let us not insist on 'the cough' which, nonetheless, contributed in no small measure to her physical and moral sufferings of the months before the illness became 'official'. It continued after she had been confined to bed, exhausting the patient day and night, especially when it was combined with intestinal pains. She suffered then 'in her whole body', except her hands.[11]

And when the coughing fits brought on crises of suffocation the patient passed through some terrible moments. It was not, moreover, just a question of a few days. For in July we read: 'She has chest pains and difficulty in breathing; at times she is positively choking. She has to inhale ether continually. At times, her breathing is so bad that the ether has no effect'.[12] Then in August: 'Her breathing difficulties also cause her the greatest fatigue'.[13] 'At eleven o'clock she again had difficulty with her breathing and it lasted the whole day until midnight'. Again, in September: 'She wanted to talk to me but was unable to do so'.[14]

Nothing is more moving, in the reading, than those points of suspension which come between the words and phrases in the *Yellow Note-Book*. Mother Agnès' transcription is as faithful as a record:

> No, I musn't talk ... But ... I believed ... I love you so much ... I'm going to be good ... Oh! little Mother![15] – ... my God! ... have pity on your little ... girl![16] – I ... can ... no longer ... even ... speak ... to you! Oh! If one only knew! – ... If I didn't love God! ... Yes, but ...[17]

Sister Marie of the Eucharist has confirmed the accuracy of this transcription: 'She had to pause a minute between each word because she had such difficulty in breathing'.[18]

As her lungs deteriorated, Thérèse had to try to find new ways to get some air: 'She was having great difficulty with her breathing. For some time now she found some sort of relief in these painful situations by making little cries like: 'Oh! là, là, or Agne! Agne![19] 'She also made little involuntary cries',[20] and sometimes reproached herself for complaining.[21]

These crises of suffocation would appear to have been the cause of Thérèse's greatest suffering. She suffered as much from their intensity and duration, as from the distress which she knew she was communicating to those around her and who were powerless to do anything for her. Several times she manifested her fear of dying by suffocation: 'I'll suffocate one night, I feel it'. '. . .Oh! yes, I wish it. Yes, but it's good! . . .' 'What?', asked Mother Agnès, 'I shall suffocate!' 'When shall I be completely suffocated! . . .' (cf. LC 21.8.2, 25.8.9, 29.9.5)

And that, in fact, was what would happen to her.

D. Emaciation

For a long time a rather strange phenomena baffled those around her. Normally the face of a person suffering from tuberculosis takes on certain characteristics, but Thérèse's face remained almost the same. Her voluminous Carmelite habit hid her thinness, and her face was full.[c] Even when confined to bed, she continued to convey the impression of good health. This amazed the two doctors. Only her very thin hands betrayed her, and gave the lie to her 'healthy look'.

This emaciation, as we know, caused various afflictions.

c   'The tuberculosis patient has a certain appearance: the cheeks and temples become hollow, the cheek-bones become ruddy, the eye lashes and brows stand out, the conjunctiva has a bluish colour.' (Dr. Dieulafoy op.cit. p.291-292)

E. Weakness, powerlessness and distress

The psychosomatic consequences of these sufferings also demand some attention. In the letters written at this time, the words, 'weakness' and 'powerlessness' recur frequently.

Although she experienced some surprising returns of vitality, Thérèse lived out her last months beneath the sign of weakness. Witnesses have left us a wealth of concrete details. From July onwards: 'She feels so very weak'. 'She can't wash her own hands any longer, it's a real effort for her and causes her suffering in all her limbs'.[22] She could no longer make the Sign of the Cross,[23] or recite the Angelus.[24]

This weakness, in one of its most trying manifestations, affected the patient's 'nerves'. The least noise, a few whispered words, or paper being crumbled, wearied her.[25] What then could be said of the conversation of her three sisters at her bedside and above all of the intoning of the 'Miserere' (even in a low tone of voice) by the whole community, on the days she received communion![26] She could no longer even bear anyone taking her pulse, or moving her bed a little. Even another's breathing wearied her.

We can also understand how, under these circumstances, her sisters' repeated questions must have added to her suffering: 'We were talking too much when the three of us were with her. This tired her out, because we were asking her too many questions at the same time'.[27] Unconsciously, they were 'harassing' her, to use her own word. Yet, willingly, she consented to Mother Agnès' desire to write down her words. On certain occasions, this must have cost her dearly.

Likewise, this general state of weakness could have been the main reason for the return of Thérèse's tears which had hardly flowed since her adolescence.

Her physical condition also gave rise to diverse forms of distress: irrational fears of 'a hypothetical spider',[28] or of being buried 'in a death-trance', 'frightful nightmares',[29] and her 'drowsiness'. All these increased as her health deteriorated.

Did the prodigious remedies, customary at that time but ridiculous today, do anything to alleviate all this suffering?

The various haemostats would have helped the coughing up of blood, but what could they have done for the vomiting? They were useless for the sporadic suffocation, and the ether was ineffectual when major crises occurred: 'She was never given oxygen', Mother Agnès said, 'I don't think it was known at that time'.

When Dr. de Cornière returned from Plombières he suggested using a sedative, but Mother Marie de Gonzague refused her permission.[d] Mother Agnès was later to say: 'She was never given a single morphine injection'. Thérèse, therefore, was given very small doses of morphine syrup only during her last days.

With reference to all these remedies the patient one day made this remark: 'The remedies which should be doing me some good, and which help other patients, do me harm'.[30] Besides, she was 'convinced of their uselessness'.[31]

At the end of this resumé of Saint Thérèse's physical sufferings we are in a better position to appreciate the unconscious irony of Sister Saint-Vincent de Paul's remark: 'Why do they speak of Sister Thérèse of the Child Jesus as if she were a saint? She has practised virtue, that's true, but she has not acquired virtue at the cost of humiliations, let alone through suffering'.

It was at the precise moment when Thérèse, in the infirmary, was suffering such cruel agony that she was told what

d   This refusal has been misinterpreted.

had been said of her: 'The more interior the suffering is and the less apparent to the eyes of creatures, the more it rejoices you, O my God', she had written in June.

Others, who were closer to her during this period, have categorically contradicted this assertion of Sister Saint-Vincent de Paul who was relying solely on appearances.

We must be grateful to Mother Agnès for the discreet way in which she recorded her sister's words, for it makes her own very brief comments all the more eloquent. 'I was coming to a point where I desired her death so that she wouldn't suffer any longer',[32] '. . . in the midst of her sufferings that were so great'. Expressions such as these run like a refrain through the *Yellow Note-Book*. She told Thérèse what someone had said: 'Ah! it's frightful what you're suffering'.[33]

To the Guérin family she poured out her own feelings more freely: 'I wonder how one can go on living in her condition. I assure you, having seen her suffer so much, I'll be consoled by her death. She'll be so happy'.[34]

Sister Marie of the Eucharist shared Mother Agnès' views: 'And we have even come to desire her deliverance for she's suffering a martyrdom'.[35]

In their brevity the doctors' comments also carry great weight. Dr. de Cornière, on September 20, was amazed at her unshakable patience and said: 'She's suffering terribly; don't wish to prolong her agony'. And Dr. La Néele, after his visit of August 30, said: 'Understand, Mother, that this little sister is suffering a veritable martyrdom'.

Thérèse herself has told very plainly of her sufferings. She did not act the stoic, but admitted quite simply what she was feeling. Over the four-month period her words about her physical sufferings do not appear very numerous, but they provide ample proof of her ascent to Calvary. We shall quote only a few: 'I have suffered very much for several days now'.[36] 'Ever since July 28 these are big sufferings'.[37] 'For the last three days it's true that I've suffered very much'.[38] 'I feel at this moment I couldn't suffer any more'.[39] 'Last night, I couldn't take any more!'[40] 'Never would I have believed I could suffer so much, and yet believe I'm not at the end of my pains'.[41] 'If only you knew what I am suffering',[42] etc. . . .

She said that she was 'ground down through suffering',[43] 'exhausted',[44] 'like a harassed traveller who falls',[45] 'crushed'.[46] Let us listen finally to what one of the witnesses had to say on this subject:

> Three days before she died I saw her in such pain that I was heartbroken. When I drew close to her bed, she tried to smile, and, in a strangled sort of voice, she said: 'If I didn't have faith, I could never bear such suffering. I am surprised that there aren't more suicides among atheists. (Sister Marie of the Trinity, Christopher O'Mahony, op.cit. p.254)

2. Sufferings of 'heart and soul'[47]

> If one judges by appearances, is there a soul less tried than mine?[48]

Today we understand better how the physical condition affects the moral, and vice versa. We are not competent to make a detailed study of psychosomatic or psychological problems of patients suffering from tuberculosis. Yet it is certain, for example, that Thérèse's extreme weakness had a part in the diverse moral and spiritual sufferings she experienced.

We put forward this distinction because Thérèse herself made it, and it gives us a practical method of analysis. On August 3, she asked for a piece of paper and wrote these lines:

O my God, how kind you are to the little victim of your merciful Love! Now even when you add bodily suffering to my soul's anguish, I cannot say 'The sorrows of death surrounded me'; but I cry out in gratitude: 'I have gone down into the valley of the shadow of death, yet will I fear no evil, for you, Lord, are with me!. (3/8/1897)

She had desired 'martyrdom of heart or of body, or rather both'.[e] Her prayer was heard, for her moral and spiritual sufferings were as numerous and varied as her bodily sufferings.

A. Terminal stages of the disease

I am a child of contradiction.[49]

When Thérèse became ill she knew that she would soon die, but she suffered from a prolonged indefiniteness, which became harder to bear as the time passed concerning her real condition. She was convinced that she was terminally ill, yet she was aware that the nuns who did not know her well, and who were ignorant of the symptoms of her disease would have difficulty in taking her for a dying person.

For a time, at least, she therefore suffered because she was not taken seriously. 'They don't believe I'm as sick as I am. So it makes it all much harder to be deprived of Holy Communion, the Divine Office'.[50] Fifteen days later, after certain comments 'had caused her pain', she returned to this subject: 'I understand very well that they don't believe I'm sick, but it's God who allows this'.[51]

Already, in May, Thérèse had compared herself to a little child who is presented with a cake that is withdrawn each time 'the child tries to take it',[52] to the child 'who misses

e   Profession note 8/9/1890.

the train',[53] to a person 'who has a lottery ticket' but whose number never comes up.[54] She no longer relied on her illness for it was 'too slow a guide'.[55]

After the alarm of the first days of June, on the 9th, she believed she had reached port. Then suddenly the situation changed. On the 10th, there was an improvement and she could 'no longer understand anything' about her sickness.[56] She was disappointed, and on the last day of the Novena in honour of Our Lady of Victories, June 14, she said: 'I'm a cured little girl'. [57] 'The hope of death is all used up'.[58]

It was like some kind of game:[f] 'Last week, I was up and around and some found me very sick. This week I can no longer stay up. I'm exhausted, and they think I am getting better!'.[59]

When the haemoptyses began she was reassured and rejoiced: 'At last, I could give him the impression that I'm really sick. Never shall I forget the scene this morning when I was coughing up blood. Dr. de Cornière had a puzzled look'.[60] On July 8 some thought it time to administer the Last Sacraments: 'I fear only one thing: that all this will change'.[61] It was a justifiable fear. 'I want to be anointed very much; let them laugh at me afterwards if they want to'.[62] (She knew that some of the sisters did not think she was in danger of death).

It was not only some of the sisters, but the superior of the Carmel himself. Yet in fairness to him, we must emphasise that Thérèse, because of the efforts she made not to sadden those around her, hardly presented the image of someone at death's-door. Canon Maupas said to her: 'Oh! You're only trying to mislead us. You're not going to die,

---

f   An unusual medical situation: the patient improves: she is disheartened, the doctor rejoices. The condition worsens: Thérèse rejoices, the doctor is dismayed. That was to continue for some weeks.

very soon you'll be running in the garden. You don't look like a person who is dying. Give you Extreme Unction? But the sacrament wouldn't be valid. You're not sick enough!'[63]

Thérèse became prey to doubts, and this is a more subtle form of suffering. Perhaps *she* was mistaken and had deceived everyone:[g] 'It came into her head that she wasn't seriously ill, that the doctors were mistaken about the state of her health. She told me (Mother Agnès) about these trials and added: "– But these changes only touch the surface of my soul ... Ah! nevertheless, they are great trials!"'.[64]

It must be admitted that the progress of the disease threw outsiders off the scent, since it amazed the doctor himself. Three days after she was taken down to the infirmary, Dr. de Cornière seems to have shared Canon Maupas' opinion. He found her 'better than usual' ... Thérèse informed the family of these sudden improvements: 'Tell them ... that I'm a child of contradiction. They think I am dying, and I don't faint away; then they think I'm alive and I'm on the threshold of death. I am a real contradiction'.[65]

On July 13 she was sure that her Spouse was at the door and had only a few more weeks to live.[66] She reminded the Guérins of the paradox: 'One day Dr. de Cornière looks so dismayed that I think I am at heaven's gate, and the next day he goes off quite happy, saying: 'Why, you're on the road to recovery'.[67]

At the end of July there were fresh doubts: 'I'm not about to die'.[68] It's too bad if no one can any longer understand anything, or if she is 'misunderstood'.[69]

---

g   This was a situation all the more painful than the childhood episode which was the source of deep interior conflicts: 'For a long time after I was cured I believed that I had made myself ill and this was a real martyrdom for my soul! (Cf Ms A p.62).

Thérèse grew somewhat tired of the frequent discussion and the morbid game of prognosis which often took place in her presence as to when she was going to die.[h]

In August the uncertainty continued. No one could any longer understand the progress of the sickness. She herself had misgivings about her imminent death. Like Robinson Crusoe on his island, she could not see the ship that she had been told was coming to save her: 'I said to myself: "They've deceived me! I'm not going to be leaving!"'[70] She would have found recovery a great sacrifice, for 'to go so far and then return! ...'.[71]

On the 23rd she said: 'God gives me no premonition of an approaching death',[72] and she then compared herself to the 'half-dead' traveller in the Gospel story of the Good Samaritan. But which way would the scales go?

At the beginning of September she was surprised by her doctor-cousin's words: 'You are like a ship that neither goes forward nor goes back'. 'You see how it changes', she said to Mother Agnès. She no longer had any confidence in these contradictory diagnoses: 'They say and then they retract!'.[73] But she was worn out by this game of hide-and-seek with 'the Thief'.

Uncertainty would be her companion until her last hour. When she was in her agony she still declared: 'You see the strength I have today! No, I'm not going to die! I still have strength for months, perhaps years!'.[74] Thérèse's acceptance of this possibility was to be her last act of abandonment to the divine will. 'I will not be sure of success until I have taken the final step and shall see myself in God's arms'.[75]

h   Would it be 'a feast day'? (2.9.1). And different feasts were mentioned: 16 July (15.7.1.), 6 August (31.7.1.), 24 September (23.9.2.) or even 'after communion', (15.7.1.)?

B. A burden on others

Thérèse had a deep fraternal love for her community and these ups-and-downs brought with them additional sufferings. She knew what the cost of a long illness would mean to a poor community. And what would happen if she were to be bed-ridden like this for years? She was concerned about this at the beginning of the Novena which was made to obtain her cure: 'The Blessed Virgin will have to cure me, or carry me off to heaven because I would find it very unfortunate for you and the community to have to care for a sick young religious'.[76] And in May she said: 'There was a time when I had trouble taking expensive medicines'.[77] She thought less of herself than of the pain she was causing her sisters, and especially her own three sisters who were suffering because of her illness. She wanted to spare them that: 'Oh! I would like ... I would like ... To cause my sisters no more pain, and in order to do this, to go very quickly'.[78] 'My good Blessed Virgin, this is why I want to leave: I tire out my little sisters, and I cause them pain when I am so sick ...'.[79] She also spoke about those 'long-term illnesses that often tire the infirmarians out and are often a cause of great suffering to the patients who are aware of this'.[80] And she was one of them: 'I give this poor little Sister Geneviève sleepless nights'.[81]

C. 'Pin-pricks'

We must not forget those 'pin-pricks' which, either directly or indirectly through a second person, still wounded Thérèse in the infirmary. She was not unaware that 'certain sisters' did not share the sentiments of the 'Martin clan".

On May 19 she confided that she felt these 'little pains very sharply' and told Mother Agnès of some painful humiliations certain sisters had given her.[82] On August 22 someone thought that she was 'imperfect'. Conversations were repeated to her. She was told that Sister Saint-Vincent de Paul, disedified at her refusal to take some broth, had said to another nun: 'Sister Thérèse of the Child Jesus is no saint, she is not even a good religious'.

Another sister came and said to her: 'If you only knew how little loved and appreciated you are here!' The humiliation was then redoubled by the cruel 'naivety' of the one who came and relayed these kind words!

And above all there was Mother Marie de Gonzague's difficult temperament which must have tried Thérèse most. Mother Agnès has left us this incident:

> On several occasions Thérèse was made to feel her jealousy which flared up because the novices often went to the infirmary. Just a few days before she died, Mother Marie de Gonzague spoke to her so coldly and made her visits so brief that Sister Thérèse of the Child Jesus asked one of the novices: 'Do you know what I have done to upset our Mother?' 'I know', replied the novice, 'I did not wish to tell you lest I caused you pain. Our Mother has noticed that I love you very much and that I am very happy when I can come and see you and she said to me: If I had known of your close ties with Sister Thérèse of the Child Jesus and how she suffices for you in everything, I would not have worried about you'. Sister Thérèse of the Child Jesus replied simply to the novice: 'Ah! That's the reason. Thank you.

On another occasion, August 30, after a visit from Dr. Francis La Néele who had spoken harshly to the prioress, the latter 'created a scene, lost her patience and railed out against the whole family, including the patient, but Thérèse remained calm'.

D. The effects of weakness

On certain occasions, in situations in which formerly she would have easily overcome herself, Thérèse suffered from the powerlessness that resulted from her physical weakness. To have known perfect self-control and to see oneself going back to base was a trial for a Carmelite, but the sick nun came through it with her usual tactic: abandonment. But that does not mean that the pain and the humiliation, which were often manifested by tears, were wiped out.

Even though she had been a model of patience, she now uttered this cry: 'Little sisters, pray for the poor sick nun who is dying. If only you knew what happens. How little it takes to lose one's patience. I would not have believed this before'.[83] On the evening of May 28, when she was running a very high temperature, a sister came and asked her immediate assistance with a piece of painting. Mother Agnès saw her sister's struggle. That same evening, Thérèse wrote her the following note: 'Your little girl has been shedding more tears, ... Ah! this evening I showed my virtue, my TREASURES of patience! And I, who am so good at preaching to others. I am glad you saw my imperfection'.[84]

> During her last illness there were plenty of occasions when she might well have been annoyed or impatient. But she hardly ever showed the slightest feeling. When she did, she admitted her weakness, and asked the person concerned to forgive her and pray for her.[i]

Then there were the interior sufferings that were more painful. 'I accept everything for love of God, even all sorts of extravagant thoughts that come into my mind'.[85] (We can only conjecture what these thoughts may have been). On August 19, shedding 'big tears', she told Mother Agnès: 'I'm perhaps losing my wits. Oh! If they only knew the weakness

---

i An example of one of these occasions: 'On July 29 1897, when she was very sick in the infirmary, one of the nuns, thinking that she would please her, brought along, to distract her, a little child's toy. But she, quite surprised, accepted it without any enthusiasm and said: 'What do you want me to do with this?' The sister, somewhat hurt, let her know that she did not find her very kind. Then, with deep humility, the Servant of God replied: 'You are right, oh! how imperfect I am! ...'

I'm experiencing. Last night, I couldn't take any more and I begged the Blessed Virgin to hold my head in her hands so that I could bear my sufferings'.[86] In the introduction to the *Green Note-Book* we find this more specific statement: 'It's like going out of one's mind'. This is a confidence which reveals much . . .

E. Temptations

The patient's state of physical weakness gave rise to different kinds of temptations.

Firstly, there were thoughts of gluttony, which were a further humiliation, not all that dangerous, we believe, which can be seen as an irony of destiny. Little Thérèse who 'has never liked the things you eat',[87] who, strangely, had never understood 'the custom of inviting one's friends to meals'[88] found herself, when dying of hunger, experiencing all sorts of fancies for food. 'She was unexpectedly assailed by a real temptation of gluttony'.[j] Her imagination put before her all sorts of choice foods and she was obsessed by the desire to have them. The *Yellow Note-Book* gives us more precise information: 'It's quite incredible! Now that I can no longer eat, I have a desire for all sorts of things, for example, chicken, cutlets, rice, tuna, fish!'[89] These may not appear to us today to be 'choice' dishes, but for a Carmelite, accustomed to a meatless diet and monastic frugality, they were a feast! Thérèse accepted moreover, with simplicity, the little dishes of food her aunt made for her as a humiliation for having been thought lacking in mortification.[90]

Of a much more serious nature were the temptations against faith that tormented Thérèse.

Concerning this spiritual trial 'that is impossible to understand', Thérèse was much more reserved. If we did not have

j   'I am plunged in matter.'

the confidence given to Mother Marie de Gonzague in Manuscript C, the fifteen or so words in the *Yellow Note-Book* about this trial would have been drowned in the sea of 'pleasantries' and smiles. If we are not to rely on appearances, then it is all the more necessary that we do not do so in this case. The insufficient data contained in the *Derniers Entretiens* needs to be clarified by Thérèse's writings.

Situated in the medical context as we now know it, the trial of faith appears even more terrible. Many know what it is like to be crushed by physical suffering. Countless sick people experience the anguish of being overwhelmed by the obsession of annihilation, the temptation to despair. But to endure both at the same time ... Especially when one is Sister Thérèse, that is to say, when one is very sensitive and intensely receptive.[k] Here we are confronted by a mysterious and impassable abyss and must content ourselves with listening to what Thérèse herself has to say.

From the midst of the pleasantries, memories, advice, affectionate words which go to make up the *Derniers Entretiens*, there sometimes emerges, rising up from the depths, allusions, brief confidences which are like choking cries. 'My soul is exiled, heaven is closed to me, and on earth's side it's all trial too'.[91] 'It's upon heaven that everything is focused. How strange and incomprehensible it is'.[92]

She admitted that certain strong impressions about the love that God revealed to her were only rays — or rather flashes of lightning — in the midst of her darkness. She insists: 'But only as a flash of lightning'.[93] Someone had read something to her in the hope of easing her pain and asked if her trial

---

k   The degree of suffering is not 'measured' only by the objective suffering experienced. It is also necessary to know who is suffering. It is true that Thérèse did not know the atrocious emotional abandonment of the anonymous patient in our modern hospitals. Surrounded by her sisters, she nevertheless felt the spiritual solitude — a faint reflection of that of Jesus surrounded by his apostles in Gethsemane.

had ceased for a moment. The immediate retort was: 'No, it was as though you were singing'.[94]

It was therefore a continuous trial. The vice was only rarely and briefly loosened.

During the night of August 6 she had hoped that she would die, for the whole night was spent struggling against temptations. 'Ah! how many acts of faith I made!'[95] Two days later: 'I admire the material heavens. The other is closed to me more and more'.[96] On another occasion, when Mother Agnès was asking her again about heaven, Thérèse gave a deep sigh: 'You are suffering very much because of your interior trial?' 'Yes. Must one love God and the Blessed Virgin so much and have these thoughts? . . . But I do not dwell on them'.[97]

On August 15, a great feast day in Carmel, the patient was in agony. 'And then one would say that (God) wants to make me "believe" that there is no heaven! . . . Ah! I'm not pretending, it's very true that I don't see a thing. But I must sing very strongly in my heart: "After death life is immortal", or without this, things would turn out badly.' [98]

When we know of her love for the Virgin Mary, these words come as a surprise: 'I would like to be sure that she loves me, I mean the Blessed Virgin'.[99]

Seeing through the window a 'black hole' in the garden, she said: 'I am in a hole like that as far as body and soul are concerned. Ah! what darkness! But I am in peace!.[100] She spoke of 'eternal life' and said after a pause: '. . . but there is one perhaps'. Then she added: '. . . and it's even certain!'.[101] This short interpolated clause throws much light on the acts of faith that she had to keep on making in the face of her continuing doubts.

On September 24 Mother Agnès thought that her sister may have had some intuition about the day she was going to die. She received this reply: 'Ah! Mother, intuitions! If you only knew the poverty I'm in ... But my soul, in spite of this darkness, is in astonishing peace'.[102]

This enduring trial that Thérèse referred to as a 'black hole', a 'wall', a 'tunnel', 'fogs', 'night', 'darkness' made her enter into a more marked solitude. It was indescribable and incomprehensible and made her a stranger even to her own sisters. Even Mother Agnès herself, who was her confidante, could not gain access to this solitude. 'You don't understand ... God alone can understand me'.[103]

Usually she preferred to remain silent about it. Yet she did speak of it to a few persons: priests,[1] her Mother Prioress, Mother Agnès, Sister Geneviève, Sister Marie of the Trinity, Sister Thérèse of Saint-Augustine and Sister Marie of the Sacred Heart.

From the chaplain, her ordinary confessor, she received no consolation, rather the contrary: 'Abbé Youf told me with reference to my temptations against the faith: "Don't dwell on these things, it's very dangerous!" This was hardly consoling to hear, but happily I'm not affected by it'.[104] Out of obedience, she also had told Mother Marie de Gonzague, since she wrote in June: 'Dear Mother, you know about this trial: I am going to speak to you about it however ...'.[105]

The *Yellow Note-Book* shows that with Mother Agnès, Thérèse was explicit, but very discreet. Up until the period in the infirmary the 'little Mother' had only known about it vaguely.

---

1 Abbé Youf and Fr Madelaine. The latter's evidence concerns the year 1896. He saw Thérèse during the June triduum and preached the retreat in October. 'Her soul was passing through a spiritual crisis; she believed that she was damned and it was at that time that she increased her acts of confidence and abandonment to God.' Externally no one would have suspected her interior trials.

Sister Geneviève was to say at the Apostolic Process: 'She was tried by frightful temptations against the faith which assailed her two years before her death and only ended with her life. She spoke to no one about these temptations which concerned the existence of heaven for fear she would pass her own indescribable torments on to them'.[m] In *Conseils et Souvenirs*, Céline shows that she knew of this suffering. She even questioned her sister, who merely answered: 'If only you knew! If you only had these trials of mine for just five minutes'.

Sister Marie of the Sacred Heart, in her testimony at the Processes, said that she did not know about her god-daughter's temptations against the faith.

In an intimate conversation with her, (Easter 1897), she asked me if I sometimes had temptations against the faith. Her question surprised me, for I did not know about her trials against the faith. I only learned of them later when I read *Story of Soul*. I then asked her if she had any herself, but she gave me a vague reply and changed the subject. I understood then that she did not wish to say anything, for fear of passing her temptation on to me.[n]

m   This is not accurate, since seven or eight persons knew, more or less, about these temptations. It is possible that Thérèse had kept her secret for a long time and had spoken only more explicitly about them in the last months of her life. It still remains that she had discussed her suffering only with her superiors.
Cf. Sister Thérèse of Saint-Augustine: 'She once told me something in confidence, which rather mystified me. 'If only you knew the darkness I am plunged into!' she said. 'I don't believe in eternál life; I think that after this life there is nothing. Everything has disappeared on me, and I am left with love alone'. She spoke of this state of soul as a temptation'. Christopher O'Mahony, op.cit. p.195.
n   Sister Marie of the Sacred Heart has not expressed herself very clearly. She said that she had not known about her sister's temptations until after her death when she read *Story of a Soul*. Yet her very statement proves that she knew something while she was alive, since she deduced from Thérèse's silence the existence of temptations that she did not want to share with her. In another section of the *Derniers Entretiens* there is an earlier text of Marie which also shows that she knew, at least partially, of her sister's trial. She herself had asked her 8 July 1897: 'You are in the dark night of faith?'. 'Ah! she said with an affirmative gesture, I am that !!! . . . '

Despite a few differences, all these witnesses were of the same opinion: Thérèse wanted to bear this trial alone. She received no real help from her superiors, and she was prudent with those on whom she felt that she might be a burden.[o] God alone could understand her.

But, from this side also, she experienced a great solitude. It was not that she was seeking sensible consolations, for her very sure faith had always sought its strength in the sacraments, which are external signs of divine action and support. Hence her insistence to receive Extreme Unction, and her joy when it was finally administered July 30. Likewise her disappointment when Abbé Youf could not come to hear her confession. We can understand that her not being able to receive communion from August 19 until her death was a very severe trial for her. And it must have been all the more so, since it was due rather to her extreme weakness than to the very strict canonical legislation of the time: she was not able to endure the long ceremony involved in taking communion to the sick. Sister Marie of the Eucharist described the situation in a letter written August 22:

> To show that her illness is becoming worse, I will tell you that she has to deprive herself of communion. She was receiving every two or three days, but, at present, if she is able, it will be once a week. When Father brings her communion the whole community enters chanting the "Miserere" and the last time, she was so weak that just hearing us got on her nerves. She is suffering martyrdom.

Mother Agnès has given us more details about this in the *Green Note-Book*, a precious text which opens up immense horizons on Thérèse's interior sufferings:

> Holy Communion, which she wanted to receive so much before, had become a source of torment during her illness. Because

o   Her prudent questions to her Sister Marie of the Sacred Heart then seem to be all the more pathetic.

118

of her vomiting, her breathing difficulties, her weakness, she feared an accident and she would have preferred that we told her not to receive. She did not want to take this responsibility upon herself, but since she had said nothing, we believed she was pleased when we insisted that she receive communion. She continued to be silent, but that day she was unable to restrain herself any longer, and she burst into tears.

We didn't know what the cause of her sadness was, and we begged her to tell us. However, the choking produced by her sobs was so violent that, not only was she unable to answer us, but she made a sign to us not to say a word, not even to look at her.

At the end of several hours, having remained alone with her, I dared to approach her and tell her that I had guessed the source of her tears. I consoled her as well as I could; she seemed as if she was dying of sorrow. Never had I seen her in such agony.

She did not receive communion from then on until her death.

We must add that this situation scandalised some of the nuns. A Carmelite dying without the sacraments ... Thérèse had heard of the 'many comments made about this subject' on that day of intense agony, and they only increased her martyrdom. On June 6, she had said: 'Undoubtedly, it's a great grace to receive the sacraments, but when God doesn't allow it, it's good just the same. Everything is grace'.[106] Six weeks later, this conviction did not stop her suffering and shedding tears at her absolute destitution: her doubts about the next life, her abandonment by the God she could not receive while heads were shaking around her. August 20 was the day she hit rock bottom: 'That day was a day of intense agony for her and of temptations which I imagine were terrible'.[107]

The temptation to discouragement that Thérèse had spoken of: 'How easy it is to become discouraged when you are very sick'.[108] The temptation to despair that prowled round her in these times of great crisis, and especially during the hours of her last agony.

> The devil is around me, I do not see him, but I feel his presence ... he torments me, he is holding me, as it were, in an iron grip to prevent me from taking the smallest relief, he increases my pains in order to make me despair ... And I cannot pray!.

This is a most enlightening confidence, since confidences of this kind were rarely given: the devil seems to have taken Thérèse's destiny in hand; prayer appeared impossible.

On September 30, coming through the broken words of Thérèse who was very restless in her bed, the witnesses discerned the presence of possible despair. Their evidence concerning that day is unanimous.

During the afternoon, Sister Marie of the Sacred Heart, very upset, left the infirmary because she could not bear any more. Until she died she would remember 30 September 1897. Much later she was to confide:

> ... to several sisters of the monastery the extreme anguish she experienced seeing her little sister suffer so terribly, and especially the last day of her life. After visiting the infirmary and witnessing it, she hesitated to return for she wondered if she would have the strength to see her again a prey to such suffering. She prayed with all her heart to obtain for her the grace not to despair.

The valiant Mother Agnès herself, riveted to her sister's bed, left the infirmary at one time to go and throw herself at the foot of the statue of the Sacred Heart so that her sister might not fall into despair.P

p   'Sister Thérèse of the Child Jesus' three sisters said many times to the Community – I personally have heard it from their lips – that Sister Thérèse of the Child Jesus suffered terribly during the afternoon of September 30. They feared that she would fall into despair. One of them – Mother Agnès of Jesus or Sister Marie of the Sacred Heart, I am not sure which, but it was certainly not Sister Geneviève of the Holy

Sister Geneviève received the same impression: 'I thought with great sorrow: "What a terrible thing it is to die!" I went out to the cloister crying and, seeking some visible sign of her happiness I said, looking up at the rainy sky: "If only there were some stars!" and I began to cry again'.[109]

Sister Marie of the Trinity also wanted to run away: 'I left the infirmary: I could no longer bear to assist at so painful a scene'.

'Since they say that all souls are tempted by the devil at the moment of death, I'll have to pass through that too',[110] Thérèse had declared one day. And pass through it she did, although the demoniac manifestations had been above all interior.[q] When we read the words of September 30, we feel that the dying nun's insistence on God's goodness: (Ah! my good God! ... Yes, he is very good, I find him very good ...'[111], etc.) is a response to interior temptations to revolt and to doubt.

After six months of fighting, after experiencing the temptation to take one's own life, the stakes had not yet been played. Right up until the last moment, Thérèse had to struggle.

We ask your pardon if you feel saturated by this synthesis of Thérèse's sufferings. Every analysis of this kind runs the risk of distorting the perspective. The third part of this book

Face, went up to the dormitory to pray to Our Lord for the dying nun, in front of the statues of the Sacred Heart and Saint Margaret Mary. These statues were still in 1970 where they had been in 1897 and where I have always seen them: in a niche next to the first cell on the left at the top of the stairs. The statues are a plaster colour. The reason for the prayer was that Sister Thérèse would not despair ...' (Written testimony of Mother Françoise of the Child Jesus 3/9/1970) Mother Marthe-Thérèse of the Eucharist, entered Lisieux Carmel in 1924, and Sister Marie-Ange, entered 1922, did not doubt that it was Mother Agnès who went to pray.

q Thérèse does not speak often of the Evil One in the *Last Conversations*. Cf. 25.8.6; 11.9.5; 11.9.6; 29.9.3.

will situate these trials in the framework of the patient's life, in the totality of her existence. Some may have felt a certain repugnance at violating a soul's mystery. Some sufferings can be readily grasped, but it is in the silence of meditation that the reader must return to the text of the *Last Conversations*. By definition, sympathy (# to suffer with) is a better means to understanding than the story.

We must understand, in a realistic way, that Thérèse was not ignorant about the basic fundamentals of man's estate. She recognized that she had a great capacity for suffering: 'Ah! what I suffered I shall not be able to say except in heaven',[112] she had already written in 1895 when recalling the spiritual suffering of her childhood. This was even more true of September 1897, and she confirmed it herself two hours before she died: 'Never would I have believed it was possible to suffer so much! never! never!'[113].

A portrait sketch

You do not know me as I really am. (LT, 25/4/1897)

We have given only the true facts of a story, now we have to gather up the threads and attempt to sketch a portrait.

It is true that the outline began to emerge at the beginning of the last chapter. But, like the modern paintings of the saint in the impressionist style, it still needs many strokes of the brush to fill in the detail that we hope will make it more true to life.

Let us not be under any illusions ... the undertaking is a difficult one for several reasons. Firstly because of the wealth of material available. We did not wish to write a synthesis. And yet a portrait of Thérèse in the face of death gathers together all her thoughts, her whole life. Everything converges towards these decisive moments.

This task is also much more difficult than that of the first part, and also more debatable, for it will inevitably be more subjective. The same pictures, edited in different ways, produce different films.

The reader can always refer back to the texts that were used as a basis for each statement, and so correct our sketch according to his or her own point of view.

___ Chapter 1 _____
A human saint

'The holier a woman is, the more feminine she is.' When Léon Bloy was writing this sentence in 1897 he could not have known that a young Carmelite in Lisieux was proving this for him in a most convincing way. At the time, Mother Agnès of Jesus and many others in the Church had written more spontaneously: 'The holier a woman is, the more angelic she is.' Thirty years later, the prioress of the Lisieux Carmel was still writing that she 'would never be in favour of writing a book on "the human qualities of the saints". Just look at what is being done to belittle the holy Curé of Ars and others'.[a]

When Mother Agnès pronounced this severe interdict, so contrary to present-day hagiography, did she realise that she had been the first to break it by taking notes in the infirmary? Her *Yellow Note-Book* gives the lie to her remark, for it brings to life again before our eyes a Thérèse who was so real and so human. Mother Agnès was too shrewd not to have noticed that her sister was human. Did she not write to Sister Marie of the Sacred Heart: 'What a joy it is to see a little saint with backbone.' A happy victory for intuition over a debatable point!

Sanctity has nothing to lose by being considered in all its human reality. 'The saint stands before us as he or she will stand before the Judge.'

a   Letter to Sister Françoise-Thérèse (Lèonie) 29/7/1928.

125

1. An invalid like others

The laws of sickness are the same for all. Speaking of the future publication of her Memoirs, Thérèse said to her sister: 'There will be something in it for all tastes, except for extra-ordinary ways'.[1] The same could be said of her last 'con-versations': Thérèse lived quite simply the ordinary life of a seriously ill person.

Lying on her bed, she heard the convent clock strike regularly for community exercises. In her imagination she saw her sisters going to the choir, entering the refectory. She let her gaze wander round the infirmary. She looked at her pictures pinned to the curtains round the bed, the statue of the Virgin of the Smile, the patch of garden that she glimpsed through the window. She heard 'music in the distance' . . . Her eyes followed 'a pretty little white thing that flies'. Raising herself a little, she would take some bitter medicine, chase away an annoying fly, smile at the sister entering the infirmary. When she was alone, she thought of her past life, of her life as it then was. She prayed. And so her days passed by, at least the moments when she had some respite from pain.

When it did come, Thérèse, like any other sick person, suffered, groaned, cried. Then she would doze off to sleep, have nightmares, or know insomnia while all around her were sleeping. Like many others – the vast majority – there were times when she felt incapable of praying, incapable of saying or having 'beautiful thoughts', of imparting a formal will or testament, of dying like Socrates. There was no affecta-tion in this simplicity: 'I would, however, like to have a beautiful death to please you'.[2]

It was too bad if she disappointed those around her who wished to reap a harvest of 'beautiful' words. They got only these: "I don't think of anything; I'm content to go to heaven, and that's it. Since I have been ill, I don't think of anything very much".[3] "If you only knew the poverty I'm in!".[4]

This absence of thoughts at certain times is not inconsistent with other words that imply deep reflection. Thérèse 'thought'[b] often during these moments of inactivity, a common phenomenon with a person confronted with death.

In June, the writing of Manuscript C stirred up reminiscenses of recent and more distant events: "I remember sometimes certain details which are like a springtime breeze for my soul".[5] Between June and 30 September Thérèse saw her life unfold once again before her. As in 1895, when she wrote her childhood memories and had sung 'the Mercies of the Lord', Thérèse, in the infirmary, pondered again on 'all the graces God has given me'. If she could no longer write, she could speak, at least on those days when she could breathe freely. Mother Agnès encouraged and prompted these past reminiscenses by asking her sister many questions about certain periods of her life. But the very nearness of death alone was enough to bring back to her mind that surge of memories. And so the whole of Thérèse's life reappears in the *Last Conversations*.

2. The upsurge of memories
'I was thinking today of my past life.'[6]

In the pleasant childhood we glimpse the first of the depths of every suffering. That childhood which had left such an impression on Thérèse and had taken up a large section of her first manuscript came back to her mind spontaneously when she was ill.

b   Typically theresian verb: it is used 98 times in Ms C, 91 in the *Yellow Note-Book*.

Of the four and a half years at Alençon she remembered the poetry she used to recite about the blue sky, the trips to Lisieux, the little basket ...

Countless memories naturally sprang to mind of the eleven years spent at Les Buissonnets: stories, poems, songs, cantiques that M.Martin used to recite or sing in the evenings. In the infirmary, Thérèse still remembered. She recited the story of 'Puss in Boots', sang a verse. She could still hear the cries of the little child next door; she remembered the happiness she had known during the days spent at Alençon and Trouville, a bottle of Cologne, the blue-birds bought at Le Havre, the large banquets ... She recalled impressions she had had when she was a shy little girl: 'In my childhood, the great events of my life appeared to me as insurmountable mountains. When I saw little girls make their first communion, I said to myself: 'How will I do at my first communion?'[7] 'And suddenly I thought: "Alas! how little I've lived! Life always seemed short to me. My childhood days, these seem but yesterday!'[8]

And with the flood of memories that had deeply moved her, she dreamt of fields and flowers.

The statue of Our Lady of the Smile was constantly before her, reminding her of her illness and cure of 13 May 1883. She did not forget any of the great graces of her life: her first communion 8 May 1884, the grace of Christmas 1886, her father's permission to enter Carmel at fifteen, the 'transports of love' of the year 1887, the trip to Rome. She saw once again Leo XIII's piercing eyes fixed on her own!

There were also the vivid memories of her religious life. The postulancy with its great sufferings: thought to be too thin by one sister, too plump by another, the mortifications in the refectory, voluntary and involuntary, the very great trial of M. Martin's illness, the sacrifice of not pouring out her soul to her sister Agnès, the painful sessions for direction

128

with the novice mistress. But there were also happier memories, the devotion to the Holy Family, the flowers for the Infant Jesus. And then there was of course that procession of graces: the general confession to Fr Pichon 28 May 1888, the 'flight of the spirit' in July 1889 in St.Magdalene's grotto, the launching on the 'waves of confidence and love' in October 1891 by Fr Alexis Prou, the reading of St.John of the Cross when she was about seventeen, the conversations with Mother Geneviève, 'the saint of the Lisieux Carmel', the 'flu epidemic of the winter of 1891-1892, and above all, the Offering to Merciful Love of just two years before.

The whole of her life as a Carmelite flashed by: She saw herself at the office, going about her different duties, in the parlour with Céline. She recalled the little everyday events: the pruning of the chestnut trees in the garden, the new habit that did not fit properly, the incident of the iron cross, personal emotions: the possibility of going to the missions, the disappointment of Christmas 1896.

3. Childhood regained

It was not just memories that returned more or less spontaneously to mind. Her whole being, knowing that it did not have an earthly future here below, revealed, as it were in itself, the eternity that was soon to lay hold of it. Or, more profoundly, Thérèse remained the child that she was.

Let us try to explain this fine point as clearly as possible. We are not saying that Thérèse's spiritual childhood was a continuation of her early childhood. She herself says very positively that she left behind 'the swaddling bands of infancy'.

This does not mean that she did not always have that wonderful ingenuity, so acclaimed by all poets: 'I have lost childhood', wrote Bernanos, 'I will only be able to regain it through sanctity'. Thérèse never completely lost it, although her maturity was exceptional.

But how can we differentiate between what was the continuation of her childhood and what was regained through the triumph of grace? On this point, the *Last Conversations* seem to defy analysis.

Thérèse was truly herself in these last months, and did not repress anything that rose up from the depths of her being. This was not due to any relaxation, through weakness or lack of perseverance, of that strict control that she had imposed on herself during the whole of her religious life. 'Now' a threshold had been crossed. All her deepest inclinations were expressed. Moreover, the weakness that resulted from her illness no longer allowed her to stop these inclinations at will: her heart was laid bare and, in Thérèse, the heart that was revealed was the heart of a child. The *Last Conversations* reveal that simplicity and frankness that Bernanos describes so well in *Les Enfants Humiliés*:

> There are saints who absolutely cannot speak of the other side without lifting their voices, and we do not need to listen to them immediately after the Gospel. We would become deaf by comparison. These saints, I suppose, one day must have given up a part of themselves that they did not think was so precious, that they probably thought was too human, and which they were not able to regain, even at the price of countless sacrifices – a certain simplicity, a certain frankness, a gift of grace, freely given and never restored in its initial form, even at the cost of their scourgings and fasts![c]

Thérèse belongs with those saints who have never lost that fundamental part of themselves – their childhood, their zest for life.

---

c   Bernanos must have had Thérèse in mind when he wrote these lines in Brazil in 1939. *Novissima Verba* was at that time his bedside companion.

A. *Love of nature*

The love of nature has always been a characteristic trait of Thérèse's personality: 'I loved the countryside, the flowers and the birds so much'.[d] We must not forget that she spent the first twelve months of her life at Semallé nourished by the milk of the quick-witted Norman, Rose Taillé, and that her early years had been profoundly influenced by that sojourn in the country.

In the infirmary, this side of Thérèse's character was thrown into relief. When her bed was still in the corner, she leant over to admire the sunset. She rejoiced to see the stars,[9] the sky.[10] On Saturday 28 August, her bed was turned round so that she could see the garden. 'Oh! how happy I am!' She was able to admire the red virginia creeper.[11]

When she saw the fruit that she loved, she showed a child-like joy. She liked especially grapes, plums and peaches because of their soft skin: 'I get so much pleasure out of touching fruit, especially peaches, and I like to see them near me'. She counted nine pears on the tree near the window: "Fruit is very good!"[12]

'You know, dearest Mother, how much I love flowers', wrote Thérèse in 1895. 'I love flowers very much', she repeated 28 August 1897. Dying in mid-autumn, flowers were never wanting, and almost every day the sisters would bring some to the infirmary. One brought along periwinkles, another violets − ('Ah! the scent of violets!'), wild flowers, cornflowers, roses, dahlias. Often a parable would spring to mind as she contemplated these gifts: the ears of corn were symbolic of the graces that filled her soul, the little white

---

d   Ms A, 37. She emphasises the sacrifice she willingly made on entering Carmel: 'I renounced forever the joy of running in the countryside'. Ibid p.175.

flower her father had given her spoke to her of her own destiny, and the dead leaf suspended in the air by a spider's web that would fall the day she died was a sign of her life that had been cut short ...

We find something of the franciscan spirit even in her attraction towards animals. The sight of a white hen hiding its chicks beneath its wings was, for her, a parable of God's love that moved her to tears. A little sparrow fed by its parents reminded her of the story of her own life. Thérèse did not want anyone to take life. As for example, 30 August, she begged her sister not to pull out a rhododendron. She protected a wounded mouse and the little birds that spoilt the fruit in the garden.[13] These latter seemed grateful to her for this, for, on the anniversary of her profession, a robin came and hopped on to her bed, and during her agony countless birds sang outside the infirmary window.[14] She would not even let anyone kill the flies that bothered her in the hot summer.[15] The day before she died, she did not want to kill an insect that got caught in her sleeve. She knew 'these little beasts!'.[16]

It is not difficult to see here once again the little girl of Les Buissonnets, the friend of birds (linnets, tame magpies, blue-birds), gold fish, silk worms, rabbits and especially Tom, the faithful spaniel, who is unexplainably missing from Manuscript A.

B. 'Children's words'

At a deeper level, the child in Thérèse expressed itself through words with an inimitable ingenuity. Children's words, funny or sad in their depth and transparency: made-up words that amaze adults. They upset Bernanos who was searching through books for the precise reason of finding the lost language of childhood.

The *Last Conversations* contain countless examples. Let each one discover them and relish those that speak to him or her. We shall quote here the ones that appeal to us: "How strange it is to fear death! But when we're married, when we have a husband and children, this is understandable: but I who have nothing! ...'[17]

'Who could ever invent the Blessed Virgin?'[18] 'And what will happen afterwards (the Last Judgement)?' Speaking of God: 'When he misleads me, I pay him all sorts of compliments, and he doesn't know what to do with me'.[19] Gazing at Christ on her crucifix: 'He is dead! I prefer when they represent him as dead, because then I think he is no longer suffering',[20] etc.

Perhaps we have to be in tune with childhood to grasp the nuance — sometimes imperceptible — between childishness, affectation, and genuine childlikeness. Nothing is more irritating than a woman who acts like a baby. In Thérèse's time, those around her were often given to affectation, and religious affectation is even more detestable. How did Thérèse manage to escape this pitfall? In the sick nun's language we do not find false expressions of her feelings, for her love of truth protected her from these dangers.

C. Affectionate and sensitive

'Jesus has not given me an insensitive heart',[21] Thérèse wrote in June 1897. As a little girl, she cried often and was even 'much given to crying' during her pre-adolescence. 'I was really unbearable because of my extreme touchiness ... I cried for having cried. All arguments were useless and I was quite unable to correct this terrible fault'.[22] It required nothing less than 'the little miracle' of Christmas 1886, when she was almost fourteen, to cure her of her hypersensitivity. 'The source of my tears was dried up and since then has re-opened rarely and with great difficulty.'[23]

These two adverbs must not be taken too literally. After Christmas 1886, Thérèse still cried: for her 'child' Pranzini, in the confessional, when she spoke of her vocation to her father, during the trips she made to Bayeux, Paris, Rome, etc. to obtain permission to enter Carmel. Entering the monastery did not dry up all her tears, for she cried on her Veiling Day, and when Céline went to the ball she 'shed a torrent of tears'.[24] She also cried when she read her correspondence.

Yet there is a distinct difference between these tears and those which preceded her 'conversion'. If she retained a young girl's sensitivity — and it was not uncommon to shed copious tears in that neo-romantic period — Thérèse overcame it.

However we notice a recurrence of tears during the last months of her life.

The principal reason for this was that her weakness undermined her physical being. Often at the end of her strength, the sick nun could not hold back the tears that welled up after an incident or a little vexation.

On several occasions we see her shedding tears of repentance, of 'perfect contrition'. 'She began to shed copious tears for fear that she had caused me trouble in a circumstance about which I wasn't even aware.'[25]

But there were other reasons for these tears, apart from the combination of sadness and weakness. The blossoming of the purified person seemed to reopen the source of the tears.

Thérèse wept 'for joy' when a passage from the Gospel answered a heart-searching question, or when she was given a relic of her friend Théophane Vénard. She wept 'in gratitude' towards God, or towards Mother Agnès, Sister Geneviève, or her three sisters together. Tears of 'consolation' flowed when she saw Our Lady of the Smile going before her into the infirmary.

She wept above all 'of love'. She saw in Mother Agnès' smile a sign of God's love for her: 'Then the tears came. It had been many years since I cried as much as I did then. Ah! but these were tears of consolation'.[26] On 6 June she cried 'as on the day of my first communion,[27] and the remembrance of a former grace, prompted by her sister's words, caused the same reaction.

We therefore notice, in this final period, an abundance of tears, for various reasons. fixing her gaze on Théophane Vénard, Thérèse confided: 'I don't know what is the matter with me; I can't look at him without crying'.[28]

Her great sensitivity, even more refined by illness, expressed itself through these tears. Thérèse herself was surprised at this. These tears of consolation and joy brought her some comfort during her trial.

D. 'I'm always cheerful and content'[29]

This does not come as any surpise to the reader of the *Last Conversations*! The sick nun, in the midst of suffering, manifests this almost uninterruptedly by her astonishing gaiety, her manifold jokes, puns and mimicry. By her words and actions she was able to make those who were weeping at her imminent death burst out into peals of laughter. She did not want any sadness around her ...

The witnesses are unanimous on this point. Ten percent of the words in the *Yellow Notebook* come under the heading of 'humorous'. 'She was always cheerful in spite of her great sufferings of both body and soul'[30] recalled Mother Agnès. Sister Marie of the Eucharist's letters contain many references to this fact:

> With regard to her morale, it's always the same: she is gaiety itself, she makes everyone who comes near her laugh ... She began amusing herself by talking about everything that would

happen after her death. Because of the way she did this, when we should have been crying, she had us bursting out with peals of laughter, so amusing was she. She reviews everything; this is her joy, and she shares it with us in words which make us laugh. I believe she'll die laughing because she is so happy.[31]

Mother Agnès' scissors had been particularly busy in this area when she published *Novissima Verba*. Given the circumstances and situation at that time, we can understand her reaction.[e] How would the jokes of a dying saint be taken by the crowd of admirers? Would not the serious-minded be discouraged? Would not her sister's sufferings be eclipsed by these puns and laughter? An objection that can now be overruled, since some critics had said that the sanctity of the editress of *Story of a Soul* was 'too flowery'. What would they have said if they had been presented with 'that charming little patient', 'with a mischievous look' who 'knows only how to make us laugh. There are times when one would pay to be near her'. All this does not reveal a very serious kind of person.

When Mother Agnès re-edited the section of the *Last Conversations*, called the *Green Note-Book*, in response to that objection, she did not have to tamper with the truth. An account of her sister's illness was enough to convince the vice-postulator. But the theresian equilibrium becomes distorted and warped if we eliminate her cheerfulness, her humour and her joy.

The unedited edition of the *Derniers Entretiens* reveals a person who was full of life, who came out with unexpected witty retorts and joked in the most tragic situations. Such a saint cheerfully broke through the canons of a stiff and solemn sanctity that was unacceptable to those who had often been driven away from the springs of living water by grim

e   Thérèse was solemnly canonised at Rome 17 May 1925. Mother Agnès prepared *Novissima Verba* in 1926.

faces. 'Saint Louis de Gonzague was serious, even during recreation, but Théophane Vénard was always cheerful'.[32] Thérèse, as we know, preferred the second.

Until now we have known her as lovable, 'usually smiling', but we had not known that she was so full of fun, wit and 'Gallic malice'.

This aspect is not unimportant if we wish to examine the contrasts in Thérèse's temperament. After her mother's death, which had had such a marked effect on her, her 'happy disposition' changed. As an adolescent, she had a keen sense of the swift passage of time and saw herself as an exile on earth. Yet by nature, she was cheerful and spontaneous. In Mme Martin's letters we find frequent reference to her resounding laughter, amusing mimicry and songs. Thérèse herself always remembered the 'lively joys' of her childhood. At twelve and a half, tortured by scruples, her aunt described her as follows: 'Thérèse and Marie amuse themselves very much. Thérèse is charmingly cheerful. Maman told me yesterday that she had never seen Thérèse so radiantly happy'. During the trip to Italy, despite the failure of her mission to the Pope, the young fifteen-year old girl was so full of life that some of the peeved pilgrims complained of her liveliness.

Her letters and writings are not lacking in humour. She knew well how to see the funny side in a situation, an individual, and she had such a gift for mimicry that, without the curb of a vigilant charity, she could have been hurtful. In Carmel, when she was absent from recreation, the young sisters were bored.

It is the same Thérèse whom we find in the infirmary — in 'her bed of suffering'. The examples of her humour in the *Last Conversations* are manifold. It does not seem right to categorise all these manifestations of her cheerfulness. Too bad! It is the only way that we can gain an insight into the extent of Saint Thérèse of Lisieux's repertoire.

She had always loved puns, like her father who often jested with words during the happy evenings at Les Buissonnets. As an invalid, she retained this love. Their standard was on a par with the Vermont or Hachette Calendars that were so popular in homes during the last century. But, knowing now, as we do the context in which they were made, we should not judge them too harshly. We will concern ourselves rather with this gravely ill person's ease and ability to seize the given opportunities.

Interrupting a conversation, (Céline) said sadly, thinking of her death: 'I'll not be able to live without her!' she answered quickly: 'That's right, so I'll bring you two wings!' (This is a play on two French words: 'elle' and 'ailes' which have the same sound).[33]

This scene was often repeated in the infirmary. In order to combat her sisters' sorrow, Thérèse was able to transform a tragic remark with a smile. The pun aims at distracting — 'distrahere' - we will come back to that later.

Let us emphasise that such an attitude was not improvised. In the midst of suffering, a person who wanted to cheer up those around their bed, but not gifted with word-play, would not have been able to seize the occasions.[f] Words had always held a fascination for Thérèse who, to raise a laugh, was not afraid to coin or use new words, to slip in archaic forms, or to use familiar language and words of her own Norman land.

We must not forget that, when she was nursed at Semallé, she imbibed, with 'little Rose's' milk, a taste for pungent expressions. Her voice always retained something of the

---

f   She also made puns with the following words: (The numbers in brakcets refer to the date in the *Last Conversations*) agonir, agoniser (8.7.9), dates, dattes (9.7.5), semper, Saint Père (10.7.2), à la terre, Alaterre (21.9.7), none, nonne (5.8.2), bière (8.7.17), le Bon-Sauveur (p.216).

Norman accent. In the infirmary, she performed, complete with accent, a little peasant comedy, addressed to her glass of mouth-wash water. "'As soon as I go to drink, it does this to me". She coughs and says to her glass of Bottot water: "It's not for drinking!" (Aside) "It doesn't understand!" Then louder: "It's not for drinking, I tell you!"'[34]

Since she had become again 'a baby living on milk',[35] she used language befitting her state. Taken out of its context, this baby-talk could encourage serious misunderstandings about Thérèse's so-called childishness. Rather it should be seen, situated in its proper background, as a form of courage.

This invalid, without resources, had some unexpected windfalls: 'I am a little drinker without thirst'.[36] Someone spoke of a superior-general of a congregation. She preferred Mother Agnès whom she instantly promoted to 'Superior-General of (her) heart'.[37] If she called Jesus the 'Thief', it then followed logically that his mother was also a 'thief'.[38] Saint Joachim became, for her, 'grandpapa'.[39]

Such is the way children play. Do we have to hold a grudge against them if they sometimes appear forward and verge on rudeness?

Thérèse did not play only with words. She could raise a laugh out of all sorts of situations: by imitating unusual expressions,[40] by making up a story to save a wounded mouse,[41] by imagining herself in heaven and curtsying to God 'like Sister Elizabeth's little niece'.[42] For Mother Agnès she invented a sign of affection that no religious ever had, or ever would receive.[g] Several times she made up words to fit well-known tunes.

g With her bare foot, she lightly touched the face of her sister who was sitting on a low stool at the foot of the bed. (Oral Tradition, quoted in the *Derniers Entretiens*).

M. Maupas refused to give her Extreme Unction. So this was what was to happen at the next visit from this 'unmanageable' superior:

> The next time I'll not go to so much trouble. I sat up in bed to be polite, and he refused what I was asking of him! Next time I'll use a little pretence. I'll take a cup of milk before he comes because then I always look terrible. I'll hardly answer him, telling him that I'm in real agony. (Then she put on a real comedy for us). (LC 9/7/1897).

Her natural wit had always enabled her to discern the foibles and idiosyncracies of others. Without any trace of cutting irony she gave vent to undeniable humour about those who gathered round her bed. When they crowded in: 'Lots of people who have something to say'.[43] The nickname, 'Bobonne', that she gave her sister, Geneviève, was an appropriate reminder to the latter of her humble duties! Hidden beneath a smile was this slight reproach to Mother Agnès: 'Say rather that it's for yourself!'.[44]

It was a humour that readily came to the fore where men were concerned, as if 'the poor misunderstood woman'[45] was taking her revenge.

Looking at the photographs of her two spiritual brothers, she said: 'I'm much prettier than they are!',[46] and before a photograph showing the seminarian Bellière dressed in military uniform: 'To this soldier, who looks so dashing, I'm giving advice as to a little girl'.[47] h

She did not want a visit from Mgr Hugonin, and added: 'If it were only Saint Nicholas, who raised three little children'.[48]

---

h   This flash of wit says much for Thérèse's understanding of Abbé Bellière. She had, nevertheless, written at the end of June: 'I do not believe myself capable of instructing missionaries; happily, I am not as yet proud enough for that!' (Ms C p.256).

But it was above all at the expense of the doctors, especially Dr. de Cornière, whom she nicknamed Clodion Le Chevelu because of the way he wore his hair, that she exercised her wit. The diagnoses were hesitant because of the fluctuations of the disease. After the doctor had declared 'a change for the better', when she was still suffering very much, she said: 'Yes, yes, she's much better than usual! ...'[49] She was not impressed by these quickly changing diagnoses: 'They say and then they retract".[50] On 31 July her sisters were discussing the few days of life she had left. Thérèse interrupted: 'It's still the patient who knows best'.[51] [i]

Saved one day, condemned the next, she planned her revenge: 'I wanted to say to Dr.de Cornière: I'm laughing because you were not able to prevent me from going to heaven; but, for all your trouble, when I am there, I will prevent you from coming there too soon'.[52] [j]

In September she made up yet another little comedy for the benefit of the medical profession: 'If I were cured, the doctors would look at me in amazement, and I would say to them: 'Sirs, I am very happy to be cured to serve God still on earth, since it is his will. I suffered as if I had to die; well, I will begin again'.[53]

Like every true humorist, Thérèse did not spare herself, even in the most tragic circumstances. There were times when she verged on 'dark humour'.

When she had great difficulty in breathing, she uttered little cries: 'Agne! Agne!' However, this did not please her and she decided to say: 'Anne! Anne!'. 'We'll put that in your circular letter', said Mother Agnès. 'You'll make it sound

---

i   This reminds one of the famous: 'Who is dying here?' of Caesar in Marcel Pagnol's play, *César*, Livre de Poche, no.14.
j   Dr de Cornière died in 1922. He was eighty-one.

like a recipe',[54] replied the patient. At other times, obliged to move in bed by putting her weight on her hands, she compared herself to the grasshopper in the Psalms.[55]

Looking at her emaciated hands, she said: 'I'm becoming a skeleton already, and that pleases me'.[56] She added: 'I will tell you something: very soon I'm going to be dying ... It reminds me of a greased pole. I've made more than one slip, then, all of a sudden there I am at the top!'.[57]

'With a happy and mischievous air', she announced that she would 'soon be in the horrors of the tomb!' Her humbled bones would leap for joy when her little Mother would join her there.

Those around her, once again, were discussing burials. The purchase had just been made of a plot of ground for the Carmel in the Lisieux cemetery. Thérèse joined in the conversation and said, laughing:

Then I will be the first one to do honours to this new cemetery?' The doctor was surprised and told her not to be thinking of her burial. She replied: 'But it's a happy thought. If the hole is so deep, it will disturb me, because some accident could happen to those who were lowering me into it'. And continuing in this same vein: 'I already hear one undertaker crying out: 'Don't pull the cord there! Another answers: 'Pull it that way! Hey! be careful! So that's that!' They will throw some earth on my coffin and then everybody will go away (LC p.258).

Although very weak, she nevertheless told stories and retained to the full her Norman common sense. The new bells, a recent gift of Uncle Guérin to the monastery, rang out. Mother Agnès said: 'Listen to the bells ringing'. Thérèse's response, expressing her lack of enthusiasm, came out spontaneously in the Norman dialect: 'Not yet, very beautiful'. (Pas cor, instead of Pas encore. Translator's note).

From these and other words, we can perhaps gain an insight into Thérèse's artistic tastes. It seems that, with the

142

approach of death, her desire for authenticity finally opened her eyes to the religious 'art' of her day.[k] On 30 July, her condition was so grave that the sisters prepared the blessed candle, holy water and sprinkler in the adjoining room. Thérèse looked at them and said: 'When the Thief comes to fetch me, put the candle in my hand, but do not give me the candlestick. It is too ugly'.[58]

There were many reasons for her overflowing joy. We have emphasised Thérèse's natural optimism: 'I always see the good side of things'.[59] But what temperament could withstand such trials?

The source of her joy, fundamentally, came from her total acceptance of God's Will. 'Don't be sad about seeing me sick, little Mother, for you can see how happy God makes me. I'm always cheerful and content'.[60] In her second last letter to the Guérins she gave the following explanation: 'I know my sisters have told you of my cheerfulness, and it is true that I am like a finch, except when I have a temperature; luckily it usually comes only at night, at the hour when finches are asleep, their head beneath their wing. I should not be as I am if the good God did not make me see that the only joy on earth is to do his Will'.[61][l]

This joy was noticeably greater at the beginning of July when Thérèse thought that she was going to die. And so, 8 July, the day she went down to the infirmary, seemed like a true festival. She was full of joy and wanted to share it with her sisters. 'Ever since she has become convinced she is going to die, she has been as gay as a little finch',[62] wrote Sister Marie of the Eucharist to her parents.

k 2 June 1897, Thérèse gave Sister Marie of the Trinity a picture of the Infant Jesus that she had loved very much. She wept as she looked at it, for it then appeared to her to be very ugly.

l One of the very rare references to her health in her letters.

We find here again the same joy that prompted Thérèse to write when she spoke of her first haemoptysis 3 April 1896: 'I thought that perhaps I was going to die and my soul was filled with joy'.[63] Only an intense love and a longing to meet the Beloved can explain her joy that was so out of the ordinary.

Thérèse's joy was an expression also of the other side of the love that filled her heart: fraternal charity. She wrote in June: 'What banquet could a Carmelite offer her sisters except a spiritual banquet of loving and joyful charity? . . . The Lord loves a giver'.[64] And when she was in the infirmary, she said: 'When we are around the sick, we must be cheerful'.[65] In reality she could have said: 'For their infirmarians, the sick must be cheerful!' Those around her were well aware of the efforts she made, and sometimes they questioned her sincerity: 'Surely all that cheerfulness was not sincere: you were suffering too much in both body and soul'. Thérèse protested, 'with a smile': 'I never *pretend*!'.[66] That does not mean that it did not require will-power. 'Whenever I can, I do my very best to be cheerful in order to please you'.[67] As for her famous smile, it takes on a deeper meaning in the light of what she said earlier to Sister Marie of the Angels: 'When I suffer something, instead of looking sad, I smile. In the beginning, I did not always succeed, but now it is a habit I am happy to have acquired'.

Her sisters were not mistaken.

To the end of her life, Thérèse retained those childlike and charming mannerisms which made her company so pleasant and attractive. All the nuns wanted to visit her in the infirmary. Her lovable cheerfulness seemed to take on a new dimension as her suffering increased. While it was only another manifestation of her fortitude of soul, it was also the effect of her exquisite charity. She sought in this way to lighten our poignant sorrow as we thought of the impending separation. (cf CGS p.215)

In view of this evidence, it can be easily understood why we have drawn so heavily on this unpublished segment of the *Derniers Entretiens*. All these jokes, witty retorts, puns and mimicry of Thérèse when she was seriously ill shed such a radiant joy that they show the whole extent of the theresian heroism. Once again, appearances can be misleading.

Fulfillment

A study of Thérèse's profound humanness leads to a better understanding of her as a real person who was endowed with diverse possibilities. But we must go further. If she reached fulfillment at the end of the short and direct course of her life, it was because divine grace had intimately penetrated that humanity.

Let us try to enter into the depths of that life which was so caught up in the grip of Love's passion.

1. 'In the fullness of love'

I try to make my life an act of love. [a]

Thérèse offered herself to Merciful Love in June 1895 and, in September 1896, she discovered her vocation: to be LOVE. Her life had but one acknowledged goal, and that was to love Jesus and to make others love him. In July, she wrote the following:

> You know, O my God, I have never desired anything but to love you, I am ambitious for no other glory. Your love has gone before me, and it has grown with me, and now it is an abyss whose depths I cannot fathom. Love attracts love, and, my Jesus, my love leaps towards yours; it would like to fill the abyss which attracts it, but alas; it is not even a drop of dew lost in the ocean!

---

a   LT, 25/4/1897. Cf also all the letters of these last six months.

... For me to love you as you love me, I would have to borrow your own Love ... (Ms C p.256)

Her last words on September 30 – 'My God ... I love you!', uttered with her last breath, summed up the whole of her life and, in a special way, that period of her illness which marked the climax.

A. 'My God ... I love you!'

We do not wish to repeat here what has been dealt with in works such as those of Mgr Combes, but rather to point out some characteristics of Thérèse's love for God. They were present, certainly, before her last illness, but they took on, at that time and in that desperate situation, a decisive strength.

Thérèse had always loved God[b] tenderly, like a child who forgets itself in order 'to please'. This expression was especially dear to her, and it could appear childish. But, once again, let us go beyond the language to grasp the interior attitude it expressed.

'It's impossible, I know, but if God did not see my good deeds, I would not be in the least distressed about it. I love him so much that I'd like to be able to please him without his being aware of it'.[1] She had formed 'such a lofty idea of heaven' that she wondered if, when she got there, she might not be deceived: 'If I am not surprised enough, I will pretend to be surprised just to please God. There isn't any danger that I'll let him see my disappointment. I will know how to go about it so that he won't notice anything'.[2] 'Everything I did was done to please God',[3] 'I've given all to him to do with as he pleases'.[4] Etc.

---

b   The eloquence of a single statistic: the word 'God' appears 257 times in the *Yellow Note-Book*; 232 times in Thérèse's mouth. (316 times in the *Derniers Entretiens*). The names *Jesus* appears only 32 times in Thérèse's mouth in the *Yellow Note-Book*.

'To please', therefore, means to love the Other by forgetting self, by not thinking of self. 'For a long time I have not belonged to myself. Since I gave myself totally to Jesus he is therefore free to do with me as he pleases'.[5]

At a time when so many christians were carefully counting their acts of virtue,[c] hoping to capitalise and gain a heavenly reward proportionate to their merits, Thérèse loved freely, extravagantly, generously. 'When one loves, one does not calculate', she had written in her poem, '*Vivre d'Amour*'. Her whole attitude is therefore expressed in this statement: 'I'm no egoist. It's God whom I love, not myself'.[6]

It was a love that expressed itself in spontaneous childlike outbursts, in familiarities that were so unexpected and so contrary to the pervading climate of the late nineteenth century Carmels where Jansenism had impregnated hearts. Thérèse challenged the fears which paralysed her companions: 'I don't understand souls who are afraid of so loving a Friend'.[7] 'Since it has been given me to realise the love of Jesus' Heart, it has driven from my heart all fear'.[8] 'Ah! the Lord is so good to me that it is quite impossible for me to fear him'.[9] 'How can I fear one whom I love so much!'.[10] [d]

Since God was truly her Father, and she was truly his child, why not call Him 'Papa'? Without knowing it, her loving intuition had rediscovered the primitive meaning of the Aramaic 'Abba', which the most rigorous exegetical criticism has recently brought to the fore.

Anticipating the liturgical reform by some sixty years, Thérèse used the familiar form of 'Tu' (Thou) when speaking

c   Thérèse had been brought up in this climate of 'book-keeping', and was freed from it. Cf. Ms A p.25. Her Rosary of Sacrifice Beads, her preparation for her first Holy Communion. She made 1949 sacrifices and 2773 ejaculatory prayers in two months. Ms A p.73.
d   'My nature is such that fear made me recoil, with love, not only did I advance ... I actually flew'. Ms A p.174.

to Jesus. She kissed 'the face'[11] and 'both cheeks',[12] and not the feet of the crucifix as was the custom at that time. Looking at a picture of two children with Jesus, she said: 'The other little one does not please me as much; he's acting like an adult. He's been told something, and he knows he must respect Jesus'.[13] In heaven she would not be like the Seraphim who 'cover themselves with their wings before God'.[14]

The realism of love that knows how to see and how to understand! Thérèse preferred the Holy Face represented with eyes cast down: 'since the eyes are the mirror of the soul, if we had seen his soul, we would have died from joy'.[15] Likewise, she thought it was better that her crucifix represented Christ as dead, because then 'he is no longer suffering'.[16]

It was a love that had become audacious in its élan! Thérèse loved St.Mary Magdalene and St.Augustine for their 'loving audacity'[e] and she followed their example. 'I imitate the conduct of Magdalene. Her astonishing, or rather her loving audacity, which charms the heart of Jesus also attracts my own'.[17] Noticing the uneasiness of those around her who were not accustomed to such language, she asked: 'Perhaps this is boldness?' Then comes the firm answer: 'No, for a long time you permitted me to be bold with you'.[18] She even taught others to act as she did:

> I am not surprised that the practice of 'familiarity' with Jesus seems to you a little hard to manage. You cannot achieve it in a day, but I am certain that I shall aid you better to walk that delightful way when I am free of my mortal envelope. (LT 18/7/1897)

It was a love which gave itself in complete trust. This abandonment to the One who would never deceive her was to

---

e   These two saints were instrumental in Teresa of Avila's conversion. (Life Ch.9).

be, in her situation, the living expression of her passionate attachment. 'I accept all for love of God'.[19] We know now what lay hidden beneath that *all*. 'I love him so much that I'm always pleased with what he does'.[20] This childlike remark reveals the purity of her disinterested love. 'When he misleads me, I pay him all sorts of compliments, and he doesn't know what to do with me'.[21]

We could go on quoting so many extracts from the *Last Conversations*, but let us sum them all up in the following passage: 'Since my Offering, all that I do, my actions, my looks, all, is done through love'.[22] That Offering she repeats as often as she can.

B. 'When I am charitable, it is Jesus alone who is acting in me'[23]

In the long expositions on fraternal charity in her last manuscript, Thérèse clearly shows why and how her charity is rooted in her love of Jesus. We learn here that it was precisely in 'that year' she received the grace to 'understand what charity is and to sound its mysterious depths'.[24] We are not going to enlarge on this surprising statement,[f] but instead look at a few of Thérèse's words to illustrate our point.

She insists often and strongly on the importance of this love. It must above all not 'consist in feelings but in words'.[25] On some pages she returns to this four times.

'For some months now,' she has no longer had 'to struggle to practise this beautiful virtue', and she gives us the key

---

f   Thérèse said that before she had understood charity, 'but in an imperfect way' (Ms C p.219). What is meant by 'this year'? Was Thérèse referring to the current year of 1897, or to the twelve months preceding the time when she was writing her manuscript? In that case it would go back to 1896. It would be very valuable to date that important grace. It remains an open question ... Perhaps a very close study of all the theresian writings could reveal the answer.

to her success: 'When I am charitable, it is Jesus alone who is acting in me, and the more I am united to him, the more also do I love my sisters'. The sick nun insists very much on this universality: Charity must extend to 'ALL who are in the house, without distinction'.[26]

The *Last Conversations* give us a perfect illustration of statements found in Manuscript C. They prove that Thérèse truly lived out what she had written. Moreover, she herself was aware of this: 'I'm very happy. I don't offend God at all during my illness. Recently, I was writing on charity (in the exercise book of her life) and, very often, the nuns came to distract me. Then I was very careful not to become impatient and to put into practice what I was writing about'.[27]

Let us suppose for a moment that the manuscript did not exist, or that it had been destroyed. By reading only the *Last Conversations* we would be able to discover through her words and actions Thérèse's principles.

'To All who are in the house without distinction'

When her world became limited to the infirmary, she ran the great risk, easily understandable in view of her condition, of slipping into a certain free-and-easy manner of living. Surrounded by her three sisters, it would not have been difficult to let herself be coddled in the rediscovered family atmosphere. On the other hand, in such a setting, it seems natural that the charity practised might be one-way: with tenderness, signs of sisterly affection and kindness being directed towards the patient. But, in Thérèse Martin's case, general rules do not apply. The opposite happened, and the dying nun gave to all more than she received.

Her love expressed itself with an exquisite tenderness. She was not afraid to write: 'I no longer feel that I must refuse all human consolations'.^g God knows how she had struggled against her natural feelings and affections during the first years of her religious life.^h A few months before she died she knew that the sacrifices had purified her 'tenderness' ...ⁱ For 'when the human heart gives itself to God, it loses nothing of its innate tenderness; in fact, this tenderness increases when it becomes more pure and more divine'. She had written to Mother Marie de Gonzague: 'I love you, dear Mother, with this tenderness, and I love my sisters too'.[28]

What was this 'now'^j in which Thérèse was living? We shall briefly examine her attitude towards those who were in daily contact with her.

With Mother Agnès

'The little Mother', who spent the most time at her sister's bedside, certainly benefited from that fraternal charity in a unique way. When she was certain that she was soon going to die, Thérèse, who knew her older sister's affection for her, feared the consequences of her going away. How would Mother Agnès take it? With much tact, the patient sent her numerous notes to ease her pain after the revelation of May 31. Thérèse was full of joy when Mother Agnès came round

g Ms C p.237. 'I don't wish to speak, dear Mother, about the love and confidence you are giving me, but do not think the heart of your child is indifferent to these. It is only that now I feel I have nothing to fear. In fact, I can rejoice in them'. (Ms C p.206.)
h 'Ah! I knew beforehand that living with one's own sisters would be the cause of continual suffering when one wishes to grant nothing to one's natural inclinations'. (Ms C p.237.)
i 'Love is nourished only by sacrifices. The more a soul refuses natural satisfactions, the stronger and more disinterested its tenderness becomes'. '... my soul is strengthened by him whom I wanted to love alone. I can see that in loving him the heart expands and can give to those dear to it incomparably more tenderness than if it had concentrated upon one egotistical and unfruitful love'. (Ms C p.206.)
j We have stressed the importance of this adverb in Ms.C. In each case its interpretation necessitates certain nuances.

to accepting the situation, and she wrote in July to Abbé Bellière: 'Ah! how happy I would be if you could take my death as Mother Agnès of Jesus is taking it ... Our good Mother was very much afraid that her sensitive nature and great affection for me would make my going very bitter for her. It has been just the opposite. She speaks of my death as of a feast, and this is a great consolation for me'.[29][k]

How can we set down the affection that Thérèse expressed to the writer of the *Yellow Note-Book*? Ten per cent of her words form 'a litany of tenderness': 'If you knew what you were for me! But I'm always telling you the same thing'.[30] Affectionate phrases abound: 'You are my sun',[31] 'for me you're a lyre, a song',[32] punctuated with the refrain: 'Little Mother, how I love you'.[33] 'I love you very much, very much.'[34].

Knowing that it would please her, Thérèse recalled the past they had shared together: 'All the great graces of my life I have received through you'.[35] 'Oh! how much I owe you.'[36] And she also made many promises for the future: 'I'll always be with my little Mother'.[37] 'You don't know how much I love you, and I'll prove it to you! ...'[38]

Her affection was not confined to words. Thérèse knew that her long illness was taking its toll on her sister's delicate health, and so she reminded her about the medication she had to take: 'You must strengthen yourself: thirty drops tonight, don't forget!'.[39] Her gestures were no less eloquent. There were the embraces and kisses she received and gave, or even asked for like a child: 'Give me a kiss, a kiss that makes a noise; so that the lips go 'smack'! Tenderly, she leant her head on Mother Agnès' heart.[40]

---

k   It is understood that Mother Agnès did not always have these sentiments. In August, Thérèse was to say to her: '... we must abandon ourselves. I would like you to rejoice'. LC 25.8.8.

A reflection of August 9 expresses the relationship that existed between the two sisters: 'You have become for me again what you were in my childhood'.[41] Referring to herself as 'baby', she often called the one who was doubly her mother 'Maman'. After twenty years, the life at Les Buissonnets *seemed* to be relived.

If this statement of Thérèse were taken out of context, it could be interpreted as a sort of regression to childhood. But what a road had been traversed since 1883 when Pauline's departure to Carmel brought on a serious illness. All the theresian writings, together with the *Last Conversations*, prove Thérèse's emotional maturity. Very plainly, she had reminded Mother Marie de Gonzague in June that she had not entered Carmel to be with Pauline and her sisters again.[1] Right up until the very end, she strongly advised them not to live a family life in the cloister. Her love did not blind her. She saw only too well her sister's temperamental weaknesses and she was not afraid to reproach her. But she always did so with a joke or a smile so that she would not hurt her too much:

> You go to too much trouble over things that aren't worth the trouble ... when you've done something like this, you make it even worse by fearing the consequences too much ... You're like a timid little bird that hasn't lived among people. You're always afraid of being caught. (LC 10.7.6.)
>
> You waver too much, little Mother. I've noticed it many times during my life. (LC 2.8.1.)

Consisting of reproaches such as these and countless signs of affection, the *Yellow Note-Book* became a personal document of inestimable value for Mother Agnès. What food to support the sufferings of a long life! We do not know when, but did such a privilege give her the right to add two words

---

1 Ms C p.216. Thérèse had undoubtedly heard about some of the remarks or insinuations made about this subject.

to a sentence of her sister: 'You know all the inner recesses of my little soul, *you alone* . . .[42] These two words prompted a reaction from Sister Geneviève which in turn was responsible for the note of explanation – and correction – that Mother Agnès wrote 28 August 1940. Thérèse was so richly and spiritually endowed,[m] that each sister, and not only the Martin sisters, was able to think that she, personally, was the recipient of a privileged friendship.

With Sister Geneviève

The brief conversations recorded by Sister Geneviève also reveal a Thérèse who was affectionate, and, at the same time, a spiritual teacher who saw very clearly the young novice's shortcomings. Céline had scarcely entered the cloister before she became aware of the distance that separated her from the little sister who had become her 'ideal'.[n] What efforts had to be made to struggle against her natural independence, her crises of discouragement, her whole temperament! There were days when the little way seemed to her inaccessible. And the one who was teaching her was going to die! Thérèse knew all this: 'Ah! my little Sister Geneviève will feel my departure the most. Certainly she is the one I pity most, because as soon as she is in trouble she comes looking for me, and she will no longer have anyone'.[43]

To encourage her sister, Thérèse used to recall many intimate memories – anything that could rekindle the union of the two once-inseparables.[o] She was no longer sparing

---

m   Thérèse's Letters show how she adapted herself to each correspondent: 'It is impossible to act with each one in the same manner'. Ms C p.240.

n   'You are my ideal, and this ideal I cannot attain. Oh! it's so cruel!' LC 24.7.2.

o   Ms A pp.103, 104. 'Little Valerian', 'the two little ducks', LC July 1, 'two little birds', LC 4.8.4., 'two little children', LC Aug. 1, 'both on God's knees', LC 4.8.4., 'the two women in the Gospel', LC 5.8.1.

with affectionate expressions: 'Bobonne, I love you very much'. 'O my Bobonne, I have a great tenderness for you in my heart'. Etc.[44]

'All things to all men'

We can understand how Sister Marie of the Sacred Heart felt, for a time, a certain jealousy towards Sister Thérèse of Saint-Augustine. Thérèse appeared to be so friendly towards her! When Thérèse was so overjoyed to see her in the infirmary[p] how could Marie have believed that this sister displeased her 'in everything'.[45]

Although she had written, when speaking of the novices: 'I am prepared to lay down my life (for them), but my affection is so pure that I don't want them to know it'.[46] Yet she sent notes to Sister Marie of the Trinity, her 'doll': 'Know that I love you more than you think . . .' 'I suffer, too, from my powerlessness, (at not being able to speak to you) . . . You hold an immense place in my heart'.[47]

Although sick herself, she did not forget others who were also sick: Mother Hermance, who was so trying for the infirmarians. Without complaint, she submitted to the importunate visits of Sister Saint-John of the Cross who, every evening, used to go to the infirmary to look at her and laugh.[48] When Sister Saint-Stanislaus left her in a draught for a long time, Thérèse, out of obedience, had to explain to the prioress what had happened, but she did so in the most charitable way she could.[49] During the last night of her life, so as not to waken her sisters, she kept holding on to the glass in her hand. How many other similar acts were there that we do not know about?

p   'Each of my visits was a cause of fresh joy for her'. Cf. "I want to be friendly with everybody (and especially with the least amiable sisters) to give joy to Jesus'. Ms C p.246.

However this ever active fraternal charity did not limit itself to the narrow confines of the infirmary. She often broke the enclosure. A keen psychologist, she quickly saw how much Abbé Bellière, who had lost his mother at an early age, needed direction that was both firm and affectionate. The advice she sent him was sometimes more like that of a mother than of a twenty-four year old sister. The liberty of expression she adopted with this twenty-three year old seminarian is also surprising. In February 1897 she was still using the formal 'Monsieur l'Abbé', but two months later, in her fourth letter, she called him 'my dear little brother', because her heart, henceforth, refused to call him 'Monsieur l'Abbé'.[50] In July she wrote: '. . . dear little brother of my soul' and ended the letter with these words: 'Goodbye, my dear and *much loved* Brother, be assured that for all eternity I shall be your *true little sister*'.[q] (Thérèse herself underlined these words). In private she called him 'Maurice'.[51]

On his side, the seminarian called her 'his little Thérèse',[52] and this pleased her. Little did he dream what an heroic effort he was demanding of his sister when he asked her to write often during his holidays. With Mother Marie de Gonzague's permission, Thérèse replied in pencil, 'with many pauses', and at length. Nothing could lessen her affection for this soul, for it was a case of strengthening, nay of even saving a vocation.[r]

She made the same effort to write to her family whom she 'loved very much'.[53] Had she not said: 'I don't understand the saints who don't love their family'?

q   LT 18/7/1897. Many of these affectionate expressions are missing from the first edition of the Letters, Carmel, Lisieux, 1949.

r   Thérèse was very clear-sighted about this matter. She entered into that friendship, but has left very clear and precise recommendations about the subject: 'Correspondence should be very rare, and it musn't be permitted at all for certain religious, who would be preoccupied with it, etc.' LC 8.7.16. 'Without the express wish of authority, this correspondence would do more harm than good', Thérèse wrote to Mother Marie de Gonzague. Ms C p.252.

When we look at the whole of Thérèse Martin's life — knowing of the serious emotional handicaps of her early years[s] — we can but admire the blossoming she attained towards the end of her days. There was a transparency in the love she expressed and lavished on all, and a balance in her relationship with others. Thérèse had an emotional maturity that was astonishing for a young girl who had entered a small enclosed community at the age of fifteen.

2. In the fullness of wisdom

A baby who is an old man.

At an early age, Thérèse knew that she had matured quickly:

> Ah! had the learned who spent their life in study come to me, no doubt they would have been astonished to find a child of fourteen understand perfection's secrets .... (Ms A p.105)

She was only sixteen when she wrote to Céline who was just twenty:

> What memories we share ... A whole world ... Yes, Jesus has his preferences, in his garden are fruits that the sun of his love ripens almost in the twinkling of an eye ... Céline! ... let us make use of the favour shown us by Jesus, Who has taught us so much in a few years! (LT 26/4/1889).

When she began to write down her childhood memories, she prefaced them with a solemn sentence, suggesting the experience of a long life:

> I find myself at a period in my life when I can look back on the past; my soul has matured in the crucible of exterior and interior trials. (Ms A p.15).

s   Her mother's death, (she was four and a half), Pauline's departure to Carmel, (nine and a half), illness at Les Buissonnets, (ten years old), crisis of scruples (thirteen), her adolescent hypersensitivity, (up until Christmas 1886 when she was fourteen).

She was twenty-two years old!

This feeling of maturity reached its fullness in the little exercise book written as death was approaching. Now she knew that her short life was coming to an end. The remarks of those around her, who 'measure experience by years' as is the practice among human beings,[54] did not leave her indifferent. In Carmel, generally speaking, a long life of fidelity was held in higher esteem than the flashing passage of a meteor. Thérèse thought otherwise. She had already reached 'an advanced age', 'for two thousand years are no more in the Lord's eyes than twenty years ... than a single day'.[t] 'Age means nothing in the eyes of God'.[55] This was the reason, in the end, why she was not greatly concerned about being criticised. Did not King David himself complain of being 'young and despised'? She found herself in the same situation, but like him, she knew that she had 'understanding above old men'.[56] This statement, made in June 1897, is not lacking in audacity if we will forget for a moment what we know of her posthumous history.

It must be noticed, however, that Thérèse did not rely solely on her own feelings in this matter. She reminded Mother Marie de Gonzague that one day the latter had 'not hesitated to tell (her) that God was enlightening (her) soul and that he was giving (her) the experience of years'.[57][u] If this had not been so, then how could the prioress have entrusted her with the novitiate? In actual fact, the little sister's 'inexperience' and 'youth' had not frightened the prioress.

Louis de Gonzague's life, moreover, ratified Thérèse's own opinion. During the reading in the refectory, she noticed that

---

t   A familiar idea with Thérèse. 'Time is nothing to your eyes, a single day is like a thousand years. You can, then, in one instant, prepare me to appear before you'. Act of Oblation, 9.6.1895.

u   Ms C p.210. This is perfectly confirmed by the following extract of a 'portrait' of Thérèse by Mother Marie de Gonzague as early as 1893: '... a wisdom, a perfection and a perspicacity of a woman of fifty ...' (cf LC p.16).

it was said of this very young boy 'that had he lived to the age of Noah he would not have learned more or become more holy'.[58]

There were other nuns who shared Mother Marie de Gonzague's opinion. 'She is ready for heaven', wrote Sister Geneviève to Brother Simeon, 'she is only twenty-four, yet because of her ability and exceptional sanctity, our Mother has made her her assistant in the novitiate'. Sister Marie of the Sacred Heart also echoed these sentiments:

> To have covered such a long course in such a short time. Abbé Youf said to our Mother: 'You have here a second Mother Geneviève'. Yes, but she has matured early and Jesus wants to gather her up for the delights of heaven. If you knew all she has told us, all her little thoughts – they are wonderful and bear the stamp of wisdom and sanctity.

The sick nun, aware of all this, said to Jesus: 'I can't understand why you are waiting so long to take me, since I am a little grape and they tell me I'm so ripe!'[59] Sister Marie of the Sacred Heart has left us a precious confidence:

> I said to her: 'You are therefore a baby?' She then became very serious and answered: 'Yes . . . but a baby who has thought much! A baby who is an old man!.[v]

We have only to re-read Manuscript C to gauge the depth of what she wrote at the age of twenty-four. Could not one think that it had been written by an old religious passing on the experience of a lifetime? We find in it an astute analysis of enclosed contemplative life, profound teaching on fraternal charity, valuable remarks about spiritual direction, an understanding of the Church and her mission – in short, a well from which spiritual writers and theologians would

---

v   A maturity which is striking in some of the photographs of Thérèse, e.g., Thérèse holding the lilies. Let us also note that the expression, 'ripe souls are destined to go quickly to heaven', was a frequently heard cliché of the religious language of the day.

later draw. All this was written under obedience and under circumstances with which we are now familiar. It contains the fruit of personal experience without any shadow of pedantry or semblance of a didactic treatise.

This experience that was so important for Thérèse who only knew what she lived[w] and which, obviously, does not cover the whole field of human endeavour.

But first and foremost, it does impart an understanding of people and of the mysterious workings of grace in the life of each individual person. It is a fundamental understanding and experience, closely linked with her vocation as a Carmelite which, in the biblical sense, touches the heart of the human person and influences all man's vital problems. In the Pascalian sense, Thérèse is a past master in the order of charity. In her own way, she stands beside the spiritual father and the 'Staretz' of the monastic traditions of both eastern and western spirituality'.[x]

A. Novice Mistress

We do not have to consider here Thérèse in her role as novice mistress, since she was unable to exercise that duty in the last month of her life. This does not mean that, until September 30, she did not make use of the least opportunity to help her little flock.

As we have said, Sister Geneviève, because of her infirmary duties, benefitted greatly from this vigilant instruction.

---

w   It would be interesting to note all the vocabulary in the theresian writings which express experience: 'I know', 'I feel', 'I understand and I know by experience', 'I realise through experience' etc. It is something which links together two saints, Teresa of Avila and Thérèse of Lisieux, across time.

x   This wisdom of 'an old man' is expressed through sentences such as this one: 'But now I'm astonished at nothing' (Ms C p.224) which could be placed in a collection of theresian sayings.

The other novices were very sad at being separated from a mistress who was so capable, and who understood them so well. This was especially so in the case of Sister Marie of the Trinity who, relieved of her work in the infirmary because of her youth, felt this very keenly. She did not hide her disappointment and Thérèse sent her several pencil-written notes which reveal both her firmness and her tenderness: 'I have pity on your weakness ... With you one must say what one thinks on the spot. I don't want you to be sad; you know what perfection I dream of for your soul, and this is why I spoke to you so severely'.[60] In August, she again wrote to the same sister who was still sad and despondent. The patient ordered her to go and play with a top in the attic of the novitiate to distract herself and lift her spirits. Earlier Thérèse had given her a humiliating penance, and had refused to give in to her pleading.

This was how Thérèse put into practice what she had written in June. The lesson must be adapted to suit the temperament of the one concerned, and the circumstances. Pedagogy, inspired by love, does not conform to rigid rules. The day before she died, Thérèse wondered if she had upset her 'doll' by sending her away from the infirmary: a last manifestation of concern for the feelings of the youngest sister in the novitiate.

Sister Marthe also received some notes full of affectionate advice:

> Dearest little Sister, do not be a sad little girl, because you are not understood, misjudged, forgotten, but win everybody by trying to be like the others, etc.[61]

Sister Marie of the Eucharist was to remember until the day she died the last instruction her cousin gave her several days before she received the veil (June 2). The lesson bore fruit. 'Ah! what a beautiful little soul she is, and how, in fact, I have thanked God for having known her. She can no longer give us her counsel, but what remains with us, and will always remain with us, is her example'.[62] But that did not prevent the mistress taking the novices to task over the smallest points: 'You shouldn't sit sideways on the chair: it's forbidden'.[63] Or, 'You must try to be more gentle, never use harsh words, or a severe tone of voice ... for yesterday you hurt Sister X ...', etc.

In the infirmary, Thérèse did not want to be free-and-easy. Under pretext that she was living there, the novices would willingly have turned it into a 'no-man's land' where the Rule no longer applied, a place for recreation where they could joke or play with the large red balloon. The mistress protested: 'We should not call ourselves by all sorts of names. After all, it isn't religious!'[64] 'No little boys' games!'.[65]

B. Wise Counsel

Others as well as the novices benefitted from her spiritual direction. On her sick-bed we saw her 'harassed' by her sisters' and her spiritual brothers' questions. The resulting counsels, so full of wisdom, contained in the *Last Conversations* and her last letters are considerable. There is nothing stiff nor starchy in that experience which was passed on without ceremony or concern about an ordered synthesis. 'What a lesson this little girl has given us ...' exclaimed Uncle Guérin himself.

Mother Agnès was the first who eagerly drew upon her little sister's accumulated experience. She asked her advice: 'What would you have done in such a situation[66] Thérèse always answered. She warned her of the temptations that beset a prioress: she must not speak about her troubles,[67] she must not listen to a certain sister who wanted to confide in her even though she was no longer prioress;[68] the sick should be obliged to make known their needs, great vigilance should be exercised with regard to any correspondence between the nuns and young priests, etc.

Sister Marie of the Sacred Heart also asked questions, but more discreetly: 'And what must little god-mother do?'[69] On another day, her god-child advised her not to pour out her heart to Mother Agnès, unless it was for the latter's consolation.[70]

She told the 'Martin clan' that they were not to discuss the latest fashions in the parlour;[71] they were to observe the silence and not live as if they were still at home. She stressed this point, turning to Mother Agnès: 'This, Mother, is the most useful of all'.[72]

Her recommendations cover every aspect of Carmelite life and religious life in general: to remain silent when misunderstood or falsely accused,[73] to fight on, even when there is little hope of victory,[74] to never give ourselves over entirely to our tasks,[75] not to judge another in haste,[76] to go to recreation, not for ourselves, but to please others,[77] to be moderate in the use of penitential instruments,[78] and above all to exert effort.[79] Thérèse also tells us how we must act when seeking spiritual direction,[80] how to treat the sick,[81] how to observe the silence,[82] and how to keep secrets.[83]

It is understandable why the older sisters used to come on the quiet to the infirmary to consult their younger sister and ask for her advice.

C. Passing on the little way

Such a wealth of experience suffices to place Thérèse among the 'great' religious of her day. But even more important than the wealth of wisdom, is the specific message which she discovered during her years in the cloister, and which became crystallised in her 'eureka' scriptural discovery. As a result of it, since 1897, millions of people throughout the world have identified theresian wisdom exclusively with her 'way of spiritual childhood'. Yet, clearly, this idea in itself is too limited, and it mutilates the theresian genius. Conrad de Meester reminds us of this in his important work, *Dynamique de la Confiance*. Following Mgr Coombes, he has shown that the words 'spiritual childhood' never came from Thérèse's pen. Mother Agnès willingly admitted that she had inserted the expression into the long synthesis presented to the Apostolic Process. With much insight, Father de Meester had adjusted the texts of *Novissima Verba* (1927) and has deleted the words 'spiritual childhood', which do not stand up to critical examination. In fact, the belated edition of these texts had been influenced by the success of the Canonisation Cause. This criticism has been perfectly justified by the publication of *Derniers Entretiens*. The *Yellow Note-Book* now contains only one text which refers to 'the way of spiritual childhood'.[84] This text is itself the result of interpolation.

These critical findings could well seem to be of secondary importance if they did not force us to draw a conclusion that is of the utmost importance for our understanding of Thérèse. It could have been thought that Thérèse having discovered her 'little way of trust and love', became a 'spiritual guide', instructing those around her in a more or less dogmatic fashion, especially as the end was drawing near. Alas, once again, for the lovers of romantic images! Undeniably, *Derniers Entretiens* destroys one by one all stereotyped ideas. We do not see there a saint, at the point of death, gathering her disciples round her to give them a formal testament. Despite certain appearances to the contrary, Thérèse breaks this imagery. Indeed, her 'disciples' did write down what she said. But at no time whatever did she play the role of theologian.

It was not that she had given up the idea in those last months of passing on her 'way'. On the contrary, she knew that she had been entrusted with a 'mission': to make God loved as I love him, of giving my little way to souls'.[85] But her attitude remained as flexible as life, and cannot be described without nuances. The sick nun never missed an opportunity to explain her 'way' to her spiritual brothers. To Fr Roulland a simple statement was sufficient:

> My way is all of trust and love ... perfection seems easy to me. I see that it is enough to realise one's nothingness, and to give oneself wholly, like a child, into the arms of God. Leaving to great souls, to great minds, the fine books I cannot understand, I rejoice to be little; because only children and those who are like them will be admitted to the heavenly banquet.[86]

With Abbé Bellière she was insistent, because she knew his needs:

> I follow the path (Jesus) maps out for me. I hope that one day Jesus will set you on the same path as me.[87]

The following month, she again spoke of it:

> I feel that we must go to heaven by the same road – suffering joined with love. When I come into harbour, I shall instruct you, dear little Brother of my soul, how you must navigate on the tempestuous sea of the world: with the love and utter abandonment of a child who knows that his father loves him too much to forsake him in the hour of peril.[88]

Eight days later, she was even more emphatic:

> You are *barred* (this word is underlined) from going to heaven by any other way than your poor little sister's ... the way of simple loving confidence is indeed the way for you.[89]

Some days later she was amused to think that she had given 'advice' to a soldier as to a little girl: 'I'm pointing out to him the way of confidence and love'.[90]

Since Thérèse knew how to 'teach' at the time, why do we find only eight words out of seven hundred and fourteen that speak explicitly of the little way? Was not this her last chance to define and give more details about her 'doctrine' to her sisters who were attentive to her every word?

As we have already emphasised, we would misunderstand Thérèse if we thought of her setting herself up in a 'dogmatic way'. We do not want any further proof than this very revealing fact: the only so called 'beautiful' definition of her little way that is in *Novissima Verba* and so often commented on by theologians and preachers,[y] is missing from the other versions. Without denying 'the perfect theresian inspiration' of this text, is it not characteristic of Thérèse that doubt can be cast on its authenticity?

A further reason explains her discretion and relative silence about her 'way of confidence and love'. In August she knew that, now, she would not be writing any more. Soon she was to agree that: 'Everything is said'.[91] She knew that her writings contained many passages about the little way. There was no point in returning to it again. She would leave that to God. For her, it was no longer a question of speaking or of writing. She had to live and die.

That, finally, is the valuable teaching contained in the *Derniers Entretiens*, and is Thérèse's ultimate lesson. We see how she herself lived the little way, and above all, how she lived it in the face of death. In the Preface of *Novissima Verba*, 10 November 1926, M. Dubosq very fittingly wrote: 'It is the dear Saint's testament. She is indeed present in it'.

Yes, the testament of a life. There was no longer any need to speak of the 'way of childhood'. Thérèse was right, for, by looking at Thérèse herself we can understand her spirit better than by reading syntheses of spiritual theology. She suffered and offered herself, pushing confidence to its furthermost limits, discovering, ever more and more, the mercy of God at work in her illness and in her suffering. '... Thérèse

---

y   'Sanctity does not consist in this or that practice, but in a *disposition of heart* which makes us humble and little in the arms of God, conscious of our weakness, and confident even to the point of boldness in his Fatherly goodness'.

168

had reached that point in her life', wrote Fr François de Sainte-Marie, 'where her mind was often preoccupied with the idea of "experience" in relation to "theory"'. Conrad de Meester expresses the same thought in an excellent way: 'Her life and her way were one'.

This is why the *Last Conversations* will disappoint those who expect to find there sublime words, 'beautiful thoughts'[z] or scholastic definitions. Let us be satisfied with the essential: to contemplate Thérèse living out her 'way of trust and love' during the last months of her life.

3. The testament of a life or the triumph of the little way

At the beginning of Manuscript C, Thérèse sets out her 'little way that is very straight, very short and totally new',[92] and explains how she discovered it.[a] Let us try to summarise it.

Filled with immense desires, but realising her extreme powerlessness, Thérèse remains little and throws herself into the arms of God her Father who will fulfill her childlike desires beyond all hope, since he himself is the One who put them into her heart.

This is what Thérèse lived out during her illness, but with a new intensity as her powerlessness became increasingly greater. In this unprecedented situation, strengthened by her past experiences, she had to test the authenticity of her 'little doctrine'. It was to be a 'moment of truth', or rather a 'month of truth', for the experience would be prolonged. We can

---

z   'When one is very little, one does not have beautiful thoughts . . . our Beloved does not need our fine thoughts, if he wants sublime thoughts, has he not his angels', etc LT 25/4/1893. Cf. Ms C p.234 and LC 8.7.16 on 'beautiful words'.

a   We refer the reader to this very important text of Ms C p.207, which is too long to reproduce here, but essential to our point.

see what was at stake. What would her discovery be worth if it was not going to withstand the supreme test: death?[b] We know already the great desires which inspired Thérèse when she became ill: to love until she died of love, to make God loved throughout the world. Since she had discovered in St. John of the Cross the key sentence which was to become a minor premise in her reasoning: 'The more he (God) wants to give, the more he makes us desire', she knew her desires were not illusions.[c]

We find this maxim of the Spanish saint in Thérèse's Act of Oblation. During those last months she did not stop repeating it. It had become a beacon in her march to death. It recurs again at the end of Manuscript C,[d] in a letter to Abbé Bellière, dated July 13, and by an interesting coincidence on the same day in the *Yellow Note-Book*: 'He (God) has always made me desire what he wanted to give me'.[93]

Three days later she gives Mother Agnès the reasons for her confidence:

I had made a complete sacrifice of Sister Geneviève, but I can't say that I no longer desired her here. Often in the summer, during the hour of silence before Matins, when I was sitting on the terrace, I would say to myself: Ah! if only my Céline were near me! No! It would be too great a happiness for this earth! . . . And when I saw here enter here, and not only enter,

b Since the appearance of the Last Conversations one is struck by the fact that so little place has been given to the last six months of Thérèse's life in studies that are nevertheless serious.

c The little way could be expressed in a syllogism. Major: I have immense desires but I am powerless. Minor: Now God never inspires vain desires. Conclusion: Therefore, by having confidence in him, I will realise my desires (since he is the One who will fulfil them). We have not expressed the little way like this to reduce it to the level of rational logic, but to show that her love rests on a logic based on total confidence. Thus Thérèse, when a child, showed that she was logical by not being surprised at the Eucharistic mystery, since 'God is all-powerful!' Ms A p.27, 10/5/1877.

d 'He has always given me what I desire, or rather, he has made me desire what he wants to give me'. Ms C p.250.

but entrusted to me to be instructed in all things, when I saw that God was doing this, and so surpassing all my desires, I understood something of his immense love for me.

So, little Mother, if a desire that is hardly expressed is answered in such a way, it is then impossible that all my great desires about which I've so frequently spoken to God will not be completely answered.[e]

Thérèse expresses the same idea again on July 18 when she speaks of her desire to work after her death, even on the very day of her death she said: 'All my desires have been fulfilled, and this great one (to die of love) will also be granted'.

Herein lies the foundation of 'the way', the various phases of which we must now set out in detail.

A. 'Weak and imperfect'

Another surprise emerges from the *Last Conversations*. Has not a saint, at the point of death, reached perfection? In a general way one would think so. Yet we find ourselves confronted by a person who is perfectly clear-sighted about her imperfections and shortcomings, one who frequently says that she is 'weak and imperfect'. Once again Manuscript C, her letters and her last words are in complete agreement.[f]

---

e LC 16.7.2. Let us note in passing that the little way is firmly rooted in Biblical tradition. Thérèse bases her hope on past experience, like the Chosen People: in present suffering, she reminds God of his past goodness, in order to hope in the future. Cf. LC 27.5.2.

f Here we must rely only on the authentic writings. With time, Mother Agnès (eg. cf. *Novissima Verba* 27.5.2.) and many other commentators have 'rubbed out' Thérèse's childish faults referred to by Mme Martin and recognised by Thérèse herself (Ms A). The same error is to be avoided for the period of the last 'conversations'. We cannot say: 'She said that she was imperfect out of humility'. This would amount to accusing Thérèse of 'pretence', and would disprove the little way.

In June, when describing the difficulties of enclosed community life, Thérèse said she knew from experience 'those sad sentiments of nature'[94] her novices confessed. 'I have the same weaknesses as they, . . . I understand them *through experience*.[95] Sometimes she very nearly lost her patience.[96] On those occasions she thought she had been very 'imperfect'.[97] Even if she no longer had to struggle to practise charity she readily admitted: 'I don't mean by this that I no longer have any faults. Ah! I am too imperfect for that!'[98] Five months before her death she summed up her opinion of herself: 'I am weakness itself . . . and I expect each day to discover new imperfections in myself'.[99] She made this prayer: 'Lord, you know better than I do my weaknesses and imperfections'.[g]

The same thoughts are echoed in the sick nun's letters: 'O my Brother, believe me, I beg you, the good God has not given you a *great* soul for your little sister, but a *very small* and very imperfect one'.[100] To Mother Agnès she admitted: 'I am glad that you have seen my imperfection'.[101] 'We must bear our imperfections patiently'.[102]

The notes of the witnesses reveal the same sincerity in repeated avowals: 'There isn't anyone here more mistrustful of her feelings than I am'.[103] To her little Mother who had confided something to her, she said: 'I have my weaknesses also'.[104] We see some examples of this in the *Last Conversations*. Thérèse feels sad,[105] she manifests a certain distaste for the condensed milk,[106] a displeasure in 'something' that is offered to her,[107] to a particular remedy.[h] She dries her

g   Elsewhere in Ms C she says that she is still 'little and weak'. Ms C p.221. 'God has cast a veil over all my interior and exterior faults'. Ms C p.244.
h   'That day she asked pardon, with tears, of a sister whom she thought she had made sad because of a remedy. She must have made some reflections . . . I do not remember very well what it was, but the imperfection which escaped her was so minor, and she made reparation with so much humility that it became heroic virtue in my eyes'. (Green Note-Book, 1.8.7.).

172

face carefully so that it will be noticed she is perspiring a lot.[108] Some sisters noticed these things and were surprised.[i] 'Alas! agrees the patient, 'I'm still at the same place as I was in the beginning'.[109] Must one then lose hope?[j] All those lofty desires for perfection, those aspirations towards sanctity, were they to be doomed to failure? All the more so since she was so keenly aware of her own imperfections.

The revolutionary re-discovery by the saint, (for it was she who instigated it), which is one of the most profound evangelical paradoxes, is manifested here. Just as Paul of Tarsis offered his weakness to Christ so that his strength might shine forth, so Thérèse offered to God her powerlessness in order that his loving plan might be accomplished in her. From this sprang the joy of victory, the certitude of being liberated by the One who came not for the just but for sinners.

Every attentive reader of Thérèse will have noticed that we have quoted only some of the texts which illustrate the saint's weaknesses and imperfections. We have done this to emphasise more clearly a fundamental reality: where the worldly-wise would expect to hear an admission of failure, if not of despair, there unfailingly springs forth a cry of thanksgiving. Thérèse upsets accepted norms by affirming her joy in the midst of her suffering.

Let us set down these texts in order:

I have my weaknesses too, but I rejoice in them. I don't always succeed in rising above the nothings of this earth. For example, I will be tormented by a silly thing I said or did. Then I enter into myself, and I say, 'Alas! I'm still in the same place as I was formerly'. But I tell myself this with great gentleness and without any sadness. It's so good to feel that one is weak and little!'[110] 'Oh! how happy I am to see myself imperfect and

---

i   '.. several would find me very imperfect, that is true'.
j   'When I commit a fault that makes me sad, I know very well that this sadness is the consequence of my infidelity'. LC 3.7.2.

to be in such need of God's mercy at the moment of my death!'[111] 'I experience a very living joy not only when I discover I'm imperfect, but especially when I feel I am. All this surpasses all praise, which only bores me.[112]

Weakness acknowledged and accepted becomes therefore the privileged ground of mercy. 'To remain little', a theme so dear to Thérèse, does not imply a psychological regression, rather it expresses a fundamental theological attitude. Moreover Mother Agnès had asked her what she meant by this frequently repeated formula: 'To remain a little child before God'.

> To remain little, is to recognise our nothingness, to expect everything from God. It is not to be too distressed over our faults. Finally, it is not to gain riches, and not to be worried about anything. Even among the poor, as long as the child is quite small, it is given what is necessary. But as soon as it grows up, the father no longer wants to feed it and says: 'Work now, you can take care of yourself'. It is so as not to hear this that I never wanted to grow up, feeling that I was incapable of earning my living, eternal life.[k]

We can understand better then, in the light of this reply, Thérèse's insistence on the value of her 'littleness',[113] her 'nothingness'[114] of calling herself 'baby',[115] a 'little child',[116] a 'little soul',[117] a 'little saint',[118] 'little Tom Thumb',[119] to emphasise her poverty. Never does the theresian language seem to be more vulnerable than when it is expressing 'littleness'. The so-called affectation of style, so often unacceptable to those who let themselves be taken in by appearances, conceals the heart of the Christian paradox rediscovered by Thérèse of Lisieux.

Let us take but one example. Some are astonished or even upset that Thérèse should call herself 'baby' on her death-bed.

k   This is a translation of the version given in *Histoire d'une Ame, (Story of a Soul)*, 1898 edition. It is older than that given in the *Yellow Note-Book*, cf. LC 6.8.8. p.139.

But, coming from her, this word was analogous to the 'little one' of Proverbs 9,4 which had been her joyous biblical discovery. Her actual situation of a 'baby', reduced to 'milk' and 'bed' by sickness, became for her the symbol of quite a different reality: her powerlessness entrusted to paternal Mercy.[1] There is the danger of a misunderstanding arising between the saint who is at the heart of the evangelical mystery and her readers who remain on a linguistic and psychological level.[m]

B. 'I want to go on abandoning myself entirely to the good God ...' [120]

Reduced to nothing like a sick baby, Thérèse therefore abandoned herself to Merciful Love's good pleasure. Without explicitly mentioning the way of confidence and love, the *Last Conversations* contain numerous references to it. We see it expressed in her abandonment, her indifference – in the Ignatian sense –, her acceptance of the present moment, her complete confidence, and finally, in her peace and her joy. The whole Thérèse is there. Not a synthesis, not a theory, but a continuing attitude that manifests itself in all her words, her gestures and her silences. The ray that converges from all these colours forms the pure white light of the little way. Isolated, each of these 'conversations' might appear insignificant. Together, they go to make up, in the end, a wonderful life-like portrait. Let us go back and read again the *Last Conversations* and content ourselves here with a brief anthology of her abandonment and confidence.

---

l   The same symbolism applies to her place in the family: the last of the Martin children was always, until her death, referred to as the 'little Thérèse'. Cf. Allusion in the *Last Conversations*, (LC 2.9.4.), 'This big, in the family!'. But, in the end, the little one goes as leader of the group and saves the whole family, like little Tom Thumb. Another reversal of Thérèse's situation.

m   Much more could be said on the question of language. We laugh at the craze at the end of the nineteenth century of using the word 'little', but our grand-children will smile at our use of 'mini'.

In June, the writer of Manuscript C stated: 'For a long time I have given myself totally to Jesus and he is therefore free to do with me as he pleases'.[121]

Her abandonment, a fundamental attitude that she would steadfastly maintain until September 30, was subject to renewed assaults by suffering. On July 13 she knew that if her soul 'had not been filled in advance with abandonment to God's will', she would have been submerged 'by a wave of bitter grief'.[122]

Fully aware that she ran the risk of being thought useless by the community: 'As far as I'm concerned, what does it matter what others think or say? I don't see why I should be disturbed by it'.[123] Now the critics could no longer touch her: '... at this present time, reproaches and compliments glide over me without leaving the slightest trace'.[124]

Her life was no longer hers. 'After all, it's the same to me whether I live or die'.[125] 'God wills that I abandon myself like a very little child who is not disturbed by what others do to it'.[126] n The refrain is regularly repeated in the witnesses' notes: 'But, at the bottom of my heart, I am resigned to living, dying, being cured, and even going to Cochin-China',[127] 'I'm ready for everything',[128] 'Yes, I will it, I really will it',[129] etc.

Despite her sister's anxious questions, she systematically refused to be worried about the future. She wanted to live in the present moment. 'I count on him. I'm sure he will continue to help me until the end. I may become exhausted and worn out, but I shall never have too much to suffer. I'm sure of this'.[130] On July 23, she gave the profound reason why she was so firmly rooted in the present: 'We who run in the way of Love shouldn't be thinking of sufferings that

---

n   'Ah! how sweet it is to abandon oneself in his arms, without fears or desires! LT, 10/8/1897.

may come in the future. It's wanting in confidence. It's like meddling in the work of creation'.[131] And then, with her ever smiling good-sense, she added: 'Why fear before it happens? Wait at least for it to happen before you become distressed'.[132]

To the continuous concern of her entourage Thérèse offered her own experience: God indeed was helping her at each moment. 'You see until now, I haven't had any sufferings I couldn't support. We must abandon ourselves'.[133] The evening before she died, she still said: 'No, Mother, not terrible, but much, much ... just what I can bear'.[134] God gave her courage in proportion to her sufferings.[135]

From another view-point we see here again not resignation to what will happen to her, but joyous acceptance of God's will: 'I love everything that God gives me'.[136] 'The only thing that makes me happy is to do God's will'.[137] 'I love him so much that I'm always pleased with what he does'.[o]

But would not the accumulation of all the sufferings we have described give rise to despair or doubt? In such a state can one still believe in a loving God? Thérèse did not yield before this objection: if God was trying her, as he tried Job, it was so that she might give him 'further proofs of (her) abandonment and love'.[138] For 'abandonment is the delicious fruit of Love!'

This throws light on some of Thérèse's own words about suffering. They must not be taken out of the general context of voluntary and steadfast abandonment to Love, lest they arouse suspicions of masochism.

In May she said: 'I have come to a point where I can no longer suffer, because all suffering is sweet to me'.[139] Then,

---

o LC 6.7.3., 14.7.5.. 'The one cause of all my joy is therefore the thought of doing the Lord's will'. (LT 18/7/97).

in June, she explained to Mother Marie de Gonzague: 'I have suffered very much since I have been on earth, but, if in my childhood I suffered with sadness, it is no longer the way I suffer. It is with joy and peace. I am truly happy to suffer'.[140] 'Suffering itself becomes the greatest of joys when one seeks it as the most precious of treasures'.[141]

In July: 'Suffering is exactly what attracts me in life'.[142] And, in August: '... It's a suffering without any disquietude. I am pleased to suffer since God wills it'.[143] But she did not wish to ask for greater sufferings: 'If I were to ask for sufferings, these would be mine, and I would have to bear them alone, and I've never been able to do anything alone'.[144] 'I'm very happy for not having asked for anything from God; that way, he is forced to give me courage!'[145]

That peace and joy, so often affirmed because it was so truly experienced, demonstrates the truth of her 'little way of confidence and love', for 'it is not possible to give oneself such sentiments'.[146] Such a reversal of values could only have come from another source. It also shows that Thérèse remained lucid and balanced.

C. 'This sweet peace which floods my soul ...'

This does not mean that we must not feel pain and suffering. Where would the merit be if it was not felt? A person can suffer very keenly, but, by offering it to God, can find in that offering great peace in the midst of the greatest sufferings. Thérèse's confidence did not waver although her condition grew steadily worse. In her manuscript in June she had admitted that a 'sweet peace' flooded her soul. Throughout her illness she repeated this affirmation: '... there's great peace in my soul'.[147] 'I remain always in profound peace in the depths of my heart. Nothing can disturb it'.[148] 'You're suffering so much!' 'Yes, but peace, too, peace'.[149] 'Yes, what darkness! But I am in peace'.[150]

The sisters were struck by this 'unchangeable peace'. 'Peace and joy'.p The two words which came from Mother Agnès' pen describing Thérèse the moment before her death. The brevity of the sign of victory – the space of a Creed – must not underestimate its importance. Peace and joy at that final moment, did not just happen like a *deus ex machina*, as if, at the last minute, after six months of tragedy, 'everything was finally fixed up'. They shine out in all the last 'conversations', in the very midst of sufferings and not 'in spite of' them. We can even say now 'because' of them, if we have grasped the fact that these accepted sufferings were the means whereby Thérèse's love was united to the all-merciful and liberating Love.

Thanksgiving is therefore the dominant characteristic of these last months. Thérèse continued 'to sing the Mercies of the Lord', the principal theme of her autobiographical manuscripts.q Have not her biographers, who for want of evidence left these last three months of her life in the shade, seen Thérèse's abandonment in her illness as the logical consequence of her little way? But must we not henceforth rather reverse the process and say that Manuscript C receives its value only from the fact that the person who wrote it had passed through the decisive test? Illness finally convinced Thérèse of the abyss which separates the written word from the lived experience: 'O Mother, it's very easy to write beautiful things about suffering. But writing is nothing, nothing. One has to enter this dark place to understand'. 'Any sister could write what I have written ... All that could have been only 'counterfeit coin'.[151]

That 'dark place' of sickness, agony and death were the crucible from which the theresian writings derived all

---

p   Thérèse also linked these two words together: Ms C p.249.
q   Ms A p.15 beginning, Ms C pp.245, 248. Cf. 'When I think of all the graces God gave me, I have to stop myself or I would shed tears of gratitude continually'. (LC 12.8.3).

their force. On September 25, referring to what she had just lived through, she said: 'I really feel *now* that what I've said and written is true about everything'.[152] We underline the word 'now'. It was necessary to have passed through all that for the little way to become credible. We only believe witnesses who are ready to face death.

Is it necessary to repeat that nothing had been gained beforehand? We know the end of the story. How easy it is, in retrospect, to see the theresian triumph as something normal, like someone who yawns during the reading of the Passion while waiting for the Easter bells to ring out ... It is too often forgotten that the theresian victory was won, literally, at the price of blood. The *Last Conversations* are a war journal, the chronicle of a combat (which is the meaning of the word *agony*). Since their publication, the 'little doctrine' can no longer be said to be the pious reflections of a meek and mild person who coated everything she touched with sugar.[r]

D. *'I haven't any fear of the final struggles'* [153]

Let us not then be surprised to see Thérèse, when she was sick, using military terminology. 'I feel within me the vocation of the warrior ...' [154] she had written in September 1896. She was sad to think that she would die in bed,[155] and not at the stake like her sister, Joan of Arc.[s] It was, however, in that bed that she won the stripes which rank her among the heroes. She knew she was a brave soldier who had fought 'with the sword of the Spirit, which is the Word of God'.[156] 'A soldier does not fear battle, and I am a soldier.

---

r   She had taken care however to warn us: 'I prefer vinegar to sugar. My soul, too, is tired of too sweet a nourishment'. (Ms C p.244) She wrote to the Abbé Bellière: 'I felt that you must have a soul of great energy, and I was happy to become your sister'. (LT 21/6/1897)

s   In a letter dated 25/4/1897, she compares her vocation to that of Joan.

180

Have I not said that I will die 'weapons in hand'?' (She was referring here to her poem 'Mes Armes') Falling asleep during prayer time, she dreamt that there were not enough soldiers 'for a war against the Prussians,'[t] and she suddenly exclaimed: 'O Mother, how happy I would have been to have fought the heretics in the times of the Crusades. No! I would not have feared being shot. I would not have been afraid of the action'.[157]

There are not two kinds of courage, Rimbaud, who died in 1891, had said. The spiritual combat which Thérèse waged was just as arduous as any human warfare. The deep similarity between Thérèse of Lisieux and Joan of Arc was something which struck Bernanos, a good judge in matters of courage. He was not put off by the language of *Novissima Verba*, and that was why, in 1934, he did not hesitate to dedicate his *Jeanne relapse et sainte* to Thérèse 'who was, with Joan, the most heroic saint of our race, a real little French knight'.

4. In the fullness of action: Thérèse's mission

A soul on fire with love cannot remain inactive.[158]

The love which was consuming the heart of Thérèse impelled her unceasingly to action. At the time when she was reduced to nothing, when she could no longer even perform the ordinary duties of convent life, the principal work for which she had entered Carmel remained, however, within her reach: to save souls through prayer and sacrifice.[u]

---

t   Mother Agnès omitted 'against the Prussians' in the *Yellow Note-Book* and *Novissima Verba*, it is in the *Green Note-Book* 4.8.4. Thérèse had been brought up in the atmosphere of the 1870 defeat and therefore of 'revenge'. Her parents had to lodge nine enemy soldiers at Alençon in 1871.

u   'It is through prayer and sacrifice that we can help missionaries'. (Ms C p.252) Cf. LC 8.7.16, LT, 9/5/1897.

In June, she reaffirmed the fundamental objectives of her Carmelite vocation:

> Ah! it is prayer, it is sacrifice which give me all my strength; these are the invincible weapons which Jesus has given me. They can touch souls much better than words as I have very often experienced ... The zeal of a Carmelite embraces the whole world ... I want to be a daughter of the Church as our holy Mother St.Teresa was and to pray for the Holy Father's intentions which I know embrace all the world. This is the general goal of my life. (Ms C pp.241, 253-4)

From the Pranzini affair until the Oblation to Love this desire had only increased. The allocation of two missionary brothers had oriented her more positively towards the far-off apostolate. But she still suffered from her limitations. She had discovered that she would be *everything* if she was Love (Ms B), but her immense desires were not satisfied. On her sick-bed, the call to a universal mission, far from becoming faint beneath the weight of suffering, took on a renewed vigor. Her Manuscript C was not finished, when, under a great impulse, she commented on the words of the *Song of Songs* ('Draw me, we shall run in the odour of your perfumes ...') which spell out this universal mission based on prayer.

Thérèse, very tactfully, managed to pass on her little way to her immediate entourage (novices, sisters, spiritual brothers), to help a seminarian[v] or a childhood friend.[w] But that did not satisfy her. Knowing, moreover, that now she would no longer be going to the missions — although she had a vocation for it[x] — she could still share closely in Fr Roulland's ministry through more intensified sacrifice[y] and

v   Dr de Cornière's son. Cf. LC 23.8.6.
w   LT 20/7/1897.
x   Cf. Ms C p.217. 'Our Mother believes in my vocation'. (LT 19/3/1897) In May, she was still thinking about it: 'I would really love to go to Hanoi to suffer very much for God'. (LC 15.5.6)
y   Her life as an invalid was now one of sacrifice. As to her prayer, it would require a lengthy study.

prayer. She wanted little black babies to be ransomed.[z] She thought of 'poor, sick missionaries',[159] and 'walked for them'.[160]

By acting in this way, she shared in the care of the Church of her day which was sending forth her missionaries to every continent, preceding or following the explorers of empires. But, in showing herself ahead of her time, she did not forget another mission. Since she was sharing the bread of bitterness with sinners she had them all in her constant care. Moreover this did not prevent her from remembering in a special way individual cases she knew: she offered her interior trial against the faith for 'someone related to the family who had lost the faith'.[161] She offered her last communion for the ex-priest Hyacinthe Loyson.

But how she suffered from the limitations of that action! She certainly offered her sufferings for all sinners and wanted the prayers for her cure to be applied to them.[162] For in this task she wished to forget herself completely: 'I keep nothing in my hands. Everything I have, everything I merit, is for the Church and for souls'.[163] 'When I gain some spiritual treasure, feeling that at this very moment there are souls in danger of being lost and falling into hell, I give them what I possess. I have not yet found a moment when I can say: 'Now I am going to work for myself'.[164] In August, she repeated that she did not want to capitalise on merits for herself, but 'for poor sinners, for the needs of the whole Church, to cast flowers upon everybody, the just and the sinners'.[165]

This passion 'for souls' (the theresian vocabulary is couched in that of her day) allows us another insight into her attraction to suffering: 'It's only to save souls that I want to suffer more'.[166] Far from expressing a morbid concentration on

---

z   LC 21/6.5.3., 13.7.11, 30.7.5.

herself it was rather a going-out of self for the benefit of others in imitation of Christ who gave his life for all men. On the day of her death, she exclaimed: 'Never, would I have believed it was possible to suffer so much! Never, never! I can only explain it by the ardent desires that I have had to save souls'.[167]

'It's incredible how big my heart seems ...',[168] wrote Thérèse at the beginning of 1889. How could she not suffer now, aware as she was of the narrow limitations of her past and present action? She would base all her hope of embracing the whole world in a posthumous mission which would be achieved in two ways: by the publication of her little way which would reach a crowd of readers, and, above all, by direct action, a shower of roses upon the world.

A. 'A very important work!' [169]

It was during this time that the idea that the sick nun's writing might possibly be published came to birth. In his Introduction to the French edition of the Autobiography, Fr François de Sainte-Marie has shown the evolution of Thérèse's thought on the publication of her manuscripts. We do not have to re-write that chapter here, but only to emphasise Thérèse's concern, when she was sick, to pass on her message by a means somewhat unusual for a Carmelite.[a]

When she wrote her first exercise book for her sisters in 1895 she had no thought of publication. In June 1897, she knew that her little black exercise book would be used to write her circular.[b] But she never for a moment dreamt that it might become a book. Rather, she thought it more likely

a   'To think beautiful, holy thoughts, to produce books, to write lives of the saints, is not worth the act of answering when called'.
b   She did not understand sisters who did not want a circular. LC 27.5.1.

that no great importance would be attached to it and that possibly it would be destroyed.[170] However, her sisters had taken up the idea of publishing to such an extent that, in July, Thérèse, in her turn, did not brush aside the notion.

On Sunday, July 11,[c] she said to Mother Agnès: 'I have not had time to write what I would have wished. It is not finished. But listen, Mother, anything that you think should be cut out or added to the exercise book of my life, it is I who will be cutting or adding it. Remember this later on, and have no scruple about it, no doubt about the matter'. That day the conversation centred on the manuscripts. Mother Agnès asked her if she thought that 'she would do good to souls' by this means. 'Yes', she replied, 'it is the means God will use to grant my desire. There will be something in it for all tastes, except for those in extraordinary ways'.[171] [d] But how well they will understand that everything comes from God, and what I shall have of glory from it, will be a gratuitous gift from God that doesn't belong to me. Everybody will see this clearly'.[172]

Although Thérèse left the general responsibility of publication to Mother Agnès she did give her positive directions on several important points. The format mattered little provided that the essential message of her 'way' was passed on. Besides, in the state she was in, how could she be preoccupied with details? She had full confidence in her little Mother. She insisted that she include the 'story of the sinful woman who died of love: souls will understand immediately, for it's such a striking example of what I'm trying to say'.[173] On July 20, she returned to the same subject: 'Don't forget to tell the story of the sinful woman! This will prove that I'm not mistaken'.[174]

c   And not the 10th, as Fr François has written in his Introduction.
d   The *Green Note-Book* adds this interesting detail: '. . . because for some time, she understood God's design in this regard'.

One feels that she retained her care for sinners. She foresaw the objection they would raise when they read the story of her life: 'She has shown such great confidence in God because she has never sinned'. Thérèse had begun to answer them in the Manuscript when the pencil fell from her hand:

> Yes, I feel it; even though I had on my conscience all the sins that can be committed,[e] I would go, my heart broken with sorrow, and throw myself into the arms of Jesus, for I know how much he loves the prodigal child who returns to him. It is not because God, in his prevenient Mercy, has preserved my soul from mortal sin that I go to him with confidence and love ... (Ms C p.259).

What was to follow would surely have been very important. Thérèse must have been really exhausted not to have continued. On July 11, still preoccupied with this thought she firmly broached the subject again with Mother Agnès:

> One could think that it is because I haven't sinned that I have such great confidence in God. Really tell them, Mother, that if I had committed all possible crimes, I would always have the same confidence. I feel that this whole multitude of offences would be like a drop of water thrown into a fiery furnace. You will then tell the story about the converted sinner who died of love.[175]

On July 16, according to *Novissima Verba*,[f] she made another recommendation to the trustee of her wishes: 'Mother, in the exercise book, I have only touched on the subject of God's justice. But, if you wish, you will find all my thoughts on this clearly explained in a letter to Fr Roulland'.[g]

---

e   Thérèse was thinking undoubtedly of Pranzini whose 'crimes' had been in the French news for months. At the end of her life, she still remembered her 'first child'.

f   This text is not to be found in the sources and can be contested, but perhaps it was remembered later.

g   LT 9/5/1897.

Finally, on Sunday August 1, we have her last advice concerning the procedure to be followed for the publication of her texts:

> After my death, you musn't speak to anyone about my manuscript before it is published. You must speak about it only to Mother Prioress. If you act otherwise, the devil will make use of more than one trap to hinder God's work ..., a very important work! ... I will write no more now![176]

The sick nun, having done all within her power to assure the efficacy of this work, did not refer to it again except to give an estimation of its posthumous value: 'There will be something in it for all tastes, except for those living in extraordinary ways'. 'What I am reading in this exercise book reflects my soul so well! Mother, these pages will do so much good to souls. They will understand God's gentleness much better ...'[h] 'Ah! I know it. Everybody will love me'.[i]

This love of crowds, far from being an obstacle to her mission, was part of it. Let all her 'historians' be on their guard: 'It is to God alone that all value must be attributed for there's nothing of value in my little nothingness'.[177]

B. 'I will come back'

It was only in July that Thérèse, undoubtedly prompted by Mother Agnès' suggestion, began to think seriously that her writings could become the means whereby she might fulfil her mission. For a long time she had been thinking of a direct mission, on a larger scale, that would begin after her death. Now she was going to die at twenty-four! Had

---

h   This text is proper to *Novissima Verba* 1.8.2. We do not know its source and cannot understand why it is not in the *Yellow Note-Book* and the *Green Note-Book*. The reserve raises the question of its authenticity.

i   The above remark applies here also. It is in the Epilogue of *Histoire d'une ame*, 1925 edition. Did Mother Agnès find these texts important when consulting her notes to re-edit the *Yellow Note-Book*?

she not been dreaming, a prey of illusions? Were all her immense desires going to end in nothingness, just as the taunting voices of her trial said? But Thérèse, who was never discouraged,[j] had already broken through the ultimate boundary. Not only would death not stop her activity, rather it would give it its real dimension. Freed at last from the limitations of time and space,[k] Sister Thérèse would become the 'universal sister'.[l]

Therefore it was normal for her to let those around her ask for graces for themselves when she left the earth.[178] After all, it is not surprising, even though it is a relatively rare fact that a christian, on the threshold of death, should make such promises to near relatives.[m] But Thérèse was unusually insistent about it. Furthermore, she repeatedly said that she would come back herself.

To Sister Geneviève, who did not stop expressing her grief at her sister's approaching death, Thérèse reiterated untiringly: 'I will come back',[179] 'I shall come down',[180] 'I shall protect you',[181] 'You will see all I'll do for you',[182] 'I will not leave you for the space of a second'.[183] The same countless assurances were given to Mother Agnès: 'I will come

---

j   'Fortunately, I don't easily get discouraged'. (Ms C p.228) 'This does not discourage me'. (Ms C p.250.)

k   We know that this had been on her mind for several months. In a poem written January 1897, she expressed the desire to break through the limitations of space, but through the intermediary of her guardian angel: 'You who travel through space/Faster than lightning/I beg you to fly in my place/to those who are dear to me'. (À mon ange Gardien).

l   Let us remember that, at this time, he who wished to be called the 'universal brother' was living in a small wooden hut at the bottom of the garden of the Poor Clare nuns in Nazareth. (Reference to Charles de Foucauld)

m   They are all there: Léonie (LT 17/7/1897), the Guérin family (LC p.275) the La Néeles to whom she promised, unconditionally, 'the most beautiful angel from heaven', (ibid and following pages, LT 16/7/1897), Mother Agnès again (LT 13/7/1897), her novices with whom she will continue her work, (Ms C p.209), her spiritual brothers (LTs of June, July, August).

down', [184] 'Baby will come back', [185] 'I'll send you lights', [186] 'graces', [187] 'I'll always be with my little Mother'. [188] To Abbé Bellière she wrote: 'But I am not dying, I am entering into life, and all that I cannot say to you her here below I shall make you understand from heaven'. [189]

But these promises of help after her death went far beyond the circle of her family and friends. With great assurance and simplicity — like an established fact — she announced that after her death she would travel the world. This idea was on her mind very much in July, although, in June, referring to a passage she had read in a book about a beautiful woman in white appearing to a baptised child, she had said: 'Later on, I'll go to little baptised children just like that'. [190]

She made her first explicit announcement to Sister Marie of the Sacred Heart on July 13: 'If you only knew the projects I'll carry out, the things I shall do when I am in heaven . . . I will begin my mission'. Her sister questioned her as to the nature of these projects: 'Projects such as coming back with my sisters, of going over there to help missionaries, and then preventing little pagans from dying before they are baptised'. [191]

The same day she had promised Abbé Bellière, who was soon to leave for Africa, that she would rejoin him there, 'no longer in thought only', but by a closer presence 'that his faith will discover'. She foresaw his objections and answered it immediately: 'All these promises may possibly seem to you to be somewhat fanciful . . .' In fact, did they not seem to be just that *at that precise moment?*[n] She replied confidently, basing her argument on the cold logic of her little way.

n   We, who know that Thérèse kept her promises, have difficulty in grasping the quiet boldness of those words in their original outburst. 'Scandalous pride' would have been the reaction of someone like P.Blino who 'took to task' that little sister who wanted 'to love God as much as St Teresa of Avila'.

You must see now that God has always treated me as a spoilt child. It is true that his cross has gone with me from my cradle, but Jesus has made me love the cross passionately. He has always made me desire what he willed to give me.[o] Do you think then that in heaven he will begin *not* to fulfil my desires? I simply cannot believe it, and I say 'Soon, little Brother, I shall be with you'.[192]

She gave the same reasons to Mother Agnès five days later: 'God would not have given me the desire of doing good on earth after my death, if he didn't will to realise it. He would rather have given me the desire to rest in him'.[193] (We can see just how much this idea filled her mind).[p] For her, the answer was perfectly clear. She had just said something even more audacious: 'God will have to carry out my will in heaven, because I have never done my own will on earth'.[194] The words of a child, yet worthy of Joan of Arc answering her judges with the same audacity. A few centuries earlier such words would have easily sent one to the stake, but, at the end of the last century, they were enough to have you accused of mental derangement or blasphemy: 'Sister Thérèse do you realise what you are saying?'[q]

On July 14, in her last letter to Fr Roulland, this child reveals the same dogged conviction:

I am sure I shall not remain inactive in heaven, my desire is to go on working for the Church and for souls, that is what I keep asking God, and I am certain he will say yes. After all, the angels are continually occupied with us, while yet they never cease to see the Face of God, and are rapt forever in the shoreless

o   The same thought is expressed in the *Green Note-Book* on the same day.
p   The same day, Sister Marie of the Eucharist asked her to obtain 'great graces' for her when she was in heaven. Reply: 'Oh! when I am in heaven, I will do very many things, great things ... It is impossible that it is not God who has given me this desire. I am sure he will answer me! And also, when I am up there, I will follow you very closely!' (LC 18/7/1897 p.252)
q   'Anyone else but you would take me for a fool, or else someone terribly proud', to Sister Marie of the Trinity.

ocean of Love.[r] Why should Jesus not allow me to imitate them?[195]

Three days later we find the famous declaration that was destined to arouse such wide-spread interest:

I feel that I'm about to enter into my rest. But I feel especially that my mission is about to begin, my mission to make God loved as I love him, to give my little way to souls. If God grants my desires, my heaven will be spent on earth until the end of time. Yes, I want to spend my heaven doing good on earth. This isn't impossible, since from the bosom of the Beatific Vision, the angels watch over us.[s] I can't make heaven a feast of rejoicing. I can't rest as long as there are souls to be saved. But when the angel says: ' Time is no more!' then I will take my rest. I will be able to rejoice, because the number of the elect will be complete, and because all will have entered into joy and repose. My heart beats with joy at this thought.[t]

The essential point is that, in July, Thérèse was convinced. From then on she only referred to her great future mission on two other occasions. She was shown a photograph of herself taking the part of Joan of Arc in prison and, seeing in the picture the symbol of her immediate limitations, she said:

r   Let us note that Thérèse saw herself in heaven, imitating the Angels, having the same position of Novice Mistress as she had had on earth: nourishing souls 'without ever leaving your (Jesus') arms or turning my head'. (Ms C p.238)

s   The same idea about the work of angels as in the previously cited Letter to Fr Roulland. LT 14/7/1897.

t   We are quoting from the *Yellow Note-Book* version, LC 17.7. The authenticity of this text raises a problem since Mother Agnès contradicts herself. In the *Green Note-Book* she wrote: 'This is more or less what she said, for I could not write while she was speaking to me, but *immediately* after'. Then in her testimony at the Apostolic Process: 'On July 17, still on her death-bed, she spoke some memorable words which I wrote down immediately as she was speaking'. But the authenticity of the meaning is verified by three witnesses, and Thérèse said these words 'several times'.

The saints too encourage me in my prison. They tell me: 'As long as you are in irons, you cannot carry out your mission, but later, after your death, this will be the time for your works and your conquests'.[196]

Then, in September, she said:

I shall go very soon (to Saigon). If you only knew how quickly I will make my journey.[197]

We have wished to follow chronologically the development of Thérèse's thought as to the sphere of her action after her death. The coherent and steady development of that desire during her last months proves its constancy. How much more important than even the publication of her writings was this conviction that she would spend her heaven doing good on earth, right until the end of time![u]

Did her sisters, who were at her bedside and caring for her during that summer of 1897, take seriously all these words? Did they understand the literal sense they were soon to take on? Could they have suspected that they were hearing prophecies? It seems very likely that the answer is 'no', and yet, certain phrases, certain recommendations, did strike them and gave them a presentiment of mystery.

C. 'You are looking after a little saint ...'[198]

It is indeed puzzling how some of Thérèse's words seem to be hinting at something. We do not know if they should be treated as light-hearted remarks or prophecy. The witnesses were struck by them at the time, not knowing how

u 'I would want to preach the Gospel on all the five continents at the same time and even to the remotest islands. I would be a missionary, not for a few years only, but from the beginning of creation until the end of time!'. (Ms B p.193)

to take them.[v] Yet they are few in number[w] and would not suffice as a basis on which to build one of those extraordinary hagiographies depicting the dying saint as propounding prophecies. Once again we maintain the utmost discretion. Thérèse did not deliver an oracle. If she seemed to do so, she was misunderstood.[x] She said nothing about her own death. She opposed certain tendencies in those around her who were somewhat avid for the supernatural: Would she die on a feast day?[199] Would her body remain incorrupt?,[200] Would there be some sign during her agony? Would angels be seen?[201] With her unfailing common sense, she reminded them of the realism of her very ordinary 'little way'.

Yet she did throw some glimmer of light on the future. In the latter part of August,[y] Thérèse, in front of her three

v Here we have put our finger on the difficulty of linking the significance of the event to time or place. It was easy *later* for witnesses to recognise prophecies when facts verified the sick nun's words or gestures. It is an area of difficult research, for the passage of time has sometimes favoured modification of texts without changing their profound significance.

w In the strict sense we can find three in the *Last Conversations*, all in September, a few days before her death. We have trouble following Fr Piat who wrote: 'Nothing is better established than the gift of prophecy which opened to Thérèse the prospect of an apostolate which would continue until the end of time. Twenty-two pages in *Novissima Verba* clearly prove this; more than forty texts, if you include extracts from correspondence and evidence given at the Processes. A foreknowledge of such fullness and precision constitutes a unique case in the annals of hagiography'. (S.Piat, *Ste Thérèse de Lisieux à la découverte de la Voie d'enfance*, Ed. Franciscaines, 2e ed. 1965, 408 pp.) It is hard to follow Fr Piat since he does not give any references. He includes all the texts concerning Thérèse's posthumous action. The truth has many nuances — the witnesses' reactions at the time of the events prove this.

x 'Little Mother will be the last to die!' (LC 11.9.1.). In fact, it was Sister Geneviève.

y We would readily put this word between August 22 and 27 for these two reasons: 'Six weeks before her death', said Sister Marie of the Sacred Heart in her evidence, and Mother Agnès said: 'Our *very* sick little Saint', at the Process and in a letter dated 4/9/1936. Also, September 3, (a few days later). This word is referred to in the *Last Conversations*. Cf. LC 3.9.2.

sisters, said: 'You know well you are looking after a little saint!'[z] Very moved by these words, Sister Marie of the Sacred Heart left the infirmary, and did not hear her sister, after a moment's silence, add: 'And what is more you are saints too'.[202]

On September 14, unpetalling roses over her crucifix as was her wont, she said quite seriously: 'Gather up these petals, little sisters, they will help you perform favours later on ... don't lose any of them'.[a][203]

As for the famous phrase: 'It will be like a shower of roses'. Must it be taken as a prophecy in the strict sense of the word, if it is put in context in the oldest account, as given by the witness to whom it was addressed?

> I (Sister Marie of the Sacred Heart) was reading in the refectory a short account of St Louis de Gonzague's life which tells of a sick person who was asking to be cured, and who saw a shower of roses fall on his bed as a symbol of the grace that was going to be granted him. Afterwards, at recreation, she said to me: 'I too, after my death, will send down a shower of roses'.[b]

Whatever the textual problems some of these words present, we cannot deny their existence, and they force us to ask the inevitable question: What had Thérèse come to know about herself during these last days?[204] Did she have a clear and vivid presentiment of 'the storm of glory' (Pius

---

z Compare all the variations of this word in the *Last Conversations*.

a LC 14.9.1. Cf. 'With charming simplicity, she got me to save her nail clippings'. (Sister Geneviève) Abbé Bellière was to ask for such 'relics'.

b This conversation is reported in different contexts. At the Apostolic Process, Mother Agnès said: 'She added: 'After my death, you will go to the letter box and find there many consolations'. Was Sister Marie of the Sacred Heart the source of these words? She said at the Diocesan Process: 'She (Thérèse) spoke also about the numerous letters which would pour in on us on her account, after her death, and the joy which these letters would bring us'. She also warned Mother Agnès that 'later, a great number of young priests, knowing that she had been given as a spiritual sister to two missionaries, would ask the same favour'. (LC 8.7.16)

XI) that would blow over Lisieux after her death? A statement to Sister Marie of the Trinity would imply that she did:

> I have an idea that she had a revelation about her future glory. On this subject one day?[c] she said to me: 'My desires reach out to infinity ... What God has in store for me after my death, what I foresee of honour and glory surpasses all one could imagine to such an extent that I am forced, at times, to stop my thoughts. It makes my head spin'. And, laughing, she added: 'Anyone else but you would take me for a fool, or else someone terribly proud'.

In other areas, the novices sometimes felt that their young mistress used to read their hearts: 'Where do you find what you say?' Yet Thérèse calmly said that she 'was really sure that (she) didn't have the gift of reading souls...' What she added can undoubtedly throw some light on our investigation: '... and this surprised me all the more because I had been so right. I felt that God was very close, and that, without realising it, I had spoken words, as does a child, which came not from me but from him'.[205]

This sentence, written in June, enables us to understand Thérèse's attitude during her last weeks. When she was pushed to foretell the date of her death, she refused. She did not know. She even protested: 'Ah! Mother, intuitions! If you only knew the poverty I'm in! I know nothing except what you know. I understand nothing except what I see and feel'.[206] Six days before her death, this very definite statement dismisses the hypothesis of a Thérèse who had a clear knowledge of the future, but who, concealing this truth from those around her, nevertheless, did occasionally give something away. A hypothesis, moreover, which is not consistent with her love of truth and her intense dislike of 'pretence'.

Manuscript C allows us to put forward the theory that some prophetic words spoken by Thérèse in September, or

c   Unfortunately we cannot put a date to this.

before, were said 'without realising what was being said, like a child'. Words spoken without affectation and surprising the speaker, for they did not 'come from me but from him'. We will include what Sister Marie of the Sacred Heart had to say when she commented on the sentence: 'You know indeed that you are looking after a little saint':

> These words seemed to have been spoken by someone else in so far as there was a note of candour and self-forgetfulness in her look and voice. In fact, there was a striking contrast between what she said and the expression on her face. One felt that it was the Holy Spirit speaking in her just as we see so often in the lives of the saints.

If Thérèse, in her last days, received some touches of inspiration about the future that were supernatural – and we cannot deny that she did, or else how can we explain these words? It seems that they were rare.[d] For our part, we see, especially in the other words foretelling her posthumous mission, a consequence of her 'way of love and confidence' lived in absolute faith. In the midst of darkness she never doubted that her work would continue after her death, and she spoke of this quite naturally, as if she already saw herself acting in heaven. It was always the logic of a child:[e] 'Oh! I'll torment God so much, if he wanted to refuse me at first, my importunity will force him to grant my desires. This story is in the Gospel'.[207] Thérèse's knowledge of herself was therefore rooted in the little way. Why would she hide that she knew she had been chosen?

---

d   Mother Agnès cites another 'prophetic' note to Mother Hermance telling her of her approaching death. Sister Marie of the Sacred Heart tells of a word concerning Mother Agnès who 'would not have time to think of her pain, for until the end of her life she will be so busied about me, she won't even have time to do everything'. And another, foretelling frequent communion in the Carmel. Cf LC July.

e   'In the last days of her life she had a strange premonition of what is now coming to pass. She spoke to us of future events, which are a reality today, with that childlike simplicity and candid humility which were characteristic of her when she spoke of the favours she had received from God'. (Sister Marie of the Sacred Heart)

I am too *little* to have any vanity now. I am too *little* even to compose beautiful sentences in order to make you think that I have a lot of humility. I prefer to agree very simply that the Almighty has done great things in the soul of his divine Mother's child. (Ms C p.210)

So why would he not do in heaven what he had done on earth? On April 25, she wrote just as simply to Abbé Bellière:

Do not believe that it is humility that keeps me from acknowledging God's gifts. I know that 'he has done great things for me'[f] and I sing it each day with joy.[208]

And Thérèse, who had dared to write that 'for several months now[g] (she) no longer had to struggle to practise charity',[209] had the audacity to say: 'Yes, it seems to me I am humble'.[210] But she adds: 'God shows me the truth. I feel so much that everything comes from him'.[211]

'Everything comes from him'.[h] This is the ultimate explanation of these affirmations which baffle human wisdom. Yet, they were only expressing the truth. A few hours before she died Thérèse gave us this testament, sealed with her own life's experience: 'Yes, it seems to me I have never sought anything but the truth. Yes, I have understood humility of heart ... It seems to me I am humble'.[212]

Conscious of her privileges – privileges that had been freely given –[i] Thérèse had always known that she was

---

f   Thérèse had been consciously singing this Magnificat since she wrote her Manuscript A.

g   We have emphasised the frequent use of this adverb in Ms C. It expresses very well the sick nun's awareness of having crossed a threshold.

h   '... But how well they will understand that everything comes from God, and what I shall have of glory from it will be a gratuitous gift from God that doesn't belong to me. Everybody will see this clearly ...' (LC 11.7.3.) (Thérèse is referring here to her Life).

i   'O my Jesus, it is perhaps an illusion, but it seems to me that you cannot fill a soul with more love than the love with which you have filled mine'. (Ms C p.256.)

only 'an instrument'. In her manuscript, she protests against 'the terribly narrow thoughts' of creatures, and she takes up the Creator's defence: 'Since when has the Lord *no longer the right* to make use of one of his creatures to dispense necessary nourishment to souls whom he loves?'[213] She was therefore under no illusion:

> We were telling her she was fortunate in having been chosen by God to tell souls about the way of confidence. She answered: What does it matter whether it's I or someone else who gives this way to souls! as long as the way is pointed out. The instrument is unimportant.[j]

'No, I'm not a saint!'[214] ... 'I believe I'm a very little saint!'[215] These apparently contradictory statements of Thérèse make sense in the light of what she said about her role as an instrument. Those around her often fell into the trap. They admired her patience: 'It's not my patience ... you're always wrong!'[216] Yes, they were always wrong. They thought that she 'must have had to struggle a lot' in order to become perfect. 'Oh! it's not that!'[217] Thérèse herself knew what she was:

> All creatures can bow towards her, admire her, and shower their praises upon her. I don't know why, but none of it could add one single drop of false joy to the true joy she experiences in her heart. Here she sees herself as she really is in God's eyes: a poor little nothing, that's all ...
>
> They were saying that souls who reached perfect love like her, saw their beauty, and that she was among their number: 'What beauty? I don't see my beauty at all. I see only the graces I've received from God. You always misunderstand me'.[218]

Her way, her 'life' of confidence and love, made her transparent to God's action. She was now living what she had

---

j   LC 21.7.5. Cf '(God) is therefore free to use me to give a good thought to a soul, and if I think this inspiration belongs to me, I would be like 'the donkey carrying the relics' who thought the reverence paid to the saints was being directed to him'. (Ms C p.234.)

said at the moment of her second communion: 'It is no longer I who live, but Jesus who lives in me'.[k]

Thérèse's knowledge of herself is fresh proof that in the end Merciful Love triumphed in her.

D. In heaven, in the Communion of Saints

Another paradox becomes apparent to the reader of the *Last Conversations*. When Thérèse's trial is concerned precisely 'about heaven', the nearer she draws to her death the more she speaks about it,[l] and seems to be already living on an equal footing with its inhabitants. The dream of May 10 had impressed her greatly: 'Heaven is peopled with souls who really love me'.[219]

Let us leave aside the revolution Thérèse has introduced into the traditional idea of heaven as a place of rest.[m] As we have said, for her it was to be rather a place of the greatest possible action, which would end only at the Parousia. There is another statement of hers that can be a source of commentaries for theologians and, at the same time, provide meditation for contemplatives:

> I really don't see what I'll have after death that I don't already possess in this life. I shall see God, that's true, but as far as being in his presence, I am already there here on earth.[220]

This surprising statement can be interpreted in many ways. Placing it in the actual context of the *Last Conversations* we

---

k   Ms A quoting Gal. 2.10.
l   A word undeniably theresian. It is to be found 126 times in her manuscripts (34 times in Ms C), 58 times in the Letters of 1897 (more than 100 times in the rest of her Correspondence). Especially in the spiritual sense, 72 times in Thérèse's mouth in the *Yellow Note-Book*. From Poem 48 on, 14 times in her poems.
m   Over the years, she would have read this sentence painted on the wall of the stairway leading to her cell, to the linen room and to the Chapter: 'Today, a little work, Tomorrow eternal rest'.

will draw the following inference: Thérèse was going to pass from earth to heaven retaining the same attitude of boldness and confidence that had been hers during her earthly life.

'They're all my "little" relatives up there!' [221]

Away then with the idea of a boring paradise peopled with unapproachable saints grouped around the Trinity, like those royal courts, restrained by protocol, which so many of the artists have depicted for us. One feels that this child, on entering heaven with her customary familiarity and spontaneity, would somewhat upset that traditional arrangement. Thérèse's imagery must no longer deceive us, our attention should be focused rather on the attitude it reveals.[n]

For her, paradise was first and foremost one immense family: 'All the saints are our relatives'.[222] She loved them all, even if she did not know the story of their lives. In which case, they would have to tell it to her, provided it did not take too long![o] She thought she would make the joyful discovery of unknown persons to whom she owed the great graces she had received. For this family is established on communion, not on ties of flesh and blood.

> God wills that the saints communicate grace to each other through prayer, so that in heaven they love each other with great love, with a love much greater than that of a family, and even the most perfect family on earth.[p]

---

n   Thérèse was no fool. 'The Holy Innocents will not be like children in heaven. They will have only the indefinable charms of childhood. They are represented as 'children' because we need pictures to understand spiritual things ... Yes, I hope to join them! If they want, I'll be their little page, holding up their trains'. (LC 21/26.5.9)

o   On that extreme rapidity of Thérèse, and her pain at having to communicate laboriously with the help of language cf Fr François de Saint-Marie's article in *Carmel*, 1957.

p   LC 15.7.5. p.99. She was undoubtedly thinking of the Martin family.

In heaven we shall not meet with indifferent glances, because all the elect will discover that they owe to each other the graces that merited their crown for them![223]

In a family a child does not remain immobile, overcome by shyness or respect. Thérèse, herself, was at home with the saints, her 'little' relatives. St. Peter did not frighten her. She reflected on the reasons for his denial. If he had known the little way, it would never have happened to him.[224] However that did not prevent her from having very definite preferences. She showed hardly any enthusiasms for the giants of asceticism, those champions of bodily mortification:[q]

> I was speaking to her about certain saints who had led extraordinary lives, such as St. Simon Stylites. She said: 'I myself prefer the saints who feared nothing, for example, St. Cecilia, who allowed herself to be married and didn't fear'.[225]

'I prefer . . .' Beyond any doubt, it was the 'ordinary' saints who attracted her. She was delighted to think that St. John of the Cross had been regarded by some of his contemporaries as 'a religious who was less than ordinary'.[226] This also explains in part her great attraction for Théophane Vénard: 'He pleases me much more than St. Louis (Aloysius) Gonzague because the life of the latter is extraordinary, while that of Théophane is very ordinary'.[227]

Dear little Théophane

We know the keen interest Thérèse showed in this young martyr. Four months after she had written a poem in his honour, in which she envied his lot and stressed what they had in common, she wrote out her testament, making use

---

q 'I know there are saints who spent their lives in the practice of astonishing mortifications to expiate their sins, but what of it? — 'In my Father's house there are many mansions'. (LT 21.6.1897)

of sentences taken from Blessed Théophane's letters. 'They are my thoughts. My soul is like his'.

Now she was living what she had written in February. She would follow ever more closely in the footsteps of this companion, who awaited her at the end of the road he himself had walked. 'He's the one who's calling me. Oh! I would love to have his portrait. He's a soul who pleases me'.[228] What similarities of character existed between these two young people! Cheerfulness, love of family, marching towards martyrdom, privation of communion at the moment of death . . . [229]

Thérèse was overjoyed when Mother Agnès gave her a 'portrait'[r] of the martyr. She immediately put it with the other pictures that were pinned to her bed-curtains. She admitted that this gave her 'extremely great consolation' for she liked him and found him amusing: 'But what he was able to do so very well does not please me . . . He is so '*very* pleasant', he is so 'very lovable'.[230] (These were expressions she had heard, and they amused her). This picture was to evoke countless signs of affection. She spoke to him,[231] stroked him 'on both cheeks' because she could not kiss him,[232] came to his rescue,[233] offered him flowers and, in the end, could not look at him without crying.[234] On September 6 there were fresh tears of joy when she was given something better still: a relic of her friend![235] A few moments before she died, she gently touched him again. And so, although he arrived a good last among the group of saints, Thérèse's friends, 'dear little Théophane' was given a privileged place.

The group of young people

Yet for all that, he did not overshadow the old friendships. Cecilia, 'the saint of abandonment'[s] was also there in a

r   This was a picture which had been mounted.
s   Poem written 28/4/1894. Cf Ms A p.131, LT 20/10/1893, LT 26/4/1894, LC 30.6.1, LC 13.7.11.

miniature pasted onto the bottom of the picture of Théophane Vénard.

Another young girl held a still more important place. There was no need to pin up her picture. Thérèse kept in her breviary the 'photograph' of her friend — herself, dressed as Joan of Arc — which made the identification between the two complete. It would be well one day to examine the prophetic sense of that friendship.[t]

Here we shall be content to sketch out briefly the stages.

Like so many other little French girls of her day, Thérèse Martin dreamt of the glorious destiny of the young girl from Lorraine.[236] In April 1897 she still remembers this:

> When I began to learn the history of France, the story of Joan of Arc's exploits thrilled me. I felt in my heart the desire and the courage to imitate her. It seemed to me that the Lord destined me for great things too.[u]

This meditation on Joan's destiny continued in Carmel and found expression in a prolific written output. In June 1897, we know that Thérèse reread her second play, which contained all her thoughts on death. In July, she pointed out two more analogies of situations which drew her closer to 'her sister'. Like her, she was 'plagued with questions',[237] and her work triumphed 'in spite of the jealousy of men'.[238]

With great care Thérèse had noted the death of Fr Mazel, twenty-six, who was cruelly put to death at Tonkin 1 April

---

t Bernanos often linked together the destiny of these two young French girls: 'Christians, the advent of Joan of Arc in the twentieth century takes on the character of a solemn advent. The wonderful fortune of an unknown little Carmelite seems to me to be a still more powerful sign'. (*Les Grands cimetières sous la lune*, Plon, 1938, p.271). 'Is it not moving to think that, at this very time when the Church of our country, which has given herself up more than ever to all the cold speculations of senile prudence, raises so high two young girls, St Joan of Arc and St Thérèse of Lisieux?' (*Lettre aux Anglais*, NRF, 1946, p.133)
u LT 25/4/1897, to Abbé Bellière.

1897.[v] She had been struck by the fact that he had died 'without having any apostolate whatsoever, without having to go to the trouble, for example, of learning Chinese. God gave him the palm of desire'.[239] Eight days later she expressed her reaction to Fr Roulland: 'Learning of the death of this young missionary, whose name I was hearing for the first time, I felt drawn to invoke him. I seemed to see him in heaven in the glorious choirs of martyrs'.[240]

Finally, there was another young figure who seemed to have caught Thérèse's attention when she was sick: Sister Constance – Jeanne-Marie Meunier – twenty-nine, who was the last of the sixteen Carmelites of Compiégne to mount the scaffold. According to a pencil-written note – faded and hardly legible – of Mother Agnès of Jesus in the Green Note-Book, Thérèse must have spoken of Constance on July 17, the anniversary of the Carmelites' martyrdom.[w] Sister Constance, a novice, walking to martyrdom. What chords that scene must have struck in the heart of Thérèse, the youngest in the Carmel![x]

Why these preferences at the moment of death? Why do the 'great saints' appear so rarely in the *Last Conversations?*[y]

---

v   'Fr Mazel, born at Rodelle (Aveyron) 22 September 1871, entered Seminary 21 October 1891 – ordained priest 28 June 1896 and left the following July 29 to be martyred in his Chapel of Lo-Li – Vicar Apostolic Mgr Chouzy, Bishop of Kongang-Si. Blessed Martyr, pray for me! . . . (1 May 1897)'. This note was written by Thérèse in pencil. Let us note her detail and interest in dates. Cf LT 30/7/1896.

w   Thérèse had a great affection for the sixteen Carmelites of Compigne. For the Centenary of their martyrdom (17.7.1894) she had made banners to decorate the chapel of the Compiègne Carmel. 'I was witness to her enthusiasm and the devotion she showed on that occasion. She could not contain her joy and she said to me: 'What happiness if the same destiny were ours! What a grace!' (Sr Thérèse of Saint-Augustine). At the beginning of September 1896, she heard a conference in the parlour by Mgr Teil, the Postulator for their Beatification Cause, and she came out full of enthusiasm. She had three pictures of the Carmelite martyrs.

x   The author of *The Dialogue of the Carmelites* unfortunately did not know the facts which so delighted Thérèse.

y   St John of the Cross himself is only mentioned five times in the *Last Conversations.*

We have only to list side by side the names of those 'saints'[z] whom Thérèse preferred. At once the points they had in common and which had captivated the sick nun become apparent: Cecilia, Joan, Constance, Théophane and Fr Mazel were all young people who had died giving their life for Jesus Christ.[a] Attracted to these young people who were similar to her in temperament and situation, the sick nun, a martyr of love who was coughing up blood, needed their special help in the trial she was undergoing. Heaven seemed closed to her. She relied on the existence of her invisible friends. She knew the happy outcome of their short life of suffering and martyrdom. Very realistically, she joined their cohort, and this identification with them was, at one and the same time, a guarantee and an anticipation of her own victory. They had attained the goal and would draw her on. She called on them, sought their help, and relied on them: 'The saints know me, love me, smile upon me, and invite me to join them'.[241]

Their lives illustrated perfectly the passage in Wisdom which she had used in her play, *Jeanne d'Arc*, and which praises the premature death of the just man. In the infirmary, she reread this text and discovered the meaning of her own destiny in the light of that of her young friends. In this way Thérèse lived the Communion of Saints, and her subsequent mode of acting since her own canonisation verifies the cogency of her attitude.

To these special preferences of hers must be added those other inhabitants of heaven who were so dear to her heart: her four little brothers and sisters who had died in infancy and whose photographs also adorned her curtains, and her father to whom she prayed.[242] But in this very real invisible

---

z   With the exception of Cecilia, none of the others had been *canonised* in 1897.

a   If we were to say that Cecilia was fifteen at the time of her death, (we can only suppose this), the average age of those five young people is twenty-five years — the same age as Thérèse!

world, in which she felt perfectly at ease, and which proved to her despite all her temptations the existence of heaven, there was someone who held a place apart: the Saint of saints, the Virgin Mary.

'The Blessed Virgin ... she is my Mother!'

A place apart because of her predominance – five per cent of the words of the *Yellow Note-Book* speak of Mary.[b] A place apart, above all, because the Blessed Virgin is Thérèse's Mother. That phrase – or rather that cry – which she had put on the lips of St Stanislaus Kostka in February, expressed perfectly her own attitude.[c] In May, she had written all that she had wanted to say about Mary in her revealing poem, '*Why I love you, Mary!*' In the infirmary, she recalled it when she outlined the plan of a sermon that she would have liked to have given, if she had been a priest. 'Finally, in my poem, *Pourquoi je t'aime, Marie*, I have said everything I would preach about her'.[243]

This is not the place to develop that Marian theology, as Thérèse understood it,[d] however great her interest. Faithful to our method, we will just look at the sick nun living with her Mother.

In the infirmary, her eyes never left her: two pictures and her statue made her present. Many of the spontaneous reflections in the *Last Conversations* were the result of this actual situation:

b 'During her last illness, she did not cease to speak of the Blessed Virgin'. (Sister Geneviève).
c 'You then love Mary very much? Oh! then tell me about her', asked Brother Augusti. St Stanislaus with indescribable tenderness replied: 'The Blessed Virgin! ... Ah! what could I say about her? ... She is my Mother!!!' (Play written 8/2/1897) 'What a joy it is to think that this Virgin is our Mother!' (LT 9/5/1897).
d In many ways, she announced the Marian theology of Vatican II.

When I was looking at the statue of the Blessed Virgin this evening I understood ... that she had suffered not only in soul but also in body ... Yes, she knew what it was to suffer. But it's perhaps wrong to wish that the Blessed Virgin suffered? And I, who love her so very much.[244]

One feels that Thérèse clung to this thought, which, in her own situation of suffering, united her more closely to her Mother. Elsewhere she had said:

Meditating on your life in the Gospels
I dare to look at you, to draw near to you.
It is not difficult for me to believe that I am your child,
For I see you mortal and suffering like me ...

Once again, the *Last Conversations* reflect perfectly what Thérèse had written in Manuscript C: 'I love the Blessed Virgin so much ... If I find myself anxious or in a difficult situation, I turn very quickly to her, and as the most tender of Mothers she always takes care of my interests'.[245] During her illness, this was what she constantly did, with childlike spontaneity: 'I've asked the Blessed Virgin that I be not so tired and withdrawn as I have been these past days ... This evening she answered me'.[246] 'However, I do so want to go ... I've told the Blessed Virgin. She can do as she wishes!'[247] She asked her to 'arrange things':[248] to stop her coughing, so that Sister Geneviève might get to sleep,[249] 'to hold her head in her hands',[250] so that she could endure her suffering when it became unbearable, etc. She gave the following explanation for these repeated prayers:

Asking the Blessed Virgin for something is not the same thing as asking God. She really knows what is to be done about my little desires, whether or not she must speak about them to God. So it's up to her to see that God is not forced to answer me, to allow him to do just as he pleases in everything.[251]

A little later she said: 'the Virgin always carries out my messages very well'. She would give her more! But if she was not heard, she would not worry: 'When we pray to the

Blessed Virgin and she doesn't answer, that's a sign she doesn't want to. Then we must leave her alone and not worry about it'.[252] However, although in July she had declared: 'No, the Blessed Virgin will never be hidden from me ...',[253] in August, in a moment of great distress, she uttered this complaint: 'I would like to be sure that she loves me – I mean the Blessed Virgin'.[254] A passing doubt, which did nothing to change her childlike attitude and usual familiarity. 'The Blessed Virgin isn't a thief by nature'.[255] 'I believe it isn't the Blessed Virgin who is playing these tricks on me! ... She is forced to do so by God![256] ... etc. Again she breaks the image of the saint, the model in all things: 'When I think of how much difficulty I've had all my life trying to recite the rosary'.[257] e

Her last 'work' on earth was to make two crowns out of cornflowers to 'please' the Virgin.[258] Three days later it was to her she penned the last lines she would ever write: 'Mary, if I were the Queen of Heaven and you were Thérèse, I should want to be Thérèse that you would be the Queen of Heaven!!!'[259] She would die with her eyes fixed just above the statue, after having invoked her throughout her long agony: In May, she had written:

> Soon I will see you in heaven.
> You came and smiled on me in the morning of my life,
> Come and smile on me again ... Mother ...
>   for it is evening.
> I no longer fear the light of your great glory
> I have suffered with you, and now I wish
> To sing on your lap, Mary, why I love you
> And to repeat for ever that I am your child ... f

e   The same thought is found in Ms C p.242. '... but when alone (I am ashamed to admit it) the recitation of the rosary is harder for me than the wearing of an instrument of penance ... I feel I have said this so poorly! I force myself in vain to meditate on the mysteries of the rosary. I don't succeed in fixing my mind on them'.

f   The last verse of the poem. Sister Marie of the Sacred Heart recited it to her, July 8, in the infirmary.

In this way Thérèse would enter heaven into eternal communion with her friends, the saints. In her turn, she too would be declared a saint and take her 'official' place with that immense cloud of witnesses. The story after her death clearly shows that she still acts like a spoilt child of God, often playful,[g] doing 'all that she wishes'. In her last letter to Abbé Bellière she describes the role that would one day be hers:

> I believe that the blessed in heaven have great compassion for our wretchedness. They remember that when they were frail and mortal like us they committed the same faults, endured the same struggles, and their love for us becomes greater even than it was on earth, this is why they do not stop protecting us and praying for us.[260]

5. In the fullness of truth: the mysterious Thérèse

Who could claim to have penetrated all the secrets of that mysterious smile?[h] Having finished the portrait sketch of Thérèse at the gates of death, we will not attempt any synthesis which would appear as depersonalising as the picture of a robot. We admit our limitations without any regret. Rather there is a certain sense of joy that comes from feeling oneself overwhelmed by the inexpressible reality, namely the truth, the simplicity, the transparency of a human life, where deception had no part.

The sense of fulfillment which Thérèse gives us is rooted in the very ground of her being. 'What contrasts there are

---

g The seven volumes of *A Shower of Roses* (an anthology of graces received by different ones and sent to the Lisieux Carmel) contain miracles somewhat out of the 'ordinary', which manifest a humour and stamp which correspond so well with Thérèse's temperament and her promises.

h Blanche Monteveille concludes her book with these words: 'Thérèse henceforth is for us no longer a mystery'. Mgr Combes has refuted this statement in his Introduction to *The Spirituality of Saint Thérèse of the Child Jesus*, by devoting twenty-three pages to *The Theresian Mystery*. Five years later, he wrote: 'The soul of Thérèse is an abyss which I cannot claim, after years of research, to have plumbed'.

in my character!'[261] That acknowledgement can be applied to the whole of the *Last Conversations*. Throughout her illness and her agony, Thérèse defied all logic. There is a final proof of the absolute authenticity of the evidence of the witnesses. Never could Mother Agnès, such as we know her, have invented those pat answers. We must be forever grateful to her for having dared to write them down faithfully, just as they were spoken.

To a serious question, one would expect a 'profound' answer, worthy of a model contemplative. A witty retort is given. A sister's remark is thought to be irritating and devoid of interest, Thérèse seizes this occasion to take the heat out of the discussion. At the stage she had now reached one would not expect to find her almost scrupulous about little details,[i] while at the same time incarnating sovereign liberty.

So unsophisticated and full of fun is she that there are times when we think we are listening to a young girl, a child. A second later, she expresses herself with the wisdom of a very mature woman. This 'baby who is an old man'. She praises littleness, but cherishes 'immense desires'. She calls herself a 'little nothing', but wants to be 'all' and to travel the world until the end of time. If she experienced an ardent desire for heaven, 'for heaven is Jesus himself', never did she despise creation and its beauties. Her realism was rooted in the Norman soil.

A warrior maid, she did not fear death, but trembled at the very thought of confronting a spider. She mortified herself, depriving herself of a drink, but wanted very much to

i   She did not dare to remove the cover which made her too hot, she wondered if she had done the right thing in touching the fruit, (LC 24.7.2) she practised little mortifications (18.8.3.), but she could not understand a priest who was doing unusual mortifications, (LC 1.8.6.), and she did not forget her 'little devotions', (LC 11.9.5.).

eat 'a chocolate éclair'.[j] Beneath her 'angelic' appearance, she manifested an uncommon vitality. It would take several months of terrible sufferings to bring down the 'little Thérèse'. Energetic, a fighter, her 'method' was to abandon herself at each moment, never to play the stoic. If she has enriched christian martyrology with noble achievements it is in her own 'little way'.

Shy in the parlour, she could show a reckless audacity when her love was at stake: 'I have never feared anyone. I have always gone wherever I pleased'.[262] Alone, without support, she went beyond the usual frontiers of the christianity of her day. She did not challenge anything but brought everything back into question by following *only* the Gospel.

Suffering, experiencing the dark night, sharing the table of sinners and atheists, she continued to jest, and remained in great peace. Would she die without the sacraments? She, alone, did not become upset. 'What did it matter? Everything is grace'.[263] 'How can all these contrasts be reconciled?'[264] Only life can do this. Not some vague animistic principle, but that life of the Spirit which breaks down all the boundaries we wish to erect around the saints.

> Sanctity has no formulae or, rather it has them all … Each saint's life is like a new flowering, the outpouring − in a world which, by the heredity of sin, is enslaved by its dead − of a miraculous, paradisian simplicity.[k]

Unclassable, unique, free. Free, because true. From March 1877 when Mme Martin wrote: 'The little one will be all right too, for she wouldn't tell a lie for all the gold in the world',[265] until 25 September 1897, four days before her death, when Thérèse said: 'I really know now that what I've

---

j That chocolate éclair merits to become as famous in the annals of sanctity as St John of the Cross' asparagus, the sweets St Francis of Assisi requested of Madame Jacqueline and St Thomas of Aquinas' herring.

k G.Bernanos, *Saint Dominique*, NRF, pp. 10 and 12.

said and written is true about everything . . .'[266] The path of her life was directed towards authenticity. 'The work of the saint is his very life, and he or she is wholly present in that life'.[1]

Truth conquered, for her natural timidity inclined her rather towards submission to her family and religious milieu. But the force of her love made her break through the 'what-will-people-say' which is so inhibiting in community life. 'I tell the whole truth, and if anyone doesn't wish to hear the truth, don't let her come looking for me'.[267]

By temperament, Mother Agnès was more diplomatic. She asked her sister to 'say a few edifying and friendly words to Dr de Cornière. She met with a kind but very positive refusal: 'Ah! little Mother, that isn't my style. Let Dr de Cornière think what he wants. I love only simplicity. I have a horror of 'pretence'.[268] I assure you that to do what you want would be to act in bad faith on my part'. Certain practices in her monastery aroused her indignation: 'Oh, what poisonous praises I've seen served up to Mother Prioress! How necessary it is for a person to be detached from and elevated above herself so as not to be harmed by them'.[m] She did not want to close her eyes. She wanted to see people and 'things in their proper light',[269] and she wanted others to act in the same way with her.

> I've never acted like Pilate, who refused to listen to the truth. I've always said to God: O my God, I really want to listen to you. I beg you to answer me when I say humbly: What is the truth? Make me see things as they really are. Let nothing cause me to be deceived.[270]

The same truth motivated her actions: 'I always act without any 'pretence'.[271] She was of the opinion that the

l   G.Bernanos, op.cit. p.8.
m   LC 14.7.7. The only objection at the Process was prompted by Thérèse's strong disapproval of a flagrant injustice of Mother Marie de Gonzague when she was novice mistress. (Sister Marie of the Trinity).

struggle between what is and what *appears* is not equal, for 'truth always triumphs',[272] even if, on this earth it sometimes seems doubtful.

'The truth will make you free',[n] she read in the Gospel of St John, which was particularly dear to her in her last months. This expresses perfectly one of the most essential secrets of the simple and mysterious Thérèse ...

n   Jn, 8, 32.

_____ Chapter 3 _____

The passion of Sister Thérèse
of the Holy Face

'To live for love is to climb Calvary with Jesus ...

When Thérèse, in June 1897, reread her play, _Jeanne d'Arc,_
a prisoner condemned to death, she found expressed there
her own thoughts. Many of the phrases must have touched
her deeply, especially this one: 'Oh how consoled I am to
see that my suffering is like that of my Saviour'.

What else had she wanted, above all in the last two years
of her life, but to follow her Beloved Jesus in his Passion?
Every christian life, which has been signed with the seal of
Baptism, leads to a sacramental participation in Christ's
death and resurrection. With St Paul it can also be said that
the Passion of Jesus continues in the members of his Body,
which is the Church. Five months before his death, Bernanos, the poet inspired by 'the most Holy Agony', wrote
in his diary: 'Just as he lays down his life on each altar where
Mass is celebrated, so he begins to die again in each man
as he undergoes his agony'.

The Passion, which has such prominence – quantitatively
and qualitatively – in the Gospels, has always been at the
heart of the meditation of the saints. It is the unfathomable
abyss, the only crucible wherein the reversal of all values
can take place: the All-Powerful One, the Master of Life,
dies there, and goes down to the depths of hell to raise man
up once again to his Life.

Thérèse's constant desire for martyrdom sprang from the
intuition of a lover: to share as closely as possible in the fate

of the Beloved. Reserved for some who are called to this particular vocation, martyrdom is a visible reactualisation of the passion of the Suffering Servant. Sister Thérèse of the Holy Face ardently wanted to be counted among that small number. She was heard. She who loved so much to make the Way of the Cross[a] did in actual fact walk it, not in a liturgical, 'figurative' way, but in reality.

> When she haemorrhaged, she rejoiced to think that she was shedding her blood for God. 'It could not have been otherwise', she said, 'I knew that I would have the consolation of seeing my blood spilt, for I am a martyr of love'.[b]

Before we look at her following in the footsteps of Jesus in Gethsemane and on to Calvary, let us examine the development of her own thoughts about death.

1. In the face of death

At an early age, little Thérèse had been confronted with death. Not only when she herself had been snatched away from it with great difficulty several times[c] after her birth, but, also, because she had grown up in a family which had been visited often by death before her own birth. Four of the children had died in infancy, and there had been numerous family funerals.[d] How many times she had heard the family speak about her little brothers and sisters who were so sadly missed! Yet she does not seem to have been unduly affected by this atmosphere. If she wanted her parents to die — she was not yet three years old when she expressed this wish — it was only because she saw that as the necessary condition for them to go to heaven![1]

a   Christopher O'Mahony, op.cit. p.242
b   Ibid, p.158.
c   Alarm as early as 17 January 1873 (she was fifteen days old), and especially from 28 February till 10 March — the day she nearly died.
d   Counting grand-parents' deaths, seven funerals in eleven years, from 1859 – 1870. There were two funerals in the years 1868 and 1870.

Everything said by these words of a child is based on logic. How can death be feared when it is associated with the idea of an immediate encounter with God, that is, with eternal happiness? In fact, right up until her last illness, it does not seem that Thérèse had ever feared death. Even her mother's departure, which had affected her so much, did not make her fearful or distressed. In her, life was stronger.

At a later date, when Thérèse and her father were out walking in the countryside around Lisieux, they were caught in a storm and she saw lightning strike a short distance away. She was not at all frightened, but rather 'thrilled with delight' and said: 'God seemed to be so close to me'.[2]

Five months after she entered Carmel, learning of the death of a cousin whom M. Guérin had helped to make his peace with God, she wrote to her aunt: 'When we look upon the death of the just man, we cannot but envy his lot. For him the time of exile is no more, there is now only God, nothing but God.[3] She was so orientated towards eternity, that the path which led there seemed to her to be only of minor importance. Even the direct experience of death did not change these sentiments. She was eighteen years old when, on 5 December 1891, she saw the venerated Mother Geneviève, whom she had loved very much, die after years of terrible sufferings: 'It was the first time I had assisted at a death', she recounts, and she added this unexpected comment: 'and really the spectacle was ravishing! . . .'[4] A month later, when an influenza epidemic laid low almost the whole community and claimed the lives of three sisters within a few days of each other, Thérèse remained on her feet and in good health:

> My nineteenth birthday was celebrated with a death, and this was soon followed by two other deaths. At this time I was all alone in the sacristy because the sister in charge was seriously ill. I was the one who had to prepare for the burials, open the choir grilles for Mass, etc. God gave me very many graces, making me strong at this time, and now I ask myself how I could have done all I did without experiencing some sort of

fear. Death reigned supreme. The ones who were most ill were taken care of by those who could scarcely drag themselves around. As soon as a sister breathed her last, we were obliged to leave her alone. One morning, upon rising, I had a presentiment that Sister Magdalene was dead. The dormitory was in darkness, and no one was coming out of the cells. I decided to go into Sister Magdalene's cell since the door was wide open. I saw her fully dressed and lying across her bed. I wasn't in the least afraid![5]

She concluded this period with these words:

The dying easily passed on to a better life, and immediately after their death an expression of joy and peace was seen on their faces and you would have said that they were only asleep.[e]

Influenced by this experience, the thought of her own death did not cause her any anxiety. However, we know that from her earliest years she had had a presentiment that she would die young. She had even desired it. It was a desire which came from the logic of her childhood wish: if one had to die in order to see God, she was ready to give her life. A desire, reinforced by another hope: to love until death, to die of love.

We understand then why Thérèse, when seriously ill in April, May and June 1897, was going to her death with astonishing cheerfulness. She gave a clear explanation to her sisters who, like the rest of men, could not understand this hurry:

It's not 'death' that will come in search of me, it's God. Death isn't some phantom, some horrible spectre, as we see represented

e   Cf Mother Agnès: 'I was saying that I feared she would suffer death's agonies: Thérèse replied: 'If by the agonies of death you mean the awful sufferings which manifest themselves at the last moment through signs which are frightful to others, I've never seen them here in those who have died under my eyes. Mother Geneviève experienced them in her soul but not in her body'. (LC 20.7.4.)

in pictures. It is said in the catechism that 'death is the separation of the soul from the body, and that is all it is'.[f]

During June and July, those months of waiting, very often she exclaimed: 'Oh! little sisters, how happy I am! I see that I'm going to die very soon, I am sure of this now'.[6] The chaplain asked her if she was resigned to die: 'Ah! Father, I feel I need resignation only to live. For dying, it's only joy I experience'.[7] She was not like Joan of Arc who 'was afraid for a moment' and tore out her hair. In a letter dated July 31, Sister Marie of the Eucharist stressed this unusual attitude: 'It's quite impossible to understand her joy at dying. She is like a little child who wants to go with all her heart to see her Father again. Never was anyone seen to die with such calmness. She says: 'What do you expect? Why should death frighten me? I've never acted except for God'.[8]

There is no boasting, either here, in this remark, or elsewhere. However, that does not permit us to state categorically that Thérèse was not afraid of death. In fact, she did experience moments of wavering, of sudden dread. She acknowledged this, and we would distort the truth if we disregarded those words:

> One morning during thanksgiving after communion, I felt the agonies of death ... and with it no consolation ...[9]

In September we have another confidence:

> ... I'm afraid I've feared death. But I have not feared what will happen after, for sure! And I'm not sorry for having lived. Oh! no. It's only when I ask myself: 'What is this mysterious separation of the soul from the body?' It's my first experience of this, but I abandon myself to God.[10]

Several times during her illness she wondered about this mysterious passage, and how she would pass through it: 'I

---

f   LC 1.5.1. This date does not seem accurate, since a letter written 16.7. says that this was said 'not long ago' by the sick nun.

wonder how I'll go when dying. I would like, nevertheless, to come off 'with honour'! But I believe this doesn't depend on oneself'.[11] 'What is baby to do in order to die? But what shall I die from?'[12] and on 29 September: 'What must I do to die?'[13] We must take into account all these nuances. Thérèse was not adopting a pose for posterity. Each word expressed just what she was experiencing at that moment. She only spoke the truth. When some of the older nuns around her saw her so determined to face death, they could not help attributing it to the ardour of youthful illusion. Someone said to her that she would be afraid:

> This could very well be true. There isn't anyone here more mistrustful of her feelings than I am. I never rely on my own thoughts. I know how weak I am. But I want to enjoy the feeling God gives me at this moment. There will always be time to suffer the opposite.[14]

And in July, undoubtedly after another remark of this kind, she said:

> ... Why should I be protected more than anyone else from the fear of death? I won't say like St Peter: 'I will never deny you.[15]

Lucid and abandoned, Thérèse was therefore ready for all. Still wanting 'to please', she did not discard the possibility of a 'beautiful death' as her sisters hoped — she even asked the Blessed Virgin for it.[16] But she wanted above all to leave that to God. He would do as he wished. In the end, she had only one real desire. It was always the same: to die of Love.

2. 'To love until death ...'

The origin of this great desire, repeated so often, is to be found in the works of St John of the Cross. In 1890-1, 'when she was about seventeen or eighteen years old',[17] the young Carmelite earnestly set herself to reading the great Spanish mystic, and she took him for her guide. At that time, she begged God to accomplish in her what she was reading about in *The Living Flame*, especially in the commentary on stanza 1, line 6. The Carmelite Doctor explains there how souls consumed by Divine Love die of that very Love which causes the soul to be separated from the body:[g]

> The death of such persons is very gentle and very sweet, sweeter and more gentle than was their whole spiritual life on earth. For they die with the most sublime impulses and delightful encounters of love, resembling the swan whose song is much sweeter at the moment of death.[h]

In the infirmary, Thérèse was not separated from the works of her spiritual guide. She reread them and took notes. It would be of the utmost interest to reread those texts over her shoulder, especially the passage we have just quoted. But there are others, such as the following:

> It is vital for a person to make acts of love in this life so that in being perfected in a short time he may not be detained long, either here on earth or in the next life, before seeing God.[i]

This was what she read when she was still in the dark night of faith. She still hoped, although she was experiencing anything but those 'sublime impulses' and 'delightful encounters of love'. Her desire 'to die of love' was always present. The importance of this subject requires the compilation of an extensive inventory of her writings and words relating to it.

In June, two days after she had begun Manuscript C, Thérèse wrote to Sister Marie of the Trinity: 'I no longer

---

g   Thérèse had been very struck by the story of the converted sinner who 'died of love' and was adamant that it be added to her unfinished Manuscript.

h   'The Living Flame of Love', St John of the Cross, trans. K.Kavanaugh o.c.d. and O.Rodriquez o.c.d., I.C.S. 1973, p.592.

i   Ibid, p.594.

rely on sickness, it is too slow a guide. I now *rely only on love*.[18] The next day, posing for a last photograph and holding in her hands the two pictures which symbolise her name and her vocation, she silently proclaims her hope. Around the picture of the Holy Face these words are written: 'Divine Jesus, fulfil my dream: To die of love . . .'[j] Two days later, the second anniversary of her Oblation to Divine Love, she wrote in her little black exercise book: 'It seems to me now that nothing can stop me flying away, for I no longer have any great desires except that of loving to the point of dying for love'.[19] The following day she repeated her heart's desire: 'Now I would want to be sick all my life if this pleased God, and I even consent to a very long life. The only favour I desire is that it be broken through love'.[20]

At the end of July she quoted a passage from *The Living Flame* to Mother Agnès:

'Tear through the veil of this sweet encounter!' I've always applied these words to the death of love that I desire. Love will not wear out the veil of my life. It will tear it suddenly. With what longing and what consolation I have repeated from the beginning of my religious life these other words of St John of the Cross: 'It is of the highest importance that the soul practise love very much'.[21]

On August 31, the sick nun made a link between the shortness of her life and the death of love. She said once again that God had answered her beyond all her desires:

Ah! it is incredible how all my hopes have been fulfilled. When I used to read St John of the Cross, I begged God to accomplish in me what he wrote, that is, even if I were to live to be very old, to consume me rapidly in Love, and I have been answered!.[22]

The Martin sisters, perfectly well aware of their dying sister's desires, and familiar with the writings of St John of

j   From Thérèse's poem, 'To Live for Love', 26/2/1895.

the Cross, fully expected to see the literal realisation of the famous pages of *The Living Flame*. On July 7, Sister Geneviève wrote to Brother Simeon: 'Her sickness is love ... It is nothing else but 'dying of love', as she has desired so much'. At the sick nun's bedside therefore, the 'gentle sweetness and transports' described by St John of the Cross were recalled: 'I shall have to say that the 'joy and transports' are at the bottom of my heart. It would not be so encouraging to souls if they didn't think I suffered very much'.[23] Mother Agnès was surprised, and said: 'How I sense your agony! And yet a month ago you were saying such beautiful things about the death of love!' Thérèse was still of the same mind: 'What I was saying then, I would say right now'.[24]

But experience had taught her to free herself from the imagery of St John of the Cross in order to return to the central message of the Gospel: the Passion of Jesus Christ.

3. 'The most beautiful death of love ...'

Thérèse's persistent rejections of her sisters' pious thoughts brought about a major reversal. Without doubt, sickness had taught the saint many basic truths in keeping with reality.

On June 4, at that solemn moment when Thérèse had gathered her three sisters around her, she gave some important recommendations. First and foremost: to remain firmly rooted in faith which is the foundation of her way.

> Don't be astonished if I don't appear to you after my death, and if you see nothing extraordinary as a sign of my happiness. You will remember that it's 'my little way' not to desire to see anything.[25]

She ended with this important statement about the famous 'death of love':

> Don't be troubled, little sisters, if I suffer very much, and if you see in me, as I've already said, no sign of happiness at the

223

moment of my death. Our Lord indeed died as a Victim of
Love, and you see what his agony was! . . . All this says
nothing.[26]

In this way Thérèse, from June onwards, distinguished
the death of love from the signs which accompany it. She
had clearly moved away from the text of St John of the Cross.
One argument alone, solid, irrefutable, drawn from the
Gospel, satisfied her: the death of the Saviour himself. If
such had been the death of Jesus of Nazareth, she did not
hope for another.

> Our Lord died on the Cross in agony, and yet this is the most
> beautiful death of love. This is the only one that was seen. No
> one saw the Blessed Virgin die. To die of love is not to die in
> transports.[k] I tell you frankly, it seems to me that this is
> what I am experiencing.[27]

A major avowal. The progress of the disease, the dark night
of faith, seemed to give the lie, little by little, to the immense
desires. Those around her became anxious. Was this the
death of love? Did not Thérèse herself experience doubt?
Was she mistaken? Then she looked at her crucifix which
never left her, and the answer slowly impressed itself upon
her: what more beautiful death of love than that of the
Crucified? Yes! in her humble clear-sightedness, based on
her instinct of faith, she identified herself with her Beloved.
Are we to be guided then by the audacity of this dying young
Carmelite, who prefered to follow her own experience, ('I
understand something of it from what I'm experiencing
myself'[28]) rather than the teaching of the Master of Carmel?
No, she was not challenging it. She was happy to follow her
own pain. She renounced what is seen for what is. 'It is not the
pain it appears to be (dying of love), I only hope it is it!'[29]

---

k   Note that Thérèse is taking here the opposite view to that expressed
    in *The Living* Flame. Let us not forget however St John of the Cross'
    description of Christ's forsaken death in *The Ascent of Mount Carmel*,
    Bk.2 Ch.vii. But had Thérèse read this?

Once again, the possibility of a somewhat spectacular 'beautiful death' was suggested to her: after communion, or on the feast day of Our Lady of Mt Carmel. (That would read so well in her circular, and how 'it would edify souls'!)

> Oh! that wouldn't resemble my 'little way'. I would be then leaving it to die? Dying after receving communion would be too beautiful for me. Little souls couldn't imitate that.[30]

And so Thérèse's death of love was in perfect harmony with her 'little way'. She had to remain in the 'night of faith'. For it was there that she rediscovered the basic teaching of St John of the Cross.[1]

4. Sister Thérèse of the Holy Face

> ... her Spouse is not a Spouse who will lead her to festivals, but up the hill of Calvary. [31]

On 10 January 1889, the day she received the habit, Sister Thérèse of the Child Jesus ended a note to Sister Marthe with a new signature: 'Sister Thérèse of the Child Jesus and of the Holy Face'.[32] This addition took on a very profound meaning when she was undergoing the great trial of her life, the illness of her father whose face was 'veiled' in imitation of the 'Adorable Face of Jesus which was veiled during his Passion'.[33] It was at the beginning of July 1890 that she quoted the passage from Isaiah 53 which was to take on such a dominant place in her spirituality.

It would be interesting to follow the development of this discovery from 1890 until 1897.[m] Let us say only that

---

l   We are leaving aside the theological problems and different interpretations of Thérèse's 'death of love'.

m   Cf. quotations from Isaiah in her Letters, 18/7/1890, 7/9/1890, 8/9/1890, 23/9/1890, 19/10/1892, 20/2/1893, 2/8/1893, Prayer to the Holy Face (1896), Consecration to the Holy Face (1895). Plays: *The Angels at the Crib*, (25/12/1894) where the Angel of the Holy Face is speaking with the Angel of the Child Jesus and quotes Is. 53. Letter dated 9/1/1897. Six plays, etc.

Thérèse's intuitive genius is once again manifested. Instinctively, she went directly to an essential Old Testament text, which modern exegesis has shown to be of fundamental importance. Jesus often quoted the Songs of the Suffering Servant which were important prophecies concerning his mission. But they were forgotten – consciously or unconsciously – by his disciples who rebelled at the idea of a Messiah who would be persecuted, rejected by his people and crucified. Thérèse did not have any knowledge of this scholarly research; she did not even have a complete Bible at her disposal, yet she nevertheless declared:

> These words of Isaiah: 'Who has believed our report ... There is no beauty in him, no comeliness, etc.,' have been the whole foundation of my devotion to the Holy Face, or, to express it better, the foundation of all my piety. I, too, have desired to be without beauty, alone in treading the winepress, unknown to everyone.[34]

We cannot place too much importance on this confidence which, at that time, amounted almost to a 'last will and testament'. Here we have an inexhaustible source of study. She, whom we customarily call St Thérèse of the Child Jesus – and who, in this way, is made to symbolise only childhood – was able to say, at the moment of her death, that the *foundation of her whole piety* was nourished on the texts of Isaiah 53, concerning the 'Suffering Servant'.

When we mutilate her name, we mutilate her message, and indeed her whole life. If we rely on the testimony of Mother Agnès, given at the Beatification Process, we could justly call her Sister Thérèse of the Holy Face:[n]

> Devotion to the Holy Face was the Servant of God's special attraction. As tender as was her devotion to the Child Jesus, it cannot be compared to her devotion to the Holy Face.[o]

n   In the Chapel of Assy, Notre Dame de Toute-Grace, P.Couturier's stained-glass window features St.Thérèse of the Child Jesus and OF THE HOLY FACE (thus written): Thérèse, like a Veronica, is hidden behind the veil which bears the blood-stained Face of Christ.
o   Twice Thérèse speaks of Job, the abandoned just man, another Old Testament figure announcing Christ – once identifying herself with

When Thérèse, on June 7, allowed her photograph to be taken 'in view of her approaching death', she posed, holding the two pictures which symbolised her name and her vocation. Far from standing in opposition – the Child Jesus and the suffering Christ – they are deeply united. It is one and the same Person. From childhood he knew suffering: naked on the straw of the cave, pursued by men, fleeing into Egypt ... Therefore, there is no contradiction in Thérèse saying that her *whole* piety was based on the Suffering Servant texts.[p]

Let us note once again that the term 'devotion' to the Holy Face suggests a completely optional pious practice, left to each one's choice. In the Carmelite Ordo at that time, the feast of the Holy Face was celebrated on August 5 and Thérèse characteristically kept that day as her feast day in order to show clearly, ('or, to express better'), that *this was the foundation of her whole piety*, indeed its very foundation stone. Here we touch the heart of her life which is that of the Gospel. Let us listen again to the testimony of her novice, Sister Marie of the Trinity:

> Sister Thérèse of the Child Jesus had a special devotion to the Holy Face of Jesus. She saw in it the reflection of the humiliations and sufferings Jesus underwent during his Passion. The sight of that divine Face awakened in her soul a passionate desire to be like him which she constantly spoke about to me. She was proud to bear its name'.[q]

him (LC 5.8.8. p.135), another time referring to his hope: 'This saying of Job: 'Although he should kill me, I will trust in him', has fascinated me from my childhood'. (LC 7.7.3).

p   It would be interesting to study the development of Thérèse's understanding of the Child Jesus. Once again she touches on fundamental questions of our own day. 'The two most popular images of western Christianity illustrate perfectly what I have referred to elsewhere as the 'all-powerlessness' of God that it is surprising that so many believers can remain prisoners of a false understanding of the all-powerlessness of God. What are these two images? A baby lying in a manger, and a tortured man hanging on a cross'. (Jean-Claude Barreau, *Qui est Dieu?*, Seuil, 1971, pp.59-60).

q   She used to carry on her heart a small picture of the Holy Face with this prayer: 'Make me like you, Jesus!'.

For a long time, Sister Thérèse of the Holy Face had desired to live his Passion. On May 27, she had meditated on this text: 'The cross is the bed of my spouses. It is there that I have them taste the delights of my love'.[35] On her bed-curtains she had pinned the picture of the Holy Face from her breviary,[r] and her crucifix never left her. 'Since I have been ill, I have held our dear little crucifix in my hands practically all the time'.[36] She kissed it,[37] symbolically took out the nails,[38] unpetalled roses over it.[39] During the whole of her agony she did not let go of it.[40]

To Thérèse's great joy, the picture of the Holy Face from the choir was hung in the infirmary on August 5, the eve of the feast of the Transfiguration: 'Oh! how much good that Holy Face has done me in my life!'[41] She looked at it all through the night.[42] These pictures and pious objects were constantly before her eyes as aids to her meditation during her months of suffering. Very often, she drew a parallel between her situation and that of Jesus.

Thus she dared to make her own, with theological soundness, the words of his testament: 'I can only borrow Jesus' words at the Last Supper. He will not object, because I am his little Bride and therefore all his goods are mine'.[s] The smallest events[t] in her life sent her back to the Passion. She has a pain in her shoulder. That makes her think of Jesus carrying his cross. A sister comes and wearies her by staring at her:

> But yes, it's painful to be looked at and laughed at when one is suffering. But I think how Our Lord on the Cross was looked

r   This is the picture she is holding in the photographs of June 7.
s   Cf. Letter dated 18/7/1897 which has a quotation from Jn. 16,5,7,22. The same argument is found in Manuscript C p.255, where she quotes at length from Jn.17. In those last months, she often quoted from the Gospel of St John: 18 times in Ms.C, 7 times in the *Last Conversations*, five times in her *Letters*.
t   She interpreted the mark on the infirmary mantle in this way: (+F) 'It means that we must carry the cross (+) in order to go afterwards higher than the firmament (F)'. (LC 20.8.7.)

at in the same way in the midst of his sufferings. It was even worse still, for they were really mocking him. Isn't it said in the Gospels that they looked at him, shaking their heads? This thought helps me to offer him this sacrifice in the right spirit.[43]

Seeing her three sisters falling asleep beside her bed, she calls them: 'Peter, James and John!'[44] It was another way of identifying herself with the abandoned Christ. It was an identification which, evidently, did not exclude differences that Thérèse was happy to emphasise. She said to Mother Agnès, who was very saddened by the thought of seeing her dead: 'The Blessed Virgin held her dead Jesus on her knees, and he was disfigured, covered with blood! You will see something different!'[45]

These details must not hide the deeper bonds which united the sick nun to her crucified Beloved. Not only did she resemble him in her physical suffering, but she shared his abandonment. Her interior solitude, her spiritual trial, made her enter into the mystery of Gethsemane:

> Our Lord enjoyed all the delights of the Trinity when he was in the garden of Olives, and still his agony was none the less cruel. It's a mystery, but I assure you that I understand something of it from what I'm experiencing myself.[46]

Her agony of September 30 would be like that of Jesus, 'without any mixture of consolation'.[47] When about three o'clock,[u] she put out her arms in the form of the cross, leaning on her two sisters, gasping for breath, and trying to find some relief,[v] those around her were forcibly reminded of the Crucified: 'For us she was a striking image of Jesus on the Cross. I regarded this coincidence as full of mystery . . .' When the same witness, Sister Geneviève, was

---

u   Each day at that hour the monastery bell would ring out to recall the death of Christ.

v   Dr. Barbets' work on crucifixion has shown that a person who is crucified dies from suffocation, the lungs become congested.

speaking of her sister's little cries and groaning, she added: 'Those broken words, all bearing the stamp of perfect conformity to God's will, were heart-breaking to hear. Like Jesus, God seemed to have abandoned her'.

A person reading the *Last Conversations* would normally be left with a feeling of extreme sadness. What could be more heart-rending, more disastrous, than the gradual destruction of a young person whose cells are all calling out for life. Thérèse was spared the 'wreck of old age', but not the slow destruction of the body by illness, with its train of miseries and humiliations. It is true that she did not know the deterioration of her mental faculties. Until her last breath – like Jesus - she remained lucid and mentally alert.[w] In the strict sense, she saw herself die. She was able to make an offering of her death.

And yet that reading radiates peace. Terrible as it was, the death of Thérèse of the Holy Face cannot arouse only sorrow and tears. The reader is aware of a passage, not an annihilation. Dead, she seems to be still living. Or rather, at last living with regard to her universal mission. And so, in the Lisieux Carmel, the first anniversary of her death was, strange to say, an occasion for joy. For had she not written to Abbé Bellière:

> Yes, I am sure that after my entry into life, my dear little Brother's sorrow will be turned into deepest joy, a joy that no one will be able to take from him.[48]

Some signs of that joy – not extraordinary, but nonetheless noticed by attentive witnesses – were given as the first-fruits of the victory that was to come. Her face, which remained unchanged in a body ravaged by disease, had struck all the witnesses. Then there were those moments preceding

---

w   'In the midst of that general decline, the mental faculties usually remain unimpaired.' (Dr. Dieulafoy, op.cit.)

her death. That 'ecstasy' did not obliterate all that she had just suffered, for what is the 'space of one Creed' when compared to six months of suffering? But it did give meaning to it. The wonderful negative, taken by Sister Geneviève on October 1, bears the imprint of that moment. In death, her face, 'with its childlike expression', was again in keeping with her body which had become 'like that of a young girl'.

After death, it seemed that her spiritual childhood was expressed by this visible sign. Thérèse was once again 'a child' in her physical being. That smile of a happy conqueror, or, 'of one happy to be conquered', which no photographic plate had really been able to capture during her life, Thérèse now finally surrendered. When someone had been speaking about the contortions which sometimes occur at the moment of death, she had said: 'If this happens to me, don't be sad, for immediately afterwards I'll have nothing but smiles'.[49] Unobtrusive sign given to the witnesses, which we can now contemplate at leisure, thanks to the invention of photography. It is a face which expresses so many things: peace, serious joy, interior fervour, liberation ... It seems to say: 'I am as one risen. I am no longer in the place where they think I am ...'[50]

5. 'I am not dying, I am entering into life'

In that life, surrendered to love, the Passion did not just come about as by accident. With her whole heart and soul Thérèse freely entered into it. 'The majestic life of the saint comes to thrust him into death as into an abyss of light and sweetness'. (Bernanos, *Saint Dominique*). Thérèse herself gives us the meaning of her Passion in her last manuscript when she borrows from St John the priestly prayer of Jesus.[x]

---

x   She also quoted the words of the martyr, St Ignatius of Antioch: 'I, too, must be ground down through suffering in order to become the wheat of God'. (LC 10.8.5.)

But is it John the theologian, or John the contemplative, who has better understood and explained the hidden meaning of the Passion of Christ, and consequently that of all Passions?[y]

With solemn introduction he opens the time of the drama: 'Before the feast of the Passover, Jesus, knowing that his hour had come to pass out of this world to the Father, having loved his own who were in the world, loved them till the end'. (Jn 13,1) Fully conscious of his divine sonship, Jesus fully entered into suffering and death, just as the Word had freely become man. 'Jesus walks to his death with full knowledge of what he is doing. The Evangelist stresses this throughout his account of the Passion: no one is taking his life from him, he is giving it. He has lived with his eyes fixed on this Hour which the beloved disciple has so often pointed out. *Now* it has come. *Now* is the judgment of this world; *now* the prince of this world is going to be cast down; and I, lifted up from the earth, will draw all things to me'.[z] 'The hour is henceforth the '*Now*', as van Den Bussche has so excellently expressed it.

The Passion unfolds then like a majestic tragedy. The evangelist emphasises Jesus' perfect knowledge of what is happening, and thereby his sovereign liberty and majesty during his Passion. 'For John, the Passion is already the Glory, just as the Resurrection and the Ascension. Or rather, the Passion, Resurrection and Ascension together constitute the glorification of the Son by the Father, the manifestation

y   'The evangelist (. . .) of the brutal event, of the apparent catastrophe, brought out another meaning: it was the passage, from this vain world, unstable and under Satan, to the Father. (. . .) This way of seeing the facts in the light of their bearing on the plan of revelation and salvation, and not according to their external appearances, shows a maturity of theological thought which alone can be the basis for prolonged and serene contemplation'. (Henri van Den Bussche, *Jean, Commentaire de l'evangile spirituel*, DDB, 1967, p.374)

z   Jn. 12, 31-32. Cf this 'now' in 13,31; 15,24; 16,5; 16,28; 17,5; 17,7; 17,13.

of God's glory in the Son. The death is the 'lifting up' (hupsôsis) in the two-fold meaning of the word: physical lifting up on the cross, and glorification'.

In fear and natural revolt, Jesus cries out to his Father, and makes to him the offering of his life: 'Knowing that everything had now been completed, Jesus said: (...) "It is accomplished", and bowing his head he gave up his spirit'.(Jn 19, 28-30) It was the supreme act of a loving will, the beginning of a total revolution for mankind. One man, the bearer of all human misery, the Suffering Servant of Isaiah 53, the Innocent One who comes from another place, turns to the Father and gives his life for all his brethren. Sign of the greatest love (Jn 15, 13). The personal drama attains a universal, cosmic dimension: mankind and the material world are liberated.

This theological reading of the Passion — the central point to which the Church returns unceasingly in her liturgy and her meditation, since it is the very source of her being — allows us to understand also the Passion of every Christian,[a] and consequently that of Sister Thérèse of the Holy Face.

Manuscript C is her Holy Thursday. There she reveals the secret of her person, and the meaning of what she will live. The repetition of the word *now*[b] which we have so often emphasised takes on its full meaning: it expresses maturity, availability. It also designates the 'Hour of Thérèse'. Like Jesus, she freely gave herself up, she abandoned herself. Hence those words, about her desire to suffer which cause

a   With St John, the Church is born from the side of the crucified Christ opened by the centurian's lance.
b   Thérèse found this 'now' in John's Gospel which she was rereading, and also in her other bedside book, *The Living Flame*, Verse 1, line 6 where St John of the Cross recapitulates the whole verse: '*Now* I am so fortified in love ... tear the thin veil of this life'. (Kavanaugh and Rodriquez, op.cit. p.595). Once again the *now* expresses a fullness, a maturity: the soul which has reached this summit is ready to die.

surprise, recall how Christ's voluntary going up to Jerusalem, the place of his execution, scandalised Peter.

Finishing her manuscript, Thérèse, with the sure instinct of faith, made her own the words of Jesus' sacerdotal prayer of Holy Thursday night. Let us reread then what Thérèse herself wrote. All that we have just written in this book becomes clear in the light of these words:

I have glorified you on earth and finished the work that you gave me to do. I have made your name known to those you have given me. They were yours and you have given them to me. Now they know that all you have given me comes from you. I have given them the teaching you gave to me, they have accepted it and they believe that it was you who sent me. I pray for those you have given me, because they belong to you. I am not in the world any longer, but they are in the world, and I am coming to you. Holy Father, keep those you have given me true to your name. Now I am coming to you, and while I am still in the world I say these things so that they may have the joy which comes from YOU in all its fullness.

I am not asking you to take them out of this world, but to protect them from evil. They do not belong to the world any more than I belong to the world. I pray not only for these, but for those also who through their words will come to believe in YOU.

Father, I want those you have given me to be with me where I am, and the world to know that you have loved them as much as you have loved me.[c]

c   The following verses are given in the order in which she used them. Jn 17,4,6,7,8,9,11,13,15,16,20,24,23. They are not written in the text Thérèse wrote, but we have given them to show the adaptation which the sick nun needed to make. The text has been wisely adapted and worked on to make it fit the case of Thérèse. Mgr Combes has made the following very good comment: 'When quoting, Thérèse followed her own idea. By comparing the two texts it can be seen that she has eliminated what would be appropriate only to Jesus, and she has made several alterations which are pregnant with meaning, e.g. v.9 She eliminates: 'I do not pray for the world'. v.11 She suppresses: 'In order that they may be one as we are one'. v.13 Instead of 'the fullness of my joy', she writes, 'the joy which comes from you'. v.20 In place of 'those who will believe in me', she writes, 'those who will believe in you'.

This is the key to the Passion of Thérèse and the ultimate meaning of all her sufferings. Hardly had she finished writing those lines when her Good Friday would begin – the period of haemoptyses which began July 6.

Blessed passion, glorious passion, which in its turn, too, would open the gates of hell and set free a countless number of men and women on all continents until the end of time, by pointing out to them the way of peace and joy.

'Truly, truly I say to you: Unless the grain of wheat falls to the ground and dies, it remains but one grain, but if it dies, it brings forth abundant fruit'. (Jn 12,24) Laid in the ground in the little cemetery of Lisieux, Thérèse would soon draw crowds. Her personal destiny would go out to the ends of the earth. On 9 July 1897, Uncle Guérin, unknowingly, had prophesied when he wrote to his daughter on learning of his niece's approaching death: 'We were heart-broken, and yet this news which saddens us marks the dawn of a triumph'.

On 17 May 1925, several hundred thousand pilgrims from all over the world were present at the 'triumph' of Thérèse Martin, glorified and canonised by the Church.

While still unknown, she had written in her bed in the infirmary: 'I am not dying, I am entering into life'.[d]

d   Cf Letter to Abbé Bellière dated 9/6/1897.

Appendix I

Thérèse as her contemporaries saw her during her illness

It seems interesting to us to include here some of the opinions expressed about Thérèse by direct or indirect witnesses during her illness. They are all taken from letters[a] written between April and September 1897.

Looking back, some of these appear as true 'prophecies'. But we must not be misled by the clichés of the day: 'our angel', 'our little saint', etc. Nevertheless some witnesses were right.

'But she is suffering with admirable patience and gentleness. She's always very much herself. Oh! how very true it is to say that death is an echo of one's life! Our little saint awaits death with patience, she's no longer tormented with ardent desires for it. Each day, she finds her peace in these words of the psalm which delight her: 'You have given me delight, O Lord, in all your doings'. (Mother Agnès of Jesus, 5/8/1897).

'I cannot find words to tell you about her patience, her gaiety, her sanctity. It is impossible to describe her wonderful abandonment, her confidence is that of a child which knows that it is loved by the best of fathers. It is unbounded confidence. Ah! my little Jeanne, let us follow our little sister's example, as you said in your letter – 'in fifty years we will see things quite differently . . .' (Sister Marie of the Sacred Heart, L 15).

---

a   From the French edition: _Derniers Entretiens_.

'Her soul already is no longer on this earth, and she will go gently, joyously, to heaven. Her sickness is love ... She is simply Dying of Love as she has desired so much'. (Sister Geneviève, L 10).

'Our little Thérèse is so pure, so holy. I believe she entered Carmel with her baptismal innocence, and what ground she must have covered in so few years'. (Mme Guérin, L 16).

'What a lesson this little girl has given us. I will remember everything she said and did, and try to put it into practice until the day I die'. (M.Guérin, L 43).

'I thank God for permitting me to know this little saint, for here in the community she is loved and appreciated as such ... Hers is not an extraordinary sanctity: there is no love of extraordinary penances, no, only love for God. People in the world can imitate her sanctity, for she has tried to do everything through love and to accept all little contradictions, all little sacrifices that come at each moment as coming from God's hands'. (Sister Marie of the Eucharist, L 32).

'I do not know why they are talking so much about Sister Thérèse of the Child Jesus. She is not doing anything extra-ordinary. You do not even see her practising virtue, you would not even say that she is a 'good religious'. (Sister Saint-Vincent de Paul, words reported by Sister Marie of the Angels at the Diocesan Process.)

'I will never cure her for you, this soul was not made for earth.' (Dr de Cornière, reported by Sister Marie of the Eucharist, L 11.)

'My sister is a *saint*. Mother, would you give me some-thing of hers to keep as a *relic* after her death, ... if you could, give me some of her nails, or her hair — perhaps later these objects will procure miracles.' (Abbé Bellière, L 52.)

238

Let us quote again that remarkable description Mother Marie de Gonzague gave in 1893:

'Tall and robust, with a childlike face, and with a tone of voice and expression that hide a wisdom, a perfection, and a perspicacity of a woman of fifty ... She is a little innocent thing to whom one would give Holy Communion without previous confession, but whose head is filled with tricks to be played on anyone she pleases. A mystic, a *comedienne*, she is everything! She can make you shed tears of devotion, and she can just as easily make you split your sides with laughter during recreation.' (LC p.16.)

Was Thérèse well cared for?

Mother Marie de Gonzague's attitude

Maxence Van der Meersch's book, *La Petite Saint Thérèse*, has presented to the general public a caricature of Mother Marie de Gonzague. Yet, despite the strong and generally well documented evidence of specialists,[a] the story of a Sister Thérèse left to her sad lot, not properly cared for and even persecuted, still circulates.

The publication of the *Derniers Entretiens* confirms (sometimes corrects) and clarifies Fr Noché's work on Thérèse illness and her prioress' role at that time. If we are to come near to the truth calmly, twenty years after these polemics, it is not futile to briefly examine the point of this question, as given in the documents.

1. Was Thérèse well cared for?

The answer given by the facts is categorical. As her condition deteriorated (April 1897),[b] Dr de Cornière, the community

a *La Petite Sainte Thérèse de Maxence Van der Meersch devant la critique et devant les textes*, Editions Saint-Paul, 1950, p.562. While recognising the errors committed by Van der Meersch and his lack of understanding of Thérèse as a person and her message, we regret the manner in which ten eminent specialists treated this author. The search for truth and the value of their arguments do not justify a certain tone and constant slating of a christian brother who is mistaken. These acrid polemics about Thérèse do not appear today to be in conformity with the spirit of Vatican II, and above all with the spirit of the saint herself.
b Was she cared for *in time*? The Chapter, 'Early symptoms of the Disease' partly answers this more precise question. After 1894, Thérèse received

doctor, visited Thérèse regularly. Until he went on holidays (about 9 or 10 August), he had visited her at least twenty-six times, and after his return, from 10 to 29 September, at least six times.

2. Did Dr de Cornière make a wrong diagnosis?

'Yesterday Dr de Cornière came twice during the day. He is terribly worried. It is not tuberculosis, but an accident which has happened to the lungs, a real lung congestion' wrote Sister Marie of the Eucharist, 8 July (L 11). The day before, Sister Geneviève sent this report to Brother Simeon: 'Some congestion in the right lung had formed a lesion, but however it was not serious enough for the doctor not to hope for a cure if her weakness had not changed the situation'. (L 10). On 12 July, Mother Marie de Gonzague reechoed this diagnosis: 'We have just been through some very anxious days. Our little Sister Thérèse of the Child Jesus who has been sick for several months has had a complication, that is, congestion of the right lung. We have spent eight shattering days which have no equal but *her virtue*'. (L 19).

Two hypotheses can be considered:
(a) A wrong diagnosis: this is Fr Noché's opinion. Given the state of medical science in 1897 concerning tuberculosis, this is not an impossibility. However, it is strange that the treatment prescribed by Dr de Cornière should be the same as that given at the time to tubercular patients: the note-book of his prescriptions proves this fact.
(b) A refusal to tell the truth: to avoid upsetting the family and community, the doctor may not have used the word 'tuberculosis' earlier, for at that time the word was taboo, just as 'cancer' is today. Those around her could have thought

treatment. No one, it seems, spoke of tuberculosis of the larynx at that time. It is true that the way in which the visits were made did not assist an accurate diagnosis.

it, but not said it out aloud, as we see Céline speaking of a 'chest complaint' not yet known.

After Dr de Cornière's departure, Francis La Néele entered the enclosure four times to see his cousin (17, 30, 31 August and 5 September). He did not hesitate to use the word (at least in front of his family). 'He told us that the tuberculosis has reached its final stage,' reported his sister-in-law 26 August (L 51). But because of the advanced stage of the disease, he could do nothing. There was no cure for tuberculosis at that time. The most that could be done was to delay the inescapable progress of the disease.

3. 'One month' without a doctor?

This statement made by Sister Geneviève at the Diocesan Process[c] and often taken up by biographers is manifestly inaccurate. Unless she meant to say: 'one month without the usual doctor'. For Thérèse was without a doctor once for a period of eleven days (from 9-17 August), and then for thirteen days (from 17-30 August). It is true that this period corresponds to the worst time of her sufferings. In her condition, she should have 'seen a doctor every day', as Dr La Néele had 'brusquely' remarked to Mother Marie de Gonzague 30 August. Why then was Dr de Cornière's replacement at Lisieux not called in? Did the prioress hesitate to call in a third doctor? On the other hand, she had little

---

c   Diocesan Process: 'And so, at the end of her illness, she was a whole month without a doctor. The community doctor was away in the South, and he entrusted his little patient to Dr La Néele, our first cousin. But the prioress refused him entrance during all that time. The family protested, the doctor came once, but afterwards there was such a scene that words cannot describe it ...' (Sister Geneviève, Preparation for deposition, large black note-book). The witness is manifestly mistaken: Dr La Néele entered the enclosure four times. Also, Dr de Cornière sent from Plombières a prescription about 25 April.

sympathy for Thérèse's young out-spoken and frank cousin, who hardly troubled himself to ask for permissions.[d] He, on his side, does not seem to have had any confidence in Mother Marie de Gonzague: he said that one did not have to carry out all her commands. This gave rise to a difficult situation, to 'imbroglios', scenes and tears which caused Thérèse double suffering – she was without relief in her worst suffering and she was subject to the back-lash of her prioress' ill-temper. But it would appear very exaggerated to claim that she had been deliverately deprived of a doctor. In the absence of the official doctor, Mother Marie de Gonzague had hesitated, lost time. Much later, Sister Geneviève would write: 'Mother Marie de Gonzague gave in to her jealousy, but it was not spitefulness. It was not because of any malice that Saint Thérèse remained a long time without treatment. It was through negligence, not through malice'.

The proof of this lies in the fact that Dr de Cornière, on his return from Plombières, once again made frequent visits. He spoke of 'morphine injections, but the prioress would not allow them. She was given only, in small doses and rarely, some morphine syrup, for the prioress still had reservations about sedatives'. There is no need to accuse her of sadism, or feelings of vengeance. She was a woman of her day and suspicious of sedatives 'prohibited as shameful'.[e] Mother Geneviève was not given any sedatives in 1891. And, Mother Marie de Gonzague, when she was dying of cancer in 1904, refused this treatment for herself and only agreed to it when the sisters insisted.

d   'I had asked permission, as a matter of form, from Mother Prioress, and, without waiting for an answer lest the Rule forbade it, I took what was your right'. (Francis La Néele, L 26.6.1897). And the doctor kissed Thérèse at the beginning of the visit and as he was leaving.

e   Apostolic Process: 'We had to resort to strategy to give her some morphine syrup for Mother Marie de Gonzague had a theory that it was shameful to help Carmelites in this way. She never gave her consent to injections'. (Sister Geneviève, Diocesan Process).

Mother Marie de Gonzague's attitude in those last months shows a broad spirit despite some incidents which resulted from her jealousy and capriciousness. She freely gave permissions:

— to Mother Agnès of Jesus to remain often at her sister's bedside and write down the conversations.

— to Sister Geneviève who was practically first infirmarian as Sister Saint-Stanislas had relinquished her rights in this office.

— to the three Martin sisters who were often together with the sick nun.

— to Sister Marie of the Eucharist who could write very frequently (sometimes daily) of news to her family.

— to the Guérin family to make exceptional visits to the parlour and send little dishes of food to the sick nun.

Finally, would Thérèse have written the following passages in her manuscript, in June, if she did not think it?

'O Mother, ... I wish first of all to tell you how much all your maternal attention has touched me. Ah! believe me, Mother, the heart of your child is full of gratitude, and she will never forget what she owes you'. (Ms C p.215.)

'Ah! Mother, ever since I became sick, the care you bestowed on me has taught me a great deal about charity. No remedy appeared too expensive to you, and when it did not succeed you tried another thing without tiring. When I was going to recreation, what attention you paid in order to shelter me from draughts! Finally, if I wanted to tell all, I would never end. When thinking over all these things, I told myself that I should be as compassionate towards the spiritual infirmities of my sisters as you are, dear Mother, when caring for me with so much love'. (Ms C p.245.)

'... but I also know that my Mother would not cease to take care of me, to try to console me, if I remained sick all my life'. (Ms C p.246).

All this is confirmed by the witnesses' letters. 'Our Mother is taking care of her, no one could do more. She does not know that I am writing to you, and I beg you, please do not give any advice about how to look after her,[f] because our Mother is so good to her and does all she can'.[g]

On the first day of the Novena to Our Lady of Victories to pray for Thérèse cure, the prioress was in tears in the choir when she intoned the Salve Regina. 'It is true, on that day, our little Angel was very sick'. (Mother Agnès, L 8).

After the first haemoptysis, Sister Marie of the Eucharist told her father about the treatment that was being given, and concluded: 'She is wonderfully cared for ... our Mother has a real motherly tenderness towards all of us in the midst of the greatest of pains, for Sister Thérèse of the Child Jesus was her greatest treasure'. (L 11 8.7.1897). This was why the Guèrins responded with expressions of gratitude to Mother Marie de Gonzague.

---

f   The prioress did not want any advice from the Guérins. Dr de Cornière was the official doctor of the Carmel.

g   The following letter of Mme Guérin dated 6 June to her daughter, Jeanne La Néele, repeats information contained in an earlier letter: 'Thérèse is very well cared for. She receives with the greatest regularity all the prescribed treatment. The good Mother takes great care of that'. One feels that Mme Guérin wanted to reassure her son-in-law, Dr La Néele, who was not over confident in Mother Marie de Gonzague.

Appendix III

An example of how one of Thérèse's expressions was amplified with the passage of time

The publication of the volume of Appendices to the *Derniers Entretiens* has enabled us to go back sometimes to the *exact words* spoken by Thérèse during her illness. To some this research may appear byzantine, but the patient effort enables us to reconstruct the facts as they happened and to discover the saint's own words. Witnesses have sometimes taken these words out of their context, this has then given them a different shade of meaning, in general in the sense of amplification and giving them a more exalted meaning.

Let us take one example.

A reader may have been surprised to find omitted from our last chapter the following words given in *Novissima Verba* for September 29: 'To Sister Geneviève of the Holy Face who asked her for a word of farewell: "I have said everything ... *everything is accomplished*! It is love alone that counts'.

It is a beautiful expression and would have fitted in perfectly with our plan to show the similarity between Thérèse's Passion and that of Christ, ending with the 'everything is accomplished' of John 19,30. But we have refused to do it — beautiful and symbolic as it may be — for the following reasons:

1. These words are not in their chronological order:

There is no evidence to say that these words were actually spoken 29 September, at the beginning of Thérèse agony, for the dating differs in the various versions.

a) The principal witness, Sister Geneviève, said: 'one day' at the Apostolic Process; 'the eve of the 29 September' in *l'Esprit*. In the original version, which may have been written not long after Thérèse death (1898?), she is even more vague: 'another time . . .' Much later, although she had written: 'the day before she died', in her book *Conseils et Souvenirs*, Sister Geneviève, in a note written 28/12/1952 remains vague: 'Not long before she died . . .' This shows that at the end of her life she did not substantiate the date as being September 29, despite all that had been published.

b) Mother Agnès of Jesus, in *Novissima Verba*, borrowed these words from Sister Geneviève and dated them according to *l'Esprit*, not knowing the date herself, she had to rely on her sister.

In conclusion this can be said: these words, with time and the progress of the theresian cause, had been pushed back to September 29 where they would take on naturally a solemn meaning. Sister Geneviève could then say at the Apostolic Process: 'Like Our Lord before he died, she said to me one day very seriously . . .' That day then became September 29. But *it is the witness' interpretation.*

2. These words have been taken out of their context:

By going back to the original version, we find the following: 'Another time I said to her: Since you want to go to Saigon, perhaps when you are in heaven, I shall go in your place to complete your work, and the two of us will do a perfect work: — 'Ah! if you ever go there, don't think it's to complete something. There is no need of this. Everything is good, everything is perfect, accomplished, it is love alone that counts. If you go there, it will be a whim of Jesus, nothing more. Don't think this would be a *useful* work, it would be a whim of Jesus!'

The context appears very different to that of *Novissima Verba*. There is no question of a solemn declaration on the eve of her death, which likens Thérèse to the dying Christ on the cross, but rather an answer to a definite question about a work to be done. It is true that Thérèse, one day not long before she died, said: 'Everything is good, everything is perfect, accomplished, it is love alone that counts . . .', and that these words were applied to her own life.

When possible, this work of research into the exact meaning of all Thérèse's important words must be attempted. It takes away nothing − rather the contrary − from the value of her words and her sanctity: it makes them simpler and truer. Saints do not need any embellishment.

Thérèse's final 'ecstasy'

If we wish to discover the truth of the facts as they are given, then we have to go back over the chain of versions to reach the most original. We will examine here what happened in the infirmary, 30 September 1897 at about a quarter past seven, according to accounts given by witnesses.

The reader of *Novissima Verba* is reminded of what came to be called Thérèse's 'ecstasy'.

'The sisters had time to kneel down around the bed and witnessed the ecstasy of the final moment. The face of our saint had taken on again the lily-white colour it had had when she enjoyed good health, her eyes were fixed on a spot above, shining and expressing a bliss which surpassed all her expectations. She made certain movements with her head, as if someone, several times, had divinely wounded her with a dart of love. Immediately after this ecstasy, which lasted the space of a Credo,[h] she closed her eyes and died'.

This text, very near that of the *Yellow Note-Book*, emphasises certain facts (the colour of th sufferer's complexion, eyes fixed upwards, movements of the head, and the length of

---

h 'Some minutes', said Sister Geneviève at the Apostolic Process. The slow recitation of a *Credo* takes from one minute forty-five seconds to two minutes.

that moment) and it contains an *interpretation* (bliss which surpassed all her expectations; 'as if someone[i] had wounded her . . .' etc).

Sister Geneviève also speaks of 'ecstasy', but gives another interpretation:

'I have often tried to analyse this ecstasy since then, and tried to understand that look of hers, which was not just an expression of beatitude. There was an element of astonishment in it, and her attitude expressed a very dignified assurance. I thought we had been present at her judgement'. Interpretation confirmed at the Apostolic Process and unvaried until *Conseils et Souvenirs*.

Sister Marie of the Sacred Heart declared:

'Then she was enraptured by a heavenly vision which reminded me of the one I had witnessed when, as a child of ten, she was cured by the apparition of the Blessed Virgin. During this ecstasy, a sister held a candle very near her eyes, but her gaze remained very clear, fixed with an inexpressible peace on the object which enraptured her. This ecstasy lasted several minutes'. (Diocesan Process).

Sister Marie of the Trinity: 'I witnessed the long and beautiful ecstatic look on her face at the moment she died' (Diocesan Process), this evidence subsequently became: 'I was then witness to her last ecstasy at the moment she died' (Apostolic Process).

The same phenomenon occurs in the evidence given by Sister Thérèse of Saint-Augustine: the word 'ecstasy' only appeared at the Apostolic Process.

Sister Marie of the Angels' account differs slightly: 'Suddenly she raised her head erect with surprising energy. She

---

i   In the *Yellow Note-Book*, we read 'Quelqu'un (Someone)'. A description drawn from the transverberation of St Teresa of Avila.

opened her eyes wide and, with a magnificent expression, gazed above the statue of the Blessed Virgin. We felt at that time that she was looking at something supernatural. I thought it must have been Our Lord (Diocesan Process).

Finally Sister Marthe's testimony is very restrained: 'I was present when she died. She opened her eyes and gazed for several moments at something invisible' (Apostolic Process).

From this evidence given at the Processes, let us go back to the original texts. By chance, we have a note written by Mother Agnès of Jesus a few minutes after Thérèse died to the Guérin family who were waiting for news in the chapel of the Carmel: 'Our angel is in heaven. She gave up her last sigh at seven o'clock, pressing her crucifix to her heart and saying: '*Oh! I love you*'. She had just lifted her eyes to heaven; what was she seeing!!!'

The unusual phenomenon of the last moment is mentioned. However, in that note scribbled at that moment, Mother Agnès could not write at length. But, if she had witnessed a very spectacular 'ecstasy' she would have mentioned it. But the word is missing.

Another very valuable document is the letter Sister Geneviève wrote ten days after the events. She describes her sister's death to Brother Simeon: 'She remained conscious until the end, despite the cruel sufferings she was enduring, but her last look and her last breath were for the Blessed Virgin. Before she gave up her last breath, she seemed to be in ecstasy. The sisters thought that she had glimpsed at that moment a little corner of Paradise ...'[j]

---

j   Letter written 10/10/1897. In a letter dated 26.1.1898 from Fr Pichon to Sister Marie of the Sacred Heart, mention is made of 'that last mysterious gaze of 30 September' which she had spoken of to him in a letter which is now lost.

Sister Geneviève does not interpret the fact here in the same way as she was later to do. She leaves that to her 'sisters'. The word 'ecstasy' appears for the first time, but as a comparison: 'She *seemed* to be in ecstasy . . .'

The first version published in Chapter XII of *L'Histoire d'une Ame*[k] presents a paradox:

'Suddenly she lifted herself up, as if called by some mysterious voice, she opened her eyes and fixed them, shining with heavenly peace and inexpressible happiness, a little above Mary's statue. This look lasted for the space of a *Credo* and her blessed soul became the prey of the *Divine Eagle* and was carried away to the heavens'.

The version given in the *Green Note-Book* (1909) is also very factual: 'Her face took on again the lily-white colour it had when she enjoyed good health, her eyes, shining with peace and joy, were fixed on a spot above. She seemed to be in ecstasy. This look lasted for the space of a *Credo*. And so she went to God'.

The first use of the word 'ecstasy' by Mother Agnès, but very much toned down when seen in its context: '*she seemed to be in ecstasy*'. At the Diocesan Process, she stated: 'This ecstasy lasted at least the space of a *Credo*'. At the Apostolic Process, as we have seen, all the witnesses spoke of *the ecstasy* as of a known fact: we feel how far the cause had progressed. All this was to lead to the versions given in the *Yellow Note-Book* and *Novissima Verba* which we quoted at the beginning.

To make a sound criticism of the texts, we must stick to all the nuances in the witnesses' accounts and clearly distinguish between the facts described and the interpretations which vary greatly according to persons (transverberation, to die of love, a vision of Christ or of the Virgin, particular

---

k   The text was to remain unchanged until the last edition of 1953.

judgement, discovery of Paradise . . .). With the passage of time, what *seemed* 'like an ecstasy' became one. No one has to call by this word the brief moment during which Thérèse gazed at a certain spot in the infirmary, just above the Virgin's statue, with a fixed look which a candle did not divert. This fact, affirmed by a dozen witnesses, some of whom gave a written or oral account, cannot be denied. Should it be called an 'ecstasy' as some of these witnesses have done? That is another question.

___Abbreviations___

Ms A Autobiographical manuscript dedicated to Mother Agnès of Jesus (1895).

Ms B Letter to Saint Marie of the Sacred Heart (September, 1896).

Ms C Autobiographical manuscript dedicated to Mother Marie de Gonzague (June - July 1897).

LC Last conversations written down by Mother Agnès and others in the Yellow Note-Book, the Green Note-Book and Additional Conversations. A popular French edition, *Derniers Entretiens,* has been translated into English by John Clarke, ocd, St Thérèse of Lisieux *Her Last Conversations.*

LT Letters written by St Thérèse of Lisieux.

L Letters written by witness of St Thérèse's last months.

CSG *Conseils et Souvenirs* published by Sister Geneviève, 1952 and published in English under the title *A Memoir of my Sister St Thérèse.*

Note: *To assist the reader, unless otherwise stated, the references I have given are to the translations by ICS Publications wherever this has been possible to do so. (Translator)*

References

To assist research, the reader is referred not only to the page of the *Last Conversations*, our principal reference, but also to the date and entry.

p. without any further abbreviations indicates the *Last Conversations*. The numbers in brackets refer to the date and entry.

Example: p.143 (9.8.3) — page 143, the third entry for 9 August.

For other abbreviations, see page 257.

Foreword
1. p.134 (5.8.4)
2. Ms A, 152
3. p.134 (5.8.4)
4. p.205 (30.9)
5. p.159 (20.8.14)
   p.161 (21.8.3)
6. p.132 (4.8.5)
7. p.46 (21/26.5.1)
8. CSG 208.
9. p.194 (21.9.3)

Part I
Chapter 1 pp.19-34
1. LT 29/6/1896
2. Ms C, 237
3. Ms C, 220

4. Ms C, 225
5. Ms C, 246
6. Ms C, 233
7. Ms C, 244
8. p.16-17
9. Ms C, 244
10. p.49 (21/26.5.11)
11. Ms C, 218

Chapter 2 pp.35-43
1. p.258 (23.8.4)
2. Ms A, 171, 172
3. LT 18/7/1894
4. Ms C, 210
5. ibid
6. LT 12/7/1897
7. cf CSG 72
8. p.52 (27.5.10)

Chapter 3 pp.45-67
1. Ms A, 97
2. p.57 (5.6.2)
3. LT 28/4/1895
4. p.94 (13.7.13)
5. LT 18/7/1897
6. Ms A, 108
7. Ms A, 178
8. Ms A, 191
9. LT 16/7/1896
10. Ms B, 193
11. ibid
12. LT 26/12/1896
13. Ms B, 192
14. LT 17/9/1896
15. LT 1/11/1896
16. LT 21/10/1896
17. LT 27/1/1897
18. LT 19/3/1897
19. LT 19/3/1897
20. ibid
21. Ms C, 234

Part 2
Chapter 1 pp.71-95
1. p.47 (21/26.5.4)
2. p.45 (18.5.2)
3. p.46 (18.5.4)
4. p.51 (27.5.4)
5. p.56 (4.6.2)
6. p.272
7. p.265
8. Ms C, 215
9. LT 9/6/1897
10. LT 18/7/1897
11. p.71 (2.7)
12. p.272

13. ibid
14. p.275
15. p.102 (17.7)
16. p.281
17. p.283
18. p.273
19. ibid
20. p.276
21. p.281
22. p.102 (18.7.2)
23. p.148 (12.8.5)
24. LT 10/8/1897
25. p.290
26. p.241 (22.8)
27. p.163 (22.8.4)
28. cf. note p.162;
29. cf. note p.162
30. p.196 (22.9.6)
31. p.184 (5.9.4)
32. p.182 (4.9.2)
33. p.291
34. ibid
35. LT 8/9/1897
36. p.192 (18.9.3)
37. p.194 (21.9.6)
38. p.200 (26.9)
39. p.201 (28.9.1)
40. p.201 (29.9.2)
41. p.204 (30.9)

Chapter 2 pp.97-122
1. p.123 (31.7.13)
2. p.200 (25.9.2)
3. p.170 (26.8.3)
4. p.148 (15.8.1)
5. p.145 (11.8.3)
6. p.275

7. p.286
8. p.172 (27.8.9)
9. p.156 (20.8.6)
10. p.288
11. p.162 (22.8.2)
12. p.283
13. p.286
14. p.195 (22.9.2)
15. p.163 (22.8.7)
16. p.198 (24.9.8)
17. p.150 (16.8.1)
18. p.288
19. p.158 (20.8.12)
20. p.206 (30.9)
21. cf. p.164 (22.8.10)
    p.166 (23.8.10);
    p.168 (25.8.5);
    p.193 (20.9.1)
22. p.275
23. p.176 (31.8.3)
24. p.182 (4.9.4)
25. p.290
26. cf. p.157 (20.8.10)
27. p.155 (19.8.8)
28. p.153 (18.8.7)
29. p.131 (4.8.1)
30. p.151 (17.8.1)
31. p.47 (21/26.5.5)
32. p.108 (25.7.1)
33. p.200 (25.9.3)
34. p.288
35. p.290
36. p.56 (4.6.2)
37. p.131 (3.8.8)
38. p.117 (29.7.8)
39. p.149 (15.8.6)
40. p.154 (19.8.1)

41. p.164 (23.8.1)
42. p.203 (20.9.9)
43. p.144 (10.8.5)
44. p.152 (18.8.2)
45. p.191 (15.9.2)
46. p.200 (26.9)
47. Ms A, 157
48. Ms C, 210
49. p.274
50. p.63 (12.6.1)
51. p.68 (29.6.3)
52. p.47 (21/26.5.2)
53. p.62 (9.6.5)
54. p.51 (27.5.8)
55. LT 6/6/1897
56. p.63 (10.6)
57. p.64 (14.6)
58. p.65 (15.6.1)
59. p.62 (9.6.3)
60. p.78 (7.7.5)
61. p.79 (8.7.1)
62. p.81 (8.7.12)
63. p.274
64. p.87 (10.7.13)
65. p.274
66. LT 13/7/1897
67. LT 16/7/1897
68. p.121 (31.7.2)
69. p.124 (31.7.15)
70. p.136 (6.8.2)
71. p.153 (18.8.6)
72. p.165 (23.8.3)
73. p.187 (10.9.1)
74. p.204 (30.9)
75. p.65 (15.6.3)
76. Ms C, 215
77. p.47 (21/26.5.4)

78. p.189 (13.9.1)
79. p.174 (28.8.9)
80. p.61 (8.6.3)
81. p.172 (27.8.5)
82. p.37 (18.4.1)
83. p.130 (3.8.4)
84. LT 28/5/1897
85. p.57 (4.6.3)
86. p.154 (19.8.1)
87. LT 14-17/10/1895
88. p.142 (8.8.4)
89. p.148 (12.8.5)
90. p.183 (4.9.5)
91. p. 68 (29.6.3)
92. p.72 (3.7.3)
93. p.106 (22.7.1)
94. p.106 (23.7.2)
95. p.135 (6.8.1)
96. p.141 (8.8.2)
97. p.145 (10.8.7)
98. p.150 (15.8.7)
99. p.159 (20.8.15)
100. p.173 (28.8.3)
     cf. p.186 (8.9)
101. p.184 (5.9.1)
102. p.199 (24.9.10)
103. p.87 (11.7.1)
104. p.58 (6.6.2)
105. Ms C, 210
106. p.57 (5.6.4)
107. p.157 (20.8.10)
108. p.132 (4.8.4)
109. CSG 242-243
110. p.153 (18.8.5)
111. p.204 (30.9)
112. Ms C, 67
113. p.205 (30.9)

PART 3
Chapter 1 pp.125-145
1. p.143 (9.8.2)
2. p.55 (4.6.1)
3. p.126 (1.8.8.)
4. p.199 (24.9.10)
5. Ms C, 248
6. p.142 (8.8.3)
7. p.58 (6.6.4)
8. p.88 (11.7.5)
9. p.72 (3.7.7)
10. p.141 (8.8.2)
11. p.192 (18.9.2)
12. p.108 (24.7.1);
    p.175 (29.8.3)
13. p.91 (13.7.1)
14. p.206 (30.9)
15. p.120 (30.7.15)
16. p.202 (29.9.7)
17. p.171 (27.8.1)
18. p.177 (31.8.10)
19. p.75 (6.7.3)
20. p.154 (19.8.3)
21. Ms C, 217
22. Ms A, 97
23. ibid
24. Ms A, 176
25. p.186 (7.9)
26. p.50 (26.5)
27. p.58 (6.6.1)
28. p.152 (17.8.5)
29. p.74 (5.7.2)
30. p.194 (21.9.7)
31. pp.275, 284
32. p.52 (27.5.10)
33. cf. p.219 (4.8.3)
34. p.156 (20.8.5)

35. pp.225, 227
36. p.184 (5.9.3)
37. p.66 (19.6)
38. p.85 (10.7.4)
39. p.162 (22.8.1)
40. p.157 (20.8.9)
41. p.84 (9.7.9)
42. p.75 (6.7.3)
43. p.79 (8.7.3)
44. p.58 (6.6.5)
45. Ms A, 140
46. p.118 (30.7.4)
47. p.146 (12.8.2)
48. p.171 (27.8.2)
49. p.92 (13.7.6)
50. p.187 (10.9.1)
51. p.123 (31.7.11)
52. p.198 (24.9.5)
53. p.184 (5.9.2)
54. p.158 (20.8.12)
55. p.133 (5.8.2);
    p.189 (13.9.1)
56. p.80 (8.7.6)
57. p.80 (8.7.7)
58. CSG 221
59. p.51 (27.5.6)
60. p.74 (5.7.2)
61. LT 16/7/1897
62. p.274
63. Ms C, 210
64. Ms C, 247
65. p.191 (17.9.1)
66. p.146 (11.8.6)
67. p.185 (6.9.2)

Chapter 2 pp.147-213
1. p.43 (9.5.3)
2. p.43 (15.5.2)
3. p.118 (30.7.3)
4. p.133 (4.8.8)
5. Ms C, 218
6. p.114 (27.7.12)
7. LT 9/5/1897
8. LT 21/6/1897
9. Ms C, 250
10. p.76 (7.7.1)
11. p.109 (25.7.4)
12. p.129 (2.8.5)
13. p.74 (5.7.3)
14. p.198 (24.9.7)
15. p.134 (5.8.7)
16. p.154 (19.8.3)
17. Ms C, 258
18. Ms C, 255
19. p.57 (4.6.3)
20. p.75 (6.7.3)
21. ibid
22. p.141 (8.8.2)
23. Ms C, 221
24. Ms C, 219
25. Ms C, 222
26. Ms C, 220
27. p.66 (15.6.5)
28. Ms C, 216
29. LT 18/7/1897
30. p.144 (10.8.6)
31. p.134 (5.8.5)
32. p.187 (11.9.2)
33. p.57 (5.6.1);
    p.97 (14.7.8)
34. p.187 (11.9.2)
35. p.49 (21/26.5.11)
36. p.196 (23.9.1)
37. p.68 (27.6)
38. p.104 (20.7.5)

39. p.112 (27.7.1)
40. p.187 (10.9.2)
41. p.143 (9.8.3)
42. p.101 (16.7.4)
43. p.214 (12.7.1)
44. p.228 (27.9)
45. Ms C, 222
46. Ms C, 239
47. LT 6/6/1897
48. p.167 (25.8.1)
49. p.138 (6.8.7)
50. LT 25/4/1897
51. LT 18/7/1897
52. cf. p.193 (21.9.3)
53. p.46 (21/26.5.1)
54. Ms C, 209
55. p.51 (27.5.5)
56. Ms C, 209
57. Ms C, 210
58. p.51 (27.5.7)
59. p.111 (25.7.12)
60. LT July 1897
61. LT June/July 1897
62. p.277
63. p.154 (19.8.6)
64. p.195 (22.9.4)
65. p.110 (25.7.9)
66. p.103 (20.7.1);
    p.129 (3.8.1)
67. p.135 (5.8.10)
68. p.139 (7.8.1)
69. p.238 (13.7.4)
70. p.240 (11.8)
71. p.150 (16.8.2)
72. p.130 (3.8.6)
73. p.36 (6.4.1)
74. ibid (6.4.2)

75. p.96 (14.7.1)
76. p.36 (6.4.3)
77. p.103 (20.7.1)
78. p.130 (3.8.5)
79. p.142 (8.8.3)
80. p.111 (25.7.13)
81. p.191 (17.9.1)
82. p.137 (6.8.5)
83. p.197 (23.9.5)
84. p.94 (13.7.12)
85. p.102 (17.7)
86. LT 9/5/1897
87. LT 21/6/1897
88. LT 18/7/1897
89. LT 26/7/1897
90. p.146 (12.8.2)
91. p.155 (19.8.8)
92. Ms C, 207
93. p.94 (13.7.15)
94. Ms C, 233
95. Ms C, 240
96. Ms C, 227
97. Ms C, 226
98. Ms C, 222
99. Ms C, 224
100. LT 25/4/1897
101. LT 28/5/1897
102. LT 7/6/1897
103. p.46 (20.5.1)
104. p.73 (5.7.1)
105. p.49 (21/26.5.11)
106. p.72 (3.7.4)
107. p.116 (29.7.3)
108. p.103 (19.7.3)
109. p.73 (5.7.1)
110. ibid
111. p.116 (29.7.3)

112. p.129 (2.8.6)
113. p.74 (5.7.3)
114. p.140 (7.8.4)
115. p.67 (23.6)
116. p.111 (25.7.11)
117. LT 25/4/1897;
     LT 1/6/1897
118. p.131 (4.8.2)
119. p.180 (2.9.4)
120. p.184 (5.9.4)
121. Ms C, 218
122. p.87 (10.7.13)
123. p.64 (12.6.1)
124. p.112 (25.7.15)
125. p.45 (15.5.7)
126. p.65 (15.6.1)
127. p.47 (21/26.5.2)
128. p.169 (25.8.8);
     p.184 (5.9.4)
129. p.202 (29.9.5)
130. p.50 (27.5.2)
131. p.106 (23.7.3)
132. p.100 (16.7.1)
133. p.169 (25.8.8)
134. p.203 (29.9.11)
135. cf. p.149 (15.8.6)
136. p.148 (14.8)
137. p.175 (30.8.2)
138. p.87 (10.7.14)
139. p.52 (29.5)
140. Ms C, 210
141. Ms C, 218
142. p.108 (25.7.1)
143. p.175 (29.8.2)
144. p.145 (11.8.3)
145. p.169 (26.8.2)
146. p.147 (12.8.3)

147. p.89 (11.7.8)
148. p.98 (14.7.9)
149. p.160 (21.8.1)
150. p.129 (28.8.3)
     p.186 (8.9)
     p.199 (24.9.10)
151. p.82 (8.7.16)
152. p.200 (25.9.2)
153. p.50 (27.5.2)
154. Ms B, 192
155. p.132 (4.8.7)
156. p.142 (9.8.1)
157. p.132 (4.8.6)
158. Ms C, 257
159. p.47 (21/26.5.5)
160. p.262
161. p.181 (2.9.7)
162. p.164 (22.8.9)
163. p.91 (12.7.3)
164. p.96 (14.7.2)
165. p.153 (18.8.3)
166. p.289
167. p.205 (30.9)
168. LT 6/1/1889
169. p.126 (1.8.2)
170. cf. Ms C, 253
171. p.143 (9.8.2)
172. p.88 (11.7.3)
173. p.89 (11.7.6)
174. p.104 (20.7.3)
175. p.89 (11.7.6)
176. p.126 (1.8.2)
177. p.141 (8.8.1)
178. p.48 (21/26.5.6)
179. p.83 (9.7.2)
180. p.228 (26.9.1)
181. p.225 (5.9.1)

182. p.227 (16.9.2)
183. p.221. (5.8.3)
184. p.91 (13.7.3)
185. p.129 (2.8.5)
186. p.94 (13.7.16)
187. p.48 (21/26.5.7)
188. p.68 (27.6)
189. LT 9/6/1897
190. p.67 (25.6.1)
191. p.238 (13.7.1)
192. LT 13/7/1897
193. p.102 (18.7.1)
194. p.91 (13.7.2)
195. LT 14/7/1897
196. p.144 (10.8.4)
197. p.181 (2.9.5)
198. p.263
199. p.121 (31.7.1)
200. p.80 (8.7.8)
201. p.55 (4.6.1)
202. p.263
203. p.190 (14.9.1)
204. p.256
205. Ms C, 243
206. p.199 (24.9.10)
207. p.48 (21/26.5.7)
208. LT 25/4/1897
209. Ms C, 222
210. p.132 (4.8.3)
211. ibid
212. p.205 (30.9)
213. Ms C, 234
214. p.143 (9.8.4)
215. p.131 (4.8.2)
216. p.153 (18.8.4)
217. p.129 (3.8.2)
218. Ms C, 210; p.143 (10.8.2)

219. Ms B, 191
220. p.45 (15.5.7)
221. p.93 (13.7.10)
222. p.93 (13.7.12)
223. p.100 (15.7.5)
224. p.140 (7.8.4)
225. p.69 (30.6.1)
226. p.128 (2.8.2)
227. p.46 (21/26.5.1)
228. p.52 (27.5.10)
229. p.98 (15.7.2)
230. p.158 (20.8.13)
231. p.144 (10.8.3)
232. p.154 (19.8.5)
233. p.155 (19.8.7)
234. p.152 (17.8.5)
235. p.185 (6.9.2)
236. Ms A, 72
237. p.104 (20.7.6)
238. p.113 (26.7.6)
239. p.41 (1.5.2)
240. LT 9/5/1897
241. p.50 (26.5)
242. p.169 (25.8.7)
243. p.162 (21.8.3)
244. p.158 (20.8.11)
245. Ms C, 243
246. p.55 (4.6.1)
247. p.60 (6.6.9)
248. p.63 (12.6.1)
249. p.149 (15.8.4)
250. p.154 (19.8.1)
251. p.55 (4.6.1)
252. p.166 (23.8.8)
253. p.81 (8.7.11)
254. p.159 (20.8.15)
255. p.86 (10.7.10)

256. p.87 (10.7.14)
257. p.160 (20.8.16)
258. p.187 (11.9.3)
259. LT 8/9/1897
260. LT 10/8/1897
261. p.69 (30.6.2)
262. p.85 (10.7.8)
263. p.57 (5.6.4)
264. Ms B, 192
265. Ms A, 28
266. p.200 (25.9.2)
267. p.38 (18.4.3)
268. p.77 (7.7.4)
269. p.42 (9.5.1)
270. p.105 (21.7.4)
271. p.92 (13.7.7)
272. Ms C, 240

Chapter 3 pp.215-235
1. Ms A, 17
2. Ms A, 38
3. LT 23/8/1888
4. Ms A, 170
5. Ms A, 171
6. p.55 (4.6.1)
7. p.58 (6.6.2)
8. p.284
9. p.56 (4.6.2)
10. p.188 (11.9.4)
11. p.58 (6.6.3)
12. p.122 (31.7.4)
13. p.201 (29.9.2)
14. p.46 (20.5.1)
15. p.83 (9.7.6)
16. cf. p.55 (4.6.1)
17. Ms A, 179
18. LT 6/6/1897
19. Ms C, 214
20. Ms C, 215
21. p.113 (27.7.5)
22. p.177 (31.8.9)
23. p.148 (15.8.1)
24. ibid
25. p.55 (4.6.1)
26. p.56 (4.6.1)
27. p.73 (4.7.2)
28. p.75 (6.7.4)
29. p.97 (14.7.4)
30. p.98 (15.7.1)
31. LT 2/6/1897
32. LT 56 10/1/1889
33. Ms A, 47
34. p.135 (5.8.9)
35. p.136 (6.8.3)
36. LT 10/8/1897
37. p.109 (25.7.4);
    p.188 (11.9.5)
38. p.85 (10.7.9)
39. p.190 (14.9.1)
40. p.205 (30.9)
41. p.134 (5.8.7)
42. p.135 (6.8.1)
43. p.167 (25.8.1)
44. p.122 (31.7.7)
45. p.109 (25.7.6)
46. p.75 (6.7.4)
47. p.204 (30.9)
48. LT 18/7/1897
49. p.86 (10.7.11)
50. p.52 (29.5.1)

___Bibliography___

Clarke, John, ocd (tr.), Saint Thérèse of Lisieux, *General Correspondence* in 2 vols. (Vol. 1 1877-1890, vol. 2 1890-1897), ICS Publications, Washington DC, vol. 1, 1982, vol. 2, 1988.

Saint Thérèse of Lisieux *Her Last Conversations*, ICS Publications, Washington DC, 1977.

Story of a Soul, The Autobiography of St Thérèse of Lisieux, ICS Publications, Washington DC, 1976.

Geneviève of the Holy Face, Sister (Céline Martin), *A Memoir of my Sister, Saint Thérèse*, authorised translation of *Conseils et Souvenirs*, by the Carmelite Sisters of New York, Kenedy & Sons, New York, 1959.

Kavanaugh, Kiernan, ocd & Otilio Rodriguez, ocd, *The Collected Works of St John of the Cross*, ICS Publications, Washington DC, 1979.

O'Mahoney, Christopher, ocd (ed. & tr.), *Saint Thérèse of Lisieux by those who knew her.* Testimonies from the process of beatification. Veritas, Dublin, 1975.

Sheed, F.J. (tr.), *The Collected Letters of Saint Thérèse of Lisieux,* 1948 edition, Sheed & Ward, London, 1949.